000617

D1416040

WITHDRAWN
NOV 7 2003
LIBRARY
OF NEWFOUNDLAND

WITHDRAWN

Manager Empowerment in China

How have the economic reforms in the post-Mao era led to the spectacular rise of a new group of managerial elites? Who exactly are the members of the elite and can the Communist Party handle them?

China is a country in the midst of rapid economic change, especially in its traditional rural areas. Despite the public ownership of township–village enterprises, managers, many of whom first gained their industrial experience in commune-brigade enterprises in the collective era, are highly motivated. Their entrepreneurial skills and expertise are indispensable for the vitality and success of rural enterprises, while their ascendancy in the local community is reinforced by the growing scale and sophistication of production necessary in the further progress of rural industrialization.

Ray Yep presents detailed persuasive evidence which suggests that, contrary to the ideas of civil society theorists, managers owe their rise to their growing indispensability and not to direct confrontation with the state. Collaboration and negotiation are the managers' dominant strategies in pursuing their interests, and this symbiotic state–manager relationship is evident in the processes of political co-optation, defending autonomy in enterprise operation, and ownership reform of rural enterprise. The in-depth and sophisticated approach of this study suggests that in the post-Mao era rural industrialization depends upon continuity with, as well as departure from, the past in order to develop the state–manager relationship.

Ray Yep is Assistant Professor in the Department of Public and Social Administration at the City University of Hong Kong.

RoutledgeCurzon Studies on China in Transition
Series Editor: David S. G. Goodman

Manager Empowerment in China

HD
70
C5
Y462
2003

Political implications of rural
industrialization in the reform era

Ray Yep

RoutledgeCurzon
Taylor & Francis Group

LONDON AND NEW YORK

First published 2003
by RoutledgeCurzon
11 New Fetter Lane, London EC4P 4EE

Simultaneously published in the USA and Canada
by RoutledgeCurzon
29 West 35th Street, New York, NY 10001

RoutledgeCurzon is an imprint of the Taylor & Francis Group

© 2003 Ray Yep

Typeset in Baskerville by
Prepress Projects Ltd, Perth, Scotland
Printed and bound in Great Britain by
Antony Rowe Ltd, Chippenham, Wiltshire

All rights reserved. No part of this book may be reprinted
or reproduced or utilized in any form or by any electronic,
mechanical, or other means, now known or hereafter invented,
including photocopying and recording, or in any information
storage or retrieval system, without permission in writing from
the publishers.

British Library Cataloguing in Publication Data
A catalogue record for this book is available from the British
Library

Library of Congress Cataloging in Publication Data
A catalog record for this book has been requested

ISBN 0–415–28295–0

For Carolin

Contents

Illustrations

Tables

Figure

Preface

This book is the result of a decade of curiosity about rural China. It began when I worked as a researcher for a trading company selling fertilizers to Chinese farmers. The daily routine of intensive reading of several dozen Chinese newspapers exposed me to fascinating stories and episodes of the dramatic changes in the countryside. Although my primary responsibility was to monitor the consumption pattern and grain production in China, my political science training always pulled my attention in a different direction, toward the possible linkage between socioeconomic changes and power relationships in the countryside. Such moonlighting was fun, as I had a substantial pool of corporate resources at my disposal to finance my private research. But it soon became clear that a more serious and disciplined effort was necessary if I really desired more than a journalistic account of rural transformation.

This book is based on my doctoral thesis at Oxford, but this is a shared enterprise. A long list of individuals have provided essential support and contributed to this work. I am particularly indebted to my supervisor, Laurence Whitehead, for his guidance, patience, and encouragement. His probing questions always enabled me to see things in a larger context and to reconsider the issue with references to real-life experience. His genuine concern for humanity demonstrates that academic work can mean more than abstract theorization or egoistic fulfillment, which I think is the most precious lesson I learned during my years at Oxford. I am also grateful to my college supervisor, John Darwin, for his support through the years. His meticulous reading of my works always provoked me to base my argument on solid empirical support and clarity.

A number of people have also unselfishly shared their wisdom with me by commenting on different drafts of my thesis: Robert Bickers, Archie Brown, Jane Duckett, Jacob Eyferth, James Kung, Tak-wing Ngo, Maria Edin, Stig Thorgensen, Paul Wilding, Ian Holliday, and Federico Varese. I am also grateful for the comments of David Goodman and Frank Pieke. The support of a number of Chinese scholars was indispensable for this project. The field research would simply have been impossible without the intermediation of Chen Xiwen, Du Ying, and Chen Jianbo in particular. I was also graced with the remarkable research assistance provided by Royce Chau, Erica Chu, Vivien Leung, and Jacqueline Yu throughout the years; their steady supply of useful data and materials helped to polish the book. John Swire & Sons, the Cha Fund of St Antony's College, Oxford, and the City University of Hong Kong provided generous funding for my research. The final version of this book was written during my visiting fellowship in the Center of Northeast Asian Policy Studies, Brookings Institution. I am indebted to Mike Armacost, James Steinberg, Catharin Dalpino, and particularly Bates Gill, as they provided me with a wonderful sabbatical year in which to finish the task. I am also grateful for the excellent proofreading support of Angela Stavropoulos and Helen MacDonald. This book would not be possible without the assistance of the outstanding editorial team at RoutledgeCurzon and Prepress Projects Ltd: Annabel Watson, Joe Whiting, Ann Grant, and Rachel Saunders.

The formative stage of this book developed during my years in Nuffield College, Oxford. Nuffield is a prestigious place for academic excellence and I am proud to be associated with it. However, for an overseas student from an unknown university, who is working on a non-mainstream subject, life is not always easy. A number of friends rescued me from all forms of social isolation: May Tam, Tak-wing Chan, Man-to Leung, Makiko Nishigawa, Aurora Manrique, and Luisa Perrotti. They made my adventure in Nuffield very enjoyable and rewarding. Words alone cannot express my gratitude to a special friend, Marc Stears. He is my adviser, colleague, and teacher. He never failed me when I needed support and advice, and our friendship is one of my most treasured accomplishments at Oxford.

My greatest gratitude goes to my wife, Carolin. Her support, patience, and encouragement provided me with the strength to endure the hard times throughout the duration of this project. Her companionship and love made any progress I made in my work even more enjoyable and meaningful. Her direct contribution to the content of this work may be remote, but, without her sacrifices and love, this work would never have been accomplished. This book is dedicated to her.

Acknowledgments

The author and publishers would like to thank the following for granting permission to reproduce material in this work:

"Towards a Symbiotic State–Enterprise Relationship in Rural China: Changes and Prospect," *Hong Kong Journal of Social Science*, No. 17, Autumn 2000, pp. 1–18.

"The Limitations of Corporatism in Understanding Reforming China," *Journal of Contemporary China*, Vol. 9, No. 25, 2000, pp. 547–66. The journal can be found on line at http://www.tandf.co.uk

"Bring the Managers in: A Case of Rising Influence of Enterprise Managers in Rural China," *Issues & Studies*, Vol. 36, No. 4, July/August 2000, pp. 132–65.

"Evolution of Shareholding Enterprise Reform in Rural China: A Manager Empowerment Thesis," *Pacific Affairs*, Vol. 74, No. 1, Spring 2001, pp. 53–73.

Every effort has been made to contact copyright holders for their permission to reprint material in this book. The publishers would be grateful to hear from any copyright holder who is not here acknowledged and will undertake to rectify any errors or omissions in future editions of the book.

Abbreviations

ABC	Agricultural Bank of China (*Zhongguo Nongye Yinhang*)
CBE	commune-brigade enterprise (*shedui qiye*)
CCP	Chinese Communist Party
CRE	Commission for Restructuring the Economy (*Jingji Tizhi Gaige Weiyuanhui*)
EA	Entrepreneurs' Association (*Qiyejia Xiehui*)
ETC	Economic and Trade Commission (*Jingji Maoyi Weiyuanhui*)
FBIS	Foreign Broadcasting Information Service
FIC	Federation of Industry and Commerce (*Gongshang Lianghehui*)
GNP	gross national product
ICA	Industry and Commerce Administration (*Gongshang Guanliju*)
ILA	Individual Laborers' Association
JPRS	Journals and Periodicals Research Service
MITI	Ministry of International Trade and Industry
PRC	People's Republic of China
RCC	Rural Credit Cooperative (*Nongcun Xinyong Hezuoshe*)
REA	Rural Enterprise Administration (*Xiangzhen Qiye Guanliju*)
TVE	township–village enterprises
ZGTN	*Zhongguo Tongji Nianjian* (*China's Statistical Yearbook*)
ZGXZQYB	*Zhongguo Xiangzhen Qiyebao* (*China's Rural Enterprise News*)
ZN	*Zibo Nianjian* (*Zibo Yearbook*)
ZR	*Zibo Ribao* (*Zibo Daily*)
ZTN	*Zibo Tongji Nianjian* (*Zibo Statistical Yearbook*)
ZTZ	*Zhongguo Tongji Zhaiyao* (*China's Statistical Digest*)
ZXQN	*Zhongguo Xiangzhen Qiye Nianjian* (*China's Rural Enterprise Yearbook*)

1 Understanding rural transformation

Comrade Xiaoping, how are you?

The sudden emergence of the new force has freed us from the outdated ideas and habits formed over thousands of years of feudalistic, small-scale farming. With their faces turned to the yellow earth and their backs to the sky, our ancestors tilled the land generation after generation and endured perpetual poverty. Many peasants want to start village and township enterprises, but they are prevented from doing so by either misgivings or inexperience. This is, however, the only way for us peasants to truly achieve emancipation and stand up both economically and politically.

The sudden emergence of the new force has also broken through the tight shackles of the old system. Although totally devoid of financial and material support, as well as technical assistance and qualified personnel from the state, the new field of a market economy has emerged. Moreover, the sudden emergence of the new force has further broken through the conventionality of trying to maintain the status quo and fighting to remain one step ahead of confusion. Racing against time and with increased speed, much has been achieved. Since 1978, the total output of village and township enterprises has quadrupled, and the tax revenues returned to the state also have more than quadrupled. The emergence of the new force has brought satisfaction to peasants and stability to the society. It has contributed much to enhancing national strength and the people's wealth. It has further revitalized agriculture and contributed to agricultural modernization . . .

(Letter to Deng Xiaoping from ten rural entrepreneurs, October 1992)[1]

The rural entrepreneurs' letter to Deng Xiaoping provides a vivid illustration of the consequences of rural industrialization in post-Mao China. The rise of rural enterprises has fundamentally transformed the economic as well as social lives of the Chinese peasantry. Peasants have been liberated from total reliance on the soil and farming, and non-agricultural activities have become feasible economic options; this signals a change in the rhythm of rural life and new possibilities. However, the letter also epitomizes the ascendance of managerial elites in rural China. While rhetorically praising the wisdom of Deng Xiaoping and government policies, the managers also demonstrated their confidence and optimism in the letter:

> [W]e will stand tall and further shoulder the heavy responsibilities
> entrusted by you. Under the leadership of the party Central Committee,
> we will infuse even greater vitality into our socialist economic construction,
> and we will ensure that socialist China will shine gloriously forever.[2]

In other words, the entrepreneurs saw themselves as champions of rural
development as well as national prosperity. What happened next proved that
they were right. Within less than two decades, rural enterprises moved from
being a negligible part of the national economy into a sector contributing more
than one-third of the total national industrial output. While the social and
economic aspects of rural industrialization have been the subject of extensive
study,[3] the political implications of the process warrant more attention than
they have received so far. There has been even less interest, surprisingly little,
in the role of enterprise managers. Particularly noteworthy is the lack of interest in the rise of enterprise managers in the rural collective sector. Although
considerable efforts have been made in analyzing the background and situation
of managers in private, state, or other sectors,[4] the managers of collective
enterprises in rural China do not receive the academic attention they deserve.
Nonetheless, although the non-state sector is undergoing tremendous growth
in rural areas, collectively owned township–village enterprises (TVEs) still
predominate. The implications of the changing role and increasing political
influence of the managers of such TVEs, who have a strategic role in steering
these collective ventures toward success, will be of great significance for the
new political landscape in rural China. Yet, despite their importance, many
basic but crucial questions remained unanswered. Who are they? What is their
role in promoting the growth of TVEs, and what is their influence on the local
polity? Most important of all, how can the local state, at the rural grass-roots
level, accommodate the rise of these new economic actors, who will play an
indispensable role in delivering a steady flow of revenues and economic benefits
to local communities?

Implications of understanding rural transformation

These insights are crucial for those who are interested in rural development
in China but the interaction between managers and the local state over the
issue of TVE management and local economic development is also a reliable
reflection of the changing state–society relations in post-Mao China for various
reasons. First, the pressure on the local state machinery to reposition itself in
local economic management epitomizes the general challenges imposed on
the task of governance by the advent of economic reform. The demise of the
collective framework of the People's Commune and the imperative of a new
economic logic imposed by the changing economic environment imply the
loss of conventional or policy instruments and the emergence of the principle
of economy-first policy making. A redefinition of the state's role is necessary.
Examination of its role in the collective sector – an arena that used to be closely

regulated and supervised by local administrations – is an ideal opportunity for observing the extent of the necessary readjustment. Second, the rise of TVE managers illustrates the new opportunities and challenges unleashed by economic reform. The reason for their ascendancy is that they have the skills and knowledge that are most desirable in the age of reform. Change in institutional frameworks affects the value of different types of knowledge,[5] and the managerial skills and entrepreneurial instincts that these managers have are highly treasured in this period of economic reform, because they are necessary for transforming the resources of the local state, in this case TVEs, into a steady flow of income. Those who possess these valuable attributes seek opportunities and make the best use of them. They assume commanding positions in the local economy, and some go even further by breaking into the local political hierarchy. For local states, recognition of the significant economic contribution of TVE managers is inevitably accompanied by some degree of power sharing. The empowerment of these new social actors is itself a reflection of the changing relations between state and society, yet it may also point to further change in this direction.

However, reform in China is not only of great intrinsic interest to those concerned with the development of China, the future of socialism, or alternatives for the Third World, but is also an invaluable reference for political scientists. The dynamic and fluid nature of the transformation makes Chinese reform an excellent testing ground for theories, concepts, and frameworks that have been proposed in the study of political development. Specifically, the tremendous economic change within the short period of less than twenty years, since the death of Mao Zedong in 1976, presents itself as an ideal candidate for the re-examination of the links between economic development and political change, discussed in the classics by Moore, Polanyi, Lipset, and Lindblom,[6] in more recent literature on democratic transition,[7] and in the polemical work by Fukuyama.[8] By the mid-1990s, China had successfully transformed itself from a closed economy, predominantly state owned and tightly regulated by central planning, into a mixed economy with a strong flavor of capitalism, price control confined to strategic sectors, and extensive linkages with the world economy, epitomized by its recent admission into the World Trade Organization. An inquiry into the process of economic reform in China certainly helps to enhance our understanding of the intriguing links between economic change and political development. This is the major motivation of this study. The unique character of China's experience makes it an even more enticing choice for examining the link between economic change and political development. Although most of the existing literature on this issue bases its insights on the experience of capitalist economies, the distinct character of the socialist transformation in China can provide an extra dimension to our understanding of this matter. Analysis of Chinese reform entails a simultaneous inquiry into two important phenomena: the development of a market economy and development in the political realm. The fluidity inherent in both processes and the interaction between them are fertile grounds for a more in-depth analysis of the interconnections between economic change and political development.

Property rights theorists may discard political development as of little analytical significance. Their standard argument is that clearly delineated and specified property rights are prerequisite to economic growth, and that movement toward a market economy is inevitable. According to Smith, "a man must be perfectly crazy who, where there is tolerable security [of property], does not employ all capital stock which he commands."[9] Thus, for any state, such as China, which is eager to search for economic efficiency, the imperative of economic rationality renders the option of marketization, based upon a foundation of private property, the only genuine choice. Many practitioners of economic reform in the post-socialist regimes share a similar, if not more hard-line, view. For instance, Boycko, Shleifer and Vishny, who have been heavily involved in the Russian reform program in the post-Gorbachev era, argue that "there was no other way [but privatization] to achieve restructuring and efficient operation of firms."

The implication of an inevitable transition toward a market economy is, however, problematic. It ignores the possible political interactions involved in the process of economic transformation and, hence, fails to comprehend the dynamics of the evolution of a new economic mechanism. This kind of mechanical view leaves no place for non-economic variables. Political variables do, however, enter into the evolution of property rights in at least two ways. First, the security of property rights is contingent upon specific conditions in the sociopolitical context. As Yoram Barzel argues, the security of property rights is possibly affected by the power relations of the parties concerned, the state's capacity for enforcing rules and regulations, or the effectiveness of alternative forms of protection; hence, political factors matter.[10]

Second, it cannot be taken for granted that objective demand for a more economically rational mechanism will be automatically translated into supply. Self-interest may or may not be conducive to the emergence of a collectively beneficial outcome, especially if public goods are concerned.[11] The issue of who will supply is crucial here. If the property rights theorists are to be consistent in their intentionality paradigm, they need to explain why highly motivated yet self-interested individuals would wish to design a new system in an unbiased manner, with the sole aim of collective improvement. Even if the new system is delivered by the state, those parties of strategic importance are likely to be favored under the new scheme. The relative capacity (in terms of strategic importance – power, position, command over resources, etc.) of the actors concerned is an important determinant of the economic landscape.[12] The fundamental questions of politics – who gets what and how – seem to have analytical relevance here.

Furthermore, the complexity of the process of market reform under a socialist regime also involves the daunting task of redefining the role of the state. The essence of socialist market reform is evolution from a planned economy. The two economic mechanisms denote contrasting economic and political philosophies, and readjustment of the state is inevitable. The complexity of the readjustment process is enormous. It is not simply a matter of the Party leadership's commitment to reform; it also involves issues such as the motivation of vested interests in the old political–economic order to comply with the change, the accommodation of conflicting interests affected by the changes, and the readjustments in mindset, habits, and expectations among all parties concerned. The new market order may be forthcoming, but it is questionable whether the impact of the socialist past fully disappears. In this respect, a study of market reform in socialist China can deepen the understanding of the dynamics of institutional change, particularly the relevance of historic legacy.

Thus, a focused inquiry into economic reform in socialist China is a valuable opportunity for students of political development. It enhances understanding of the role of the socialist state in the era of economic reform, i.e. how and why it redefines its role in the face of the changing political and economic order, and reveals the prospect for the Chinese market reform program.

Defining key terms

Before beginning to evaluate the strengths and limitations of the existing theoretical analysis on rural transformation in China, several key terms need explicit definition. TVE managers are those in charge of these collectively owned enterprises. Collective ownership implies that managers are not the proprietors, or even shareholders, of these enterprises in most cases. Yet, as will be argued later, owing to the unique opportunities and incentive structures in the Chinese rural community, these individuals nevertheless perform similar entrepreneurial, as well as managerial, functions – risk-taking, innovative roles etc. – to their counterparts in the private sector. They are, in short, the rural entrepreneurs of the reform era.

The term "TVE" also needs some elaboration. It is important to note that there are many regional variations in the management and ownership of TVEs, yet a few generalizations can still be made. TVEs are collectively owned firms controlled by the local township and village administrations – the lowest tiers of the Chinese administration. Theoretically, local communities own them as a whole. Many of them were either established and controlled by agricultural collectives during the days of the People's Commune or were set up by township and village administrations during the 1980s. However, they should not be perceived as worker cooperatives, as individual members of the local community have no institutionalized channels for expressing their opinions on enterprise management.[13] In reality, the collective label implies that, although these local administrations possess all the key components of property rights over these firms – the right of residual claimancy, the right to appoint and dismiss managers, the right to transfer assets, and the right to direct control if necessary – nevertheless, as we shall see in the forthcoming discussion, these nominal rights are subject to constraints imposed by the rising importance of enterprise managers. Despite their public ownership, TVEs may be contrasted with their counterparts in the state sector in two crucial ways. First, their development is mostly outside the state plan. That is, they are guaranteed neither markets for their outputs nor the supply of inputs at subsidized prices.[14] Second, they face much tougher budgetary constraints.[15] That is, although state-owned enterprises are likely to be bailed out by the state in the case of financial crisis, the likelihood of rescue for TVEs is remote. This is mainly because of the relatively weaker financial position of local governments. They simply cannot afford to keep enterprises alive, no matter how eager they are to do so. The option of bankruptcy is more commonly adopted among loss-making TVEs than among loss-making state-owned enterprises. These two factors taken together suggest that TVEs face much tougher pressures from market competition than do their state counterparts.

The term "local state" here refers to the Party-state at county and township levels in rural China. Local states are the bottom levels of the administrative machine. This work focuses on these levels, particularly township administration, mainly because this is where there is the greatest interaction between the state and TVE managers. As the discussion is primarily focused on a single policy area – the regulation of local TVEs – the local state is generally treated in this analysis as a unitary actor, moving and acting in a coherent fashion. Nevertheless, the tensions and conflicts within the Chinese state must always be remembered. Three sources of tension are particularly noteworthy. First, there is the discrepancy between central and local interests and concerns in economic reform. Second, the coexistence of administrative units, which are under different lines of command at the same level of administration, is a major manifestation of conflicts between different tiers of government. The classic problem of *tiao* (the vertical line of command) versus *kuai* (the horizontal line of command) is evident in rural China.[16] Third, even within local administration, different policy priorities and concerns may pull in different policy directions. The local state is hard pressed to maintain fairness in distribution in the local community and to provide incentives for enterprise managers. The existence and interaction of all these contradictions and tensions are, in fact, what force the redefinition of the role of the local state, which this study attempts to explore.

Chinese state meets social scientists

In this section, several approaches that have been commonly used to explain political change in post-Mao China will be examined. The review aims to evaluate the possible contributions and limitations of these approaches in enhancing our understanding of the political future of China. Although these approaches are useful in formulating important research questions and concepts, they all fail to pay sufficient attention to the role played by social forces in the era of market reform. In the case of rural development, the imbalance caused by the limited analysis of the role of TVE managers, in particular, has to be addressed.

The state as the basic determinant of politics

The fundamental position of neo-statism is that the state is an independent variable of politics.[17] Such a position denotes an anti-pluralist view of politics and a stress on state autonomy. The atomistic universe of politics advocated by the pluralist – a reductionist perspective that regards public policy as the outcome of the resolution of vectors resulting from interests and resources in the society – is rejected.[18] "Atoms are bounded within stable molecules and compounds," the neo-statists argue.[19]

The neo-statist perspective obviously has its appeal for those who are concerned with the politics of socialist regimes. The seemingly overt authoritarian character of these regimes warrants the application of such a perspective. However, several omissions from this analytical framework are noteworthy.

First, the neo-statists fail to recognize the impact of the past on the position of the state in determining politics. The role of the state is contingent upon specific historical conditions. Historical inheritances can greatly constrain the power of the state; China is no exception to this. The communist state in Maoist China was able to produce a high degree of dependency among peasants,[20] and managed to penetrate deeper into the countryside than any of its imperial predecessors.[21] Nevertheless, despite these achievements, traditional elements could still express themselves in the communist setting. A good illustration is the persistence of the kinship system, which was targeted by the Communist Party as an object of social transformation because of the Party's distaste of its notorious parochialism.[22] The sheer size of the rural hinterlands and the Party's anxiety to achieve a prompt and smooth transition to a new political order served to reinforce the traditional institution.[23] Consequently, the traditional institutions have continued to exist, though in a less institutionalized and organized form. Endurance of this traditional pattern of intermediation between state and society in a rural polity, which relies on the support of local people, reinforced the open nature of rural administration. That is, local officials, mostly close kin of local residents, continued to play the role of the bridge between state and local society and, most significantly, remained vulnerable to societal pressure.[24] Such a connection raises the issue of potential tensions and differences between local and central state. Vivienne Shue provides the best exposition of the tensions embedded in the local polity in rural China:

> The lower levels of the state's apparatus, reflecting the parcelized or honeycomb socioeconomic structure over which it presided, had, in fact, become a maze of power pockets and vested interests manned by people who were constrained to mouth the rhetoric of revolution but who often had everything to gain by protecting and elaborating on the status quo. Far from serving as robotic handmaidens of central domination, these stubborn, savvy, and often cynical officials came to constitute a formidable obstacle to real and effective central penetration and control on the ground.[25]

This kind of honeycomb pattern of polity in its worst form could result in a local tyranny exercised by local cadres. However, through the cadres' intermediation and formalities, policies from the top were adapted to local needs.[26]

In a nutshell, the contribution of the neo-statist approach to an understanding of rural politics in China is hindered by its insufficient attention to historical specificity and hence the consequent neglect of the persistence of the past. The pattern of power brokerage at the rural grass roots also exposes a fundamental deficiency of applying the statist approach to rural politics in China: the neo-statists fail to comprehend the insightful comment made by Joel Migdal, "the role of the state is itself an object of the struggle."[27] This view challenges the neo-statist perspective of the state as an aggregate that always manages to move in a coherent fashion, and it questions the validity of the stubborn exclusion of society from the analysis. In the case of China, the picture of tensions and conflicts between different levels of the administration and the vulnerability of the lower tier to local influence, described above, seems to be in line with this challenge.

The complexity of the contemporary development of reform in China demands a more nuanced understanding of the intriguing state–society interface and has provoked genuine reflection within the statist tradition. Two trends are noteworthy: the growing popularity of the notion of corporatism and the rising concern with the developmental nature of the Chinese state. First, there is a growing interest in applying the concept of corporatism, a variant on statism, in analyzing state–society relations in reforming China. According to one of its major advocates, Schmitter, who employs this concept in analyzing business–government relations in Latin America, corporatism is defined as:

> A system of interest representation in which the constituent units are organized into a limited number of singular, compulsory, non-competitive, hierarchically ordered and functionally differentiated categories, recognized or licensed (if not created) by the state and granted a deliberate representational monopoly within their respective categories in exchange for observing certain controls on their selection of leaders and articulation of demands and supports.[28]

Though corporatism does not go so far as the pluralist view that state policy is simply reactive and responsive, the notion does imply room for negotiation and bargaining between the state and social interests. Compared with the aforementioned neo-statist view, there is more scope for the intervention of social interests in the making of public policy in this analytical framework. Nevertheless, when scholars interested in the development of Chinese politics have applied this concept in China, the major emphasis has been on the role of the state. State corporatism, used in this context, is stressed as a deliberate strategy of the state to preserve its dominance in the face of the emergence and empowerment of social interests. The empirical focus is on how the Chinese state prevents the emergence of autonomous societal groups by co-opting these new social interests into its sponsored associational networks.[29] Though there exists disagreement on the potential of these official associations to form the basis for spontaneous political participation,[30] the main concern here is on the effectiveness of this co-option strategy in enhancing coordination and diffusing potential pressure from below.

As with its counterparts in East Asia, which share a similar preference for authoritarianism, the option of state corporatism sounds appealing to the Chinese state, given its dual concerns of accommodating the new social interests, which have increasing functional importance for the modernization program, and maintaining its dominant role in the polity. However, the implicit assumption that state corporatism is a systematic and deliberate strategy by the state as part of the reform program is problematic. In the first place, the economic reform program itself is not unused to accusations of being disjointed, piecemeal, and reactive. Moreover, the coherent image of the state portrayed here is also challenged by the growing literature on the cleavages between agencies of the state, either caused by deliberate efforts at administrative and financial decentralization or the unintended consequence of economic reforms.[31] And as White, Howell, and Shao argue, even though there may be a pervasive impetus toward corporatism among state agencies at different levels, their different agendas and concerns may both integrate and disarticulate the operations of the state.[32] In other words, the assumption of a consistent state corporatist strategy overlooks the trend of growing fragmentation of the Chinese state and may mislead analysis of the changing state–society relations in the reform era.

Equally important, the preoccupation with the preservation of state dominance, which is inherent in the notion of state corporatism, may even divert attention from the more fundamental issue of the shift in the balance of power between state and society. This is ironic, as the application of the concept of corporatism to China hinges upon the premise of changing power relations between state and social interests in the reform era. If the state remains completely autonomous and independent, and social interests are subordinated to state control in all aspects of policy making, then there is no corporatism.[33] Nevertheless, although it is true that the corporatist perspective recognizes the empowerment of social interests during the reform era, this perspective, with its inherent concern with state dominance, is hardly ideal for capturing the functional reciprocity between these rising social interests and the state. In other words, social actors are not given their proper place in the analysis under this framework.

The literature on the positive role of the Chinese state in economic development similarly overlooks the role of social actor. Based mainly on the success of state-led industrialization in Japan, Taiwan, and South Korea,[34] adherents of this view claim that good, growth-enhancing, relations between the state and business are possible.[35] Many China observers subscribe to this view as a possible tool for evaluating the growing involvement of the Chinese state in the economy. Blecher and Shue[36] argue that a strong development orientation can be observed in local administrations, and that these traits can be traced back to the last decade of the Mao period. Blecher[37] further distinguishes between developmental and entrepreneurial states, with the latter being directly involved in profit-seeking activities. Duckett[38] follows the same line of inquiry and suggests that, contrary to the neo-liberal view, such state entrepreneurism can be adaptable and potentially productive. Howell[39] and Ma[40] provide an alternative notion of the market-facilitating state that embodies both the developmental and entrepreneurial traits mentioned above. This positive image is even more vividly encapsulated in Oi's notion of local state corporatism, which we will discuss at greater length momentarily. A similar emphasis on the benevolent role of the state in promoting economic development can also be found in the argument of Wank[41] and Pearson[42] on the endurance of clientelism in Chinese business.

However, even if we agree that state involvement in economic transformation is a given, the question of how to avoid the possibly growth-enhancing collaboration from degenerating into collusion remains valid. Public choice literature focusing on the micro-incentives of bureaucrats provides a stern challenge on this matter. It is argued that bureaucrats are no different from ordinary self-seeking people. The logic is that dense state–business ties will only provide these self-seeking individuals ample opportunity to pursue personal gains at the expense of the developmental objectives, no matter how benevolent the state's intent.[43] Literature on developmentalism emphasizes that two major mechanisms are at work in avoiding this situation: Weberian-type bureaucracy and moral appeal. An insulated and meritocratic bureaucracy, as epitomized by MITI (Ministry of International Trade and Industry) in the Japanese case, is a strong bulwark against corruption, and a social consensus of growth and prosperity reinforced by either nationalism or a crisis mentality is also an effective deterrent against the abuse of power.[44] These are the necessary (though not sufficient) conditions for saving a positive state–business collaboration from degenerating into collusion. One does not have to subscribe to the pessimistic views of moral decay and rampant corruption in China, but it takes great optimism or naivety to argue that the Chinese state has met the "hard state" criteria required of a successful developmental state. Then how can advocates of state developmentalism justify their observation in reform China? What is missing is the discussion on the reciprocity between state and society. Exchanges are crucial for maintaining a stable relationship, whether clientelistic or developmental in nature. Those "junior" social partners in the relationship must have something to offer, e.g. support for policy implementation or contribution to economic progress, if excessive predation or abuses are to be contained. The recent effort by developmental theorists to look beyond the state dimension in analyzing the prospects of developmental states provides an important clue here.[45] According to this view, a nuanced understanding of the maintenance of positive state–society collaboration requires a balanced view of both sides of the state–society connection.

Civil society: society versus the state

Alternatively, the concept of civil society reasserts the role of social actors in the analysis of political development. The notion of civil society has been applied extensively in the analysis of democratic transition and consolidation. Schmitter suggests that an ideal type of civil society should contain the following features: dual autonomy, collective action, non-usurpation, and civility.[46] This last element of "civility" resonates with the classical meaning of the concept, which originated from concern with the fundamental tension between particular and universal interest and the need for some collective solidarity in a moral community.[47] However, the current usage of the concept puts a greater emphasis on its liberal strand; the concept of civil society is tied to liberal individualism and is seen as being in opposition to the state. In its application in the socialist context in particular, civil society is conceived as a collective, homogenized agent standing against the evil state.[48]

The concept of civil society is gaining popularity among China-watchers.[49] Again, it is the minimalist definition, with a focus on societal autonomy and collective action, which occupies the central position in the debate on changing state–society relations in the reform era. White, for instance, argues that civil society is "an organic accompaniment of the spread of market relations and the consequent emergence of a new realm of social organizations based on voluntary participation and enjoying some autonomy from the state."[50] According to this state versus society view, it is in this realm of autonomous social space that the aspirations and interests of societal actors can find an effective outlet for expression. It is hoped that it may pose a limitation on the power of the overseeing state and may create a *de facto* dispersion of political power, ultimately leading to the restructuring of political institutions or even democratization.[51]

The civil society approach certainly sheds new light on the role of social interests, neglected by the neo-statist approach. It helps to bring society back into the analysis and to focus attention on how society will respond to state encroachment. With the inevitable diversification of social interests and the likely empowerment of these forces with the advent of economic reform, the notion of civil society provides a useful perspective for analyzing the changing pattern of state–society relations. However, several caveats should be noted. First, one should be warned against the danger of overoptimism with regard to the development of civil society. As deregulation is one of the dominant themes of the Chinese economic reforms, any signs of state retreat could easily be misread as signs of the progress of civil society. This is largely a result of a misconception of the state–society relationship as a simple zero-sum game. However, if, as its advocates suggest, civil society implies not only a freedom from state intervention but also an assertion of civil society's will against the state, then, even if there is a decline in state power, it will not be automatically mean an increase in the power of society. Such ungrounded optimism is very much related to another common error committed by many "civil society" advocates: the failure to acknowledge the contingent or fragile nature of many instances of social autonomy. It would be too hasty, if not wrong, to conclude that a civil society is emerging if all the "autonomous" moves vis-à-vis the state could be reversed by the state if it chooses to do so.[52]

The assumption of the logical inevitability of the link between social autonomy and political change is most problematic, however. The implicit argument in this conception of civil society is that political change or liberalization is the logical outcome of the expansion of societal autonomy. However, the links are not fully specified. The questions of *how* and *why* those social interests that are becoming more autonomous and powerful must support further changes in the political (e.g. democratization) or economic realms (e.g. further marketization) need to be answered. This is an empirical question that needs to be explored. The danger of "incivility" in civil society, as Whitehead[53] points out, and the lack of enthusiasm for further reform exhibited by social actors with a relatively high degree of autonomy in China, as revealed by several empirical studies, suggest that further thought is needed on this subject.[54]

Closely related to this matter is the issue of collective action by social interests. The civil society argument presupposes the inclination of the empowered social interests to organize collective action to pursue their own interests. In the case of specific social interests, e.g. enterprise managers or workers, a common position and experience resulting from their similar functional role in the economy may contribute to the strengthening of horizontal ties. But the assumption that such categorical groups as these will automatically transform themselves into identity groups – groups with a clear sense of community and the willingness and capacity to organize collective action – is again a leap too far. Two important elements are missing from the analysis: potential cleavages within social interests and the vertical ties with the state. Both elements cut across the horizontal bonding among the categorical group and reduce its propensity for collective action. The latter is particularly relevant to an understanding of the socialist transformation. Reform does not start from scratch but from a planned economy.[55] The slow pace of market reform and the continuation of the Party's rule in China imply that the interaction and linkage between state and society remain pervasive and significant. The new pattern of state–society relations need not involve a more clearly delineated boundary between autonomous social actors and the demonic state; other possible forms of state–society interactions have to be envisaged. It is not necessarily a story in which civil society is cast in the role of David against the Goliath of the modern state. A dichotomous view of the state versus society is an oversimplification, which obscures as much as it illuminates.

Research focus: state–manager relations in rural China

Instead of conducting a general overview of state–society relations, this research has a more specific focus on the interaction between the state and a new economic actor at rural grass-roots level – the enterprise manager. And, as argued previously, this is based on the assumption that their interaction is an epitome of the state–society interface in the process of market transition. In other words, by this focused analysis, this study attempts to answer the following questions, which this author believes can contribute to one's understanding of general state–society interaction in the process of market transition in China: In what ways is the position of the local state in the management of the local political and economic order affected by market reforms and what is its response? Is the local state alone capable of developing the local economy? Does the new political and economic setting require new resources and skills? If so, is the empowerment of a new social category inevitable, and how does this affect the distribution of political and economic power at the local level?

Nee: declining role of local state

What has been said on this subject so far? The ideas of Victor Nee and Jean Oi are particularly noteworthy. Victor's Nee theory of market transition assigns a greater role to social actors in the analysis of state–society relations in China during the reform era. The central argument is that "the shift from hierarchies to market in a socialist economy changes the determinants of socioeconomic attainment and therefore the sources of power and privilege."[56] Nee's theory focuses on the potential erosion of state power during the economic transformation in rural China:

> The market transition theory maintains that the more complete the shift to market coordination, the less likely that economic transactions will be embedded in networks dominated by cadres, and the more likely power – control over resources – will be located in market institutions and in social networks (*guanxi*) of private buyers and sellers.[57]

The weakening of state dominance is well reflected in the declining value of "political capital" – the power and privilege of officials. Nee suggests that, given the breadth and volume of both downward and upward vertical mobility in the reform period, it is unlikely that households' chances of economic gains and losses are primarily controlled by cadres. Clientelistic politics, he contends, can only flourish when cadres can monopolize access to scarce resources and opportunities involving a small number of households, as in the Maoist era. His findings also reveal that former cadres appear to enjoy no advantage in terms of managerial success. This suggests that human capital (e.g. professional skills and managerial competence) and the household labor force composition may be relatively more important.[58] In other words, productive effort and entrepreneurial drive, which are hardly monopolized by cadres, are at least as important as official support for entrepreneurial success. Positional power alone is not a sufficient condition for economic gain.

Nee also stresses the negative impact of state intervention on the development of rural entrepreneurship, contending that these administrative interventions in enterprise operation are fundamentally counter-productive to economic growth and efficiency. Inspired by Douglas North, he argues that predictability is crucial for economic success. The local state still has a role to play during economic transformation, but it should redefine its role to focus on the provision of subsistence guarantees and the maintenance of public works essential for economic growth. Arbitrary intervention simply reduces the predictability of economic activities and, without the possibility of calculating future profits, entrepreneurs will simply stay at home. Furthermore, the common practice of investing heavily in personal connections as a means of reducing uncertainty is an expensive exercise. This will ultimately result in higher total transaction costs.[59]

In short, Nee has put rural entrepreneurs, those endowed with management know-how, at center stage in local economic development, and his theory portrays a pattern of mutual dependence between state and society during the process of rural industrialization. For Nee, the growth-concerned local state should be more restrained in its involvement in TVE operation, and hence he suggests a scenario of more dynamic interaction between state and society.

However, Nee's teleological view that post-socialist societies are progressing toward a well-defined end – some clear or ideal type of market economy – is controversial. Although Nee does concede in his more recent works that there are multiple paths of transition from state socialism to market economy, and "the trajectories of transition are shaped by previous institutional forms and the politics of market,"[60] he still insists on the inevitability and necessity of progress toward a market economy. He argues that this is needed in order to overcome all the structural imbalances in the Chinese economy caused by the hybrid forms of market economy and that, "fundamentally, this entails putting private property rights on an equal basis with other ownership forms, creating legal norms and regulations – and means to enforce them – that protect private property rights, and making further progress in instituting a market-clearing price structure."[61] The present concern here is not the economic rationality of the market or whether socialism can still be a viable alternative, but the analytical limitations inherent in this market transition perspective. Szelenyi and Kostello accurately point out the shortcomings in Nee's implicit assumptions about the possibility of building capitalism by design and of measuring the "success" of transition by contrasting the development of the Chinese economy with a pure model of a market economy. They argue that this view "precludes making discoveries about possibly new social phenomena and reduces all such variation onto a single scale with socialism at one end and capitalism at the other."[62] In a similar vein, Lin argues that this transitional view, which focuses on the value end-state rather than on the forces that operate in the present and the immediate future in the shaping of both the on-going and emerging institutions, will simply exclude "the theoretical plausibility that these forces may indeed forge institutions that may not only persist and sustain into the future but also provide insights into alternative and viable socioeconomic systems other than a totally market economy."[63] Nee, in other words, fails to realize the possibility of different types of market development; for him, there is only a difference in development stages. The growing literature on the different forms of property rights arrangements during market transition in post-socialist countries, and their persistence, seems to suggest that different types of market development are possible.[64] Most important of all, this is, after all, a matter of empirical research rather than assumption. Transformation, rather than transition, appears to be a more informative perspective.

In addition, Nee's economic approach also fails to recognize the importance of the economic transformation process's political dimension. First, the implicit assumption, inherent in transition theory, of the compatibility between the macro-efficiency of market capitalism and micro-rationality in striving for its progress is problematic. That is, even if we accept that capitalism is the most efficient economic mechanism, this still does not justify assuming the automatic mobilization of individual economic actors for this cause. Such an assumption obscures the inquiry into the supply and demand for institutional change raised previously in the discussion. Decisions by individual economic actors are likely to be determined by the availability of resources and opportunities offered by the environment or potential changes in the environment, as well as by the power relations among the parties concerned.[65] Second, Nee's prediction of the declining value of political capital also obscures the complexity of the changing state–society relations during economic reform. It may be true that the redistributive power of officialdom is declining with the advent of market reform, but this does not imply that new sources of state power are impossible. Whether the bureaucracy can readjust its role as middleman, broker, adviser or coordinator by drawing on resources, influence and connections developed previously or by absorbing new skills, knowledge or talents through the co-option of new social interests, is, again, an empirical question that warrants more in-depth research.[66]

Oi's local state corporatism – dominance of the state

Oi's notion of local state corporatism is arguably the most important contribution to the understanding of the changing pattern of state–society relations in rural China during the reform period.[67] The local state, she argues, was responsible for the tremendous growth of rural industry in the reform era, and local state corporatism – a distinct form of state-led developmental strategy – was the momentum behind this success. According to this argument, the local state was highly motivated by the financial incentives unleashed by the financial decentralization process introduced in the post-Mao era. The local state treats enterprises within its administrative purviews as one component of a larger corporate whole and it "coordinates economic enterprises in its territory as if it were a diversified business corporation."[68] According to Oi, the local state is prepared and equipped to get a firm hold over local enterprises, and its intervention is beneficial rather than harmful for enterprise development. Instead, she suggests that administrative intervention has become indispensable to enterprise success. Thus, in terms of state–society relations, the dominance of the state at the rural grass-roots level has been strengthened and "contrary to expectations that the market reforms would shift power to producers, an independent economic elite has yet to emerge in China."[69]

The notion of local state corporatism advances the understanding of state–society relations in rural China on at least three counts. First, it recognizes the impact of the institutional legacy inherited from the Maoist system and shows how the interaction between state and society during the reform era was affected by the past. Second, it transcends the dichotomy of state versus society by suggesting the possible image of the local state as the champion of local interests. The local state in Oi's conception sees lobbying on behalf of local enterprises for bank loans, resources, and administrative services as part of its duty. This view goes beyond the narrow-minded conspiracy theories that tend to explain every state action as predation by a demonic entity.[70] Oi provides an appropriate perspective for comprehending the complicated pattern of interaction during the present stage of reform. Third, Oi's disaggregated approach in dealing with the role of the state also places us at a higher level of analysis. The local state is identified as an agency, which, though under the command of the central state, has its own different interests and agenda, and "the new institutional incentives increasingly encourage local officials to carry out their regulatory functions to maximize local rather than national interests."[71]

However, the intriguing phenomenon of the coexistence of a dominant local state and vibrant entrepreneurship has to be explained. For Oi, the question seems irrelevant. She argues, "for China the issue was not whether its bureaucracy is capable of generating economic growth but whether it had the incentive to do so."[72] For her, there is no inherent reason why only individuals, as distinct from the government, can be entrepreneurs, and the post-Mao reforms have created the incentive to unleash entrepreneurship from the local bureaucracy.

What Oi's notion of local state corporatism implies is an entrepreneurial developmental state which differs from the concept of the developmental state that is commonly employed in understanding the success of the East Asian states mentioned earlier. The concept of the developmental state, as with the concept of local state corporatism, rejects the notion of a diminution of state power at the advent of reform. However, Oi and other developmental state theorists differ in their views of where entrepreneurship is found and of the relationship of the enterprise to the state. Where there is local state corporatism, the state actually undertakes entrepreneurial activity and the autonomy enjoyed by the enterprise is minimal, whereas a developmental state is confined to the macro level of planning, coordination, and the provision of infrastructure.[73]

However, the question arises of whether incentives alone are sufficient to generate good entrepreneurship. The new imperative of financial independence no doubt provides the motivation as well as the pressure for the local bureaucracy to develop the local economy. However, it is doubtful whether these highly motivated cadres can successfully readjust to their new role as managers of profit-oriented ventures in a market economy. Compared with their fellow peasants, cadres are certainly better equipped for the new task of enterprise management in terms of literacy, exposure, connections, and organizing and social skills. However, an understanding of the operation of specific industries, technical knowledge of production, and, most important of all, an ability to innovate are hardly on the standard training program of local officials. If, as suggested by Oi, the imperative of concern for revenue is the dominant explanation for the redefined economic role of the local state in the new institutional setting, it is logical to suspect that the assignment of managerial posts in TVEs is likely to be determined by the ability to translate these assets into steady supply of revenues. In other words, although, as the representative of the collective interest, the local state can designate the managers of TVEs, it remains an empirical question whether cadres fill all the managerial posts in TVEs. Although several efforts have been made to analyze the background of managers in non-public enterprises in China, the collective sector is a relatively unexplored area.[74] This study attempts to explore this area.

The possibility of an alternative source of entrepreneurship exacerbates the intensity of the local state's possible dilemma in regulating TVEs – how to maintain its control over the local economy while managing to gain the benefit of the fully expressed entrepreneurship of TVE managers. Oi's argument stresses the beneficial character of administrative intervention and its role in the reduction of transaction costs (e.g. securing supply of scarce resources, bypassing red tape etc.). However, Nee's concern with the negative impact of the arbitrary nature of these measures, as raised earlier, is relevant here. It is hard to imagine that TVE managers, either cadres or non-cadres, would bother to take the risk of innovating or exploring new markets if they knew that there was a good chance that their share of rewards could be squeezed by arbitrary and unrestrained extortion or predation by the local state. Cadre managers are more likely to swallow their frustration, as their career in the bureaucracy is at stake. However, the possibility of the inclusion of non-cadre managers requires more in-depth analysis. How can the local state contain these new social actors, whose skills are important for local economic development? Alternately, is the rise of these non-cadre managers conducive to a readjustment by the local state in its involvement in local enterprises? These questions are crucial for understanding state–society relations in rural China. Unfortunately, these issues find no place in the framework of local state corporatism.

Leaping forward: TVE development in the 1990s

Another major deficiency of Oi's description is her static view of the dominant position of the local state. Based mainly on rural development in the 1980s and early 1990s, Oi's insightful observation on state dominance is valid for the infant stage of rural enterprise development, when most enterprises are small in size and operation is confined by local boundaries with limited integration into a larger market. However, as seen in the next chapter, TVEs in China have undergone tremendous development since the early 1990s. In addition to their growing contribution to the national economy, the average size and scale of operation has also increased dramatically. A brief review here may reveal the pace of TVE development over the last two decades (Table 1.1).

These changes entail a growing sophistication and professionalism for effective management of these business ventures, and, as argued in this study, the position of those who possess these managerial skills and experience is definitely on the rise in local communities. The size of enterprise does matter. Local cadres may feel comfortable in managing a small factory operating with simple technology, a modest budget, and dozens of workers. Yet, the sophistication and professional knowledge required to run a business venture targeting a market beyond the local area and operating with several hundred staff and an asset value and annual turnover of more than a million yuan is a different matter. The extent of information asymmetry between the principal (the local government) and the agent (the manager) has increased as the production process has become more technical and professional. The growing enmeshment of managers with the details of sophisticated operation works in their favor. If, as Oi argues, revenue is the primary motive for the local state's involvement in enterprise management, it is only logical to expect a pragmatic approach

Table 1.1   TVE development in China, 1985–98

Year	Number of enterprises (million)	Average number of staff	Average asset value ('000 yuan)	Average annual output ('000 yuan)	Average annual sales income ('000 yuan)
1985	1.57	26	50	130	120
1990	1.45	32	150	430	350
1991	1.44	33	180	540	460
1992	1.53	34	–	770	–
1993	1.69	34	–	1,020	–
1994	1.64	36	–	–	–
1995	1.62	37	560	–	1,980
1996	1.55	36	720	–	2,360
1997	1.29	41	970	3,390	2,940
1998	1.07	45	1,260	4,060	3,590

Sources: *Zhongguo Xiangzhen Qiye Nianjian* (*China's Rural Enterprise Yearbook*), 1978–87, p. 569; 1991, p. 133; 1992, pp. 133; 1993, pp. 142–3 and 147; 1994, pp. 151 and 169; 1995, pp. 87–9; 1996, pp. 99 and 101–3; 1997, pp. 121–3; 1998, pp. 107–12; and 1999, pp. 111–17.

by the local state in accommodating the rise of managerial talent as long as a steady supply of revenue is guaranteed. In other words, the state–manager relation is more a dynamic interaction between the two, which is contingent upon the level of development of these enterprises and the larger economic context. In short, a more dynamic perspective is needed for understanding the changing pattern of interaction.

The discussion on the rise of managers in capitalist economy merits a recapitulation here. One should, of course, be aware of the fundamental differences between socialist and capitalist order. Yet with the growing imperative of economic progress and market transformation inherent in reform China, the literature may still be relevant for our present concerns with the manager's role in economic development. There are two major arguments for the rise of managers under capitalism: growing functional indispensability and the gradual withdrawal of the owner from management. Burnham is among the pioneers in depicting these changes:

> There is a combined shift: through changes in the technique of production, the function of management has become more distinctive, more complex, more specialized, and more crucial to the whole process of production, thus serving to set off those who perform these functions as a separate group or class in society; and at the same time those who formerly carried out what functions there were of management, the bourgeoisie, themselves withdraw from management, so that the difference in function becomes also a difference in the individuals who carry out the function.[75]

According to Burnham, the rising importance of managers is reflected not only in terms of their preferential treatment in reward allocation, but, more crucially, they have also become indispensable. Owners maintain veto power, as they are entitled to dismiss rebellious managers. However, it is another manager, with parallel knowledge in production and management, who takes his place, and takes on power, responsibility, and privilege.[76] A simultaneous development is the withdrawal of owner participation. This may take the form of retreating from an active and direct role in operation, or of losing a controlling share of the corporation. Either way, managers are the beneficiaries in terms of control over the firm. And non-owning managers are seen as having displaced their capitalist predecessors in running the capitalist economy and society.[77] Parsons and Smesler go further to argue that the business families that once controlled ownership of most of the big businesses by and large failed to consolidate their positions as the dominant class in society.[78]

We should not be detained by the empirical controversy over the extent of the dilution of the capitalist class's corporate control,[79] or by the debate over how successfully the managerial class has displaced the bourgeoisie. What concern us here are the several possible hints for our present project of evaluating the role of managers in rural China. First, one should look beyond ownership patterns in analyzing dynamics in corporate management. Put into China's context, having the local state as a *de facto* owner of collective enterprise does not automatically imply its active and dominant control over enterprise operation. Second, knowledge of technical production and operation breeds access to managerial control. Growing sophistication in management and operation, attributed either to expansion of the scale of business or to technical changes, may entail delegation of power from owners to those with the know-how. The rapid expansion of TVEs in the post-Mao era mentioned above, in other words, fully justifies our speculation of the rising role of managers in rural China. And, lastly, the literature also points to the possible connection between changes in ownership structure and patterns of interaction within an enterprise. With the prevalence of the idea of shareholding reform among China's economists and policy makers, and its experimentation in rural enterprises in the 1990s, it seems reasonable to raise our query regarding the possible change of the enterprise manager's role.

The analytical strategy

The preceding review puts the analysis of the dynamics of state–society interaction in rural China into a new light. Three major lessons can be drawn from the above theoretical evaluation. First, the homogeneity of social interest cannot be taken for granted, and this makes the fundamental inquiry on the background and formation of specific social interest a prerequisite for any attempt to evaluate the state–society relationship. Second, the presumption of harmony between state agencies also needs to be reconsidered; the potential tensions and conflicts within the state must always be remembered. Third, and most important of all, what we must keep in mind, as highlighted in James Scott's latest work, is not only the role of society and its capacity "to modify, subvert and even overturn the categories imposed upon it [by the state],"[80] but also the engagement between the two. As stressed by Bates, the relationship between state and society is mutually constitutive. That is, the state helps to define societal interests and influences their formation and development; once consolidated, these interests exert considerable impact on subsequent state action.[81] The state is not necessarily always the predominant party dictating the pattern of interaction, as depicted by neo-statists, nor are these exchanges mostly driven by the state's concern with control over society. Most of all, these encounters are not, as projected by civil society theorists, inherently antagonistic in nature. Instead, economic reform may be conducive to a scenario in which both parties simply need each other to pursue their own ends. Such interaction and engagement should not simply be interpreted as retreat, or as the weakening of the state. Such social embeddedment, as Evans puts it, can be a possible way of strengthening the state's capacity to manage the economy.[82]

Drawing on the perspectives discussed above, the approach adopted in this inquiry will exhibit several features, which, this study argues, can add new knowledge to the discussion.

This research aims to do more than simply bring society back into the analysis of the changing state–society relationship in reforming China. It also intends to capture the dynamics of how the socialist state redefined its role during its heightened engagement with social interests in the reform era. The state may enjoy certain advantages in deciding the agenda and goals for the territory, yet social resistance or, in a less dramatic fashion, the incorporation of social interests into the organization of the state (changing composition of Party membership or people's representatives, commercialization of propaganda machinery, etc.) may change the ideological and moral character of the state. Engagement with society will certainly affect the formulation of goals.[83] Deregulation, which is designated as the path to prosperity, fundamentally rests on the success of unleashing the energy and enthusiasm of society toward the goals of modernization. However, this should not be seen simply as a retreat of state power in the state versus society dichotomy. Rather, it can be conceived as a "mutually empowering process"; whereas society is gaining a more active role in the public policy-making process, the state is also establishing a new basis on which to justify its authority:

> [T]he interaction of states and other social formations is a continuing process of transformation. States are not fixed entities, nor are societies; they both change structure, goals, constituencies, rules, and social control in their process of interaction. They are constantly *becoming*.[84]

The research implication of such a perspective is that one does not have to concentrate simply on the tensions between state and society, or on how the latter is empowered to challenge the former. Instead, a focus on how the two parties interact, accommodate, collaborate, and cooperate with each other can be equally illuminating.

The proposed approach of this study also draws attention to the diversity within the state organization. The view that the state is a homogeneous entity with a unifying degree of autonomy in relation to different social interests is simply not confirmed empirically.[85] The difference in performance reveals the simple fact that, at different points of the state organization, the pressures on state agencies and officials differ markedly, depending primarily on the resources under their command as well as on the resources of the social interests concerned in that particular policy arena. This relative strength affects the pattern of engagement between state and society and eventually the position of the state in that specific policy area. However, this is not the only pressure faced by specific state agencies; pressure from supervising units, which aim at ensuring compliance with the objectives and direction imposed by higher levels, and pressure from within – i.e. opinions of those in office – matter too. In other words, differences in position in the hierarchy, intensity of administrative control, line of command, the collective and individual histories and concerns, and relative strength in relation to relevant social interests are all likely to lead to differences in purpose, in insulation from external pressure, in *esprit de corps*, and in the responses of specific units performing their roles as state agencies. This approach, which disaggregates the state into various components and emphasizes the possible tension between levels of state administration and administrative units, provides a clearer picture of the interaction between state and society in the reform era.[86]

The new institutional setting implies new constraints, new incentives, and new opportunities, and the actors concerned must adjust to these new conditions in order to pursue their interests.[87] The analysis is fundamentally based on the belief that institutional change should lead to a modification in the behavior of the actors concerned and potentially to the emergence of a new pattern of interaction. Changes in specific characteristics of political and economic institutions (the demise of People's Communes, a new three-tier administrative framework, the decentralized financial arrangements, etc.) and in the overarching state structure (the movement from a socialist economy to a partially reformed market mechanism) are conducive to potential changes in the rural political scene. History matters, however. One should be aware of the thin line between institutional constraints and institutional determinism.[88] Action can be affected by changes in rules, but it is important not to assume that outcomes can simply be read off an institutional map, that actors are merely spectators to these changes, and that their actions are nothing more than knee-jerk responses to new stimuli. The problem with such a mechanical view is obvious: the same rule can have completely different effects and meanings in different socioeconomic conditions.[89] Among all possible variables, the factor of historical legacy will be emphasized in this study. The simple fact that China's reform is growing out of socialism appears to be commonly forgotten, yet it affects the functioning and impact of the aforementioned changes in the institutional setting in two important ways: in a legacy of Maoist institutions which may obstruct the full operation of the new changes or diffuse their impact and in the persistence of a pre-reform perspective, which is likely to affect actors' identification and assessment of opportunities and benefits.[90]

Contextualizing Zibo

This analysis is based on a case study of the rural industrialization of Zibo, a prefecture in Shandong province, in the post-Mao era (since 1978). This author made five visits to the prefecture between 1995 and 1998. Zibo prefecture is one of the most industrialized and developed cities in Shandong province. Situated about 100 kilometers from Jinan, the capital city of the province, it has a population of about four million. What is remarkable about the development of rural enterprises in this area is that, within less than two decades, these enterprises have already consolidated their position as the most important component of local industrial base. In other words, they are indispensable for local development.

The choice of case study as a research strategy was determined by the research agenda and by the nature of the information needed for the analysis. The qualitative case study approach was chosen for three reasons. First, the arguments raised earlier over the unevenness of state strength and the necessity of disaggregating the state organization in analysis justify a refined and focused approach. An extensive investigation of the political development of a single locality, which provides depth in analysis and flexibility in strategy, fits well with this requirement. Second, the unique strength of the case study approach in answering questions and puzzles is also particularly important for this project. This study aims to explore the prospect of a new pattern of state–society relations in reforming China, a historical juncture that, the study argues, leaves many questions unanswered. Rather than adopting a variable-oriented approach, which in most cases starts by specifying the relevant variables, matching them to theoretical concepts, and collecting information on these variables, the complexity and indeterminacy of the transformation process and, most important of all, the limited knowledge of the subject at hand warrant an alternative approach. The qualitative case study is the right tool for this purpose. Its flexibility provides more room for readjustment of the research strategy as new knowledge and questions emerge from the puzzle. Its unique strength in studying "a phenomenon within its real-life context when the boundaries between phenomenon and context are not clearly evident"[91] also makes it a desirable tool for capturing the dynamic development in rural China during the reform period. The depth provided by this research strategy and its permissible use of different methods – interviews, observations, and secondary materials – also makes it a good choice for an explorative study.[92] Third, the diverse pattern of development of rural enterprises across China also warrants a more refined focus.[93] The contrasting patterns denote variations in the basis of state–society interaction, and therefore separate studies for each of these variations are certainly desirable when trying to capture the dynamics of political change.

Zibo is a particularly interesting focus for a case study of change in reform China for several reasons. First, the growth of rural industries has been tremendous. Table 1.2 shows that rural industries in Zibo multiplied at a high speed, with an average annual growth rate of 38.7 percent from 1980 to 1994. The pattern is consistent with the national trend of rural enterprise development in China. Between 1990 and 1994, the average annual growth in industrial output by rural enterprises in China was 47 percent.[94] Second, these rural enterprises also become the engine of local industrialization. Except in 1980, the industrial growth of rural enterprises also exceeded the overall industrial growth of Zibo, with a huge margin during this period. As shown in Table 1.3, two-thirds of local industrial output was provided by the rural sector by 1994. Lastly, collective-owned enterprises maintain a dominant role in the rural economy in Zibo. Although collective enterprises at the township and village levels constituted about 12 percent of the total 87,766 rural enterprises in the prefecture, the collective sector contributed about two-thirds of the

Table 1.2 Industrial growth rate of rural enterprises in Zibo

Year	Industrial growth rate of rural enterprises (%)	Overall industrial growth rate in Zibo (%)
1980	2.8	5.3
1981	3.9	–0.6
1982	23.5	7.1
1983	32.5	10.0
1984	42.2	8.1
1987	41.1	28.6
1988	44.1	26.6
1989	31.1	22.4
1990	31.2	13.1
1991	33.6	17.6
1992	56.5	29.3
1993	91.2	45.9
1994	69.1	40.9

Source: calculated from data available in *Zibo Tongji Nianjian* (*Zibo Statistical Yearbook*), 1994, p. 85.

Table 1.3 Rural enterprise contribution to total industrial output in Zibo, 1980–94

Year	Total industrial output (A)	Industrial output by enterprises at township level or below (B)	(B)/(A) (%)
1980	6,359	440	6.9
1981	6,324	458	7.3
1982	6,770	566	8.4
1983	7,449	750	10.1
1984	8,056	1,067	13.2
1986	10,465	2,064	19.7
1987	13,453	2,919	21.7
1988	17,025	4,207	24.7
1989	20,845	5,518	26.5
1990	23,576	7,257	30.8
1991	27,727	9,694	35.0
1992	35,864	15,168	42.3
1993	52,337	28,993	55.4
1994	73,753	49,039	66.5

Source: *Zibo Tongji Nianjian* (*Zibo Statistical Yearbook*), 1994, p. 88.

Note
Units: million yuan (at 1990 fixed price).

total rural employment of 1.02 million, two-thirds of the total output value of seventy-seven billion yuan (current price) and two-thirds of the total income of sixty-one billion yuan in 1994.[95] The dominance of the collective sector is

Table 1.4 Composition of rural industrial output by ownership in Zibo, 1992–7

Year	Collective sector			Private sector
	Total	*Township enterprise*	*Village enterprise*	
1992	81.0	21.6	59.4	19.0
1993	85.4	20.6	64.8	14.6
1995	83.7	29.3	54.4	16.3
1996	82.0	28.0	54.0	18.1
1997	80.6	26.4	54.2	19.4

Sources: calculated from data available in *Zibo Tongji Nianjian* (*Zibo Statistical Yearbook*), 1993, pp. 74–5; 1994, pp. 50–1; 1996, pp. 52–3; 1997, pp. 48–9; and 1998, pp. 66–7.

Note
Figures rounded to the one decimal place. All values are percentages.

further illustrated in Table 1.4. In spite of the substantial growth of private enterprises in the countryside, collective enterprises at the township and village levels continued to provide more than 8 percent of the total industrial output in rural Zibo.

The differences in the patterns of rural enterprise development across China suggest the possibility of a contrasting political landscape in rural China. The dynamics of political change in each scenario can be remarkably different as a result of the peculiar constellation of actors involved in each pattern. The possible inclusion of overseas investors and private entrepreneurs implies a different mix of challenges for the local administrations concerned. The relative strength of economic sectors of differing ownership, the differential in the availability of leverage and policy instruments, and the distinctive policy framework determined by the central state toward different non-state actors, will all affect the process of role redefinition for the local state with the advent of economic reforms. Observations in Zibo represent a story of political development of a locality exhibiting the distinctive features of the dominance of the local state in local economic development. Its initial points of development with an evident collective presence and legacy may not be identical to all development patterns found across rural China, but surely it is more in line with the most common scenario,[96] in which rural industrialization took off with a strong collective component and with heavy involvement of the local state. Localities with contrasting economic, and hence political, constellations may experience different complications in the negotiation process and mutual adjustment between local state and economic actors, but the Zibo lesson should also be relevant for them as it sheds new light on how local state responds to the rise of new economic actors and new requirements for effective governance – common challenges inherent in the process of economic transformation.

Key arguments

Three major lessons can be drawn from the Zibo case.

Rise of rural managers

First, into the 1990s, the rising economic importance of business ventures implies that those with the know-how to convert these resources into a steady flow of revenue and income are likely to become the most wanted personnel in the local community. Thus, it is reasonable to expect that rural managers – persons in charge of these business entities – will gain influence in the economic realm as well as in local politics. Toward the end of the twentieth century, the rapid development of rural enterprises and the changes in macroeconomic setting and national policies led to a different pattern of state–enterprise interaction, as portrayed by Oi's notion of local state corporatism. Local officials may be better equipped in terms of literacy, exposure, social and organizing skills, and connections, yet good managership requires more. Knowledge of specific industries, technical know-how, and an ability to comprehend the economic logic of business are hardly the credentials of ordinary officials. Non-political variables are likely to be as important as political factors in making a good enterprise manager, and this points to the possibility of an alternative path to power. In short, TVE managers, who have been neglected in previous analyses of rural development of China, are rising in the rural political and economic order and are having a growing impact on state–society relations in the reform era.

A symbiotic and particularistic relationship

The rise of new social interests is, however, not necessarily conducive to heightened tension between state and society. In the case of rural entrepreneurs, several distinctive features of the context for rural business may suggest the possibility of a different scenario. The local state finds managers indispensable because they are the ones who turn idle assets into a stream of income. Yet the absence of full marketization and the institutional legacy of a market-unfriendly framework inherited from the Maoist era imply that the local state's support is still necessary for reducing transaction costs for rural business. In other words, they are in a state of interdependence, and neither is yet able to get rid of the other and to grasp the whole cake. In addition, the relationship between the local state and managers remains particularistic in nature. That is, the local state adjusts its position toward individual managers according to the contribution that each makes. Autonomy in enterprise management and operation, income, and even a manager's political influence in the local community are all proportional to a particular manager's performance in delivering economic goods. The internal diversity among managers reduces their potential as collective actors.

The possibility of unorthodox economic arrangements

The intimate relationship between this new social interest and the local state affects the prospects for reform. Both the distinct opportunities and incentive structures inherent in this unique mutual dependence and the common concern with immediate, local, interests affect the cost–benefit analysis of the desirability of specific reform proposals. Proposals expected to bring macro-improvements may or may not be compatible with local actors' calculations, and the enthusiasm of empowered social interests toward further reform cannot be taken for granted. As a result of the pursuit of sectional interests, unorthodox economic arrangements may emerge and may even exhibit strong tenacity and vitality. The ultimate outcome hinges upon the interaction between the past and the present. The legacy of socialism and the demand for market reform exert contrasting pressure on the shaping of the new order. Trapped in the middle of the storm, the parties concerned – the local administrations, the central leadership, the managers, and the rural populations – are all readjusting their calculations and strategies in order to maximize their gains from the opportunities available. This is a historical juncture full of institutional possibilities, and the future is all but determined.

Structure of the book

The rest of the book will be divided into seven chapters. Chapter 2 starts with a further elaboration of the institutional context in rural China. The changes introduced in the post-Mao period will be discussed and evaluated, with recognition of the impact of the legacy of the Mao era. The basic political and economic outlook of Zibo on the eve of reform will also be provided. This should provide a clear picture of the institutional and historical context of the political interaction between state and society in Zibo, as well as rural China, during the reform era.

Chapter 3 focuses on an important issue: who the enterprise managers are. The major arguments here are that political capital alone cannot account for all managerial appointments and that the revenue imperative of the local state necessitates the accommodation of non-cadre personnel. A new social force has emerged which is asserting its presence in the local political and economic order simply by making itself functionally indispensable.

Chapters 4 and 5 examine the conditions of interdependence between managers and the local state. The former concentrates on the external business transactions of local enterprises and the latter centers on internal enterprise management. The discussion will reveal the dilemmas faced by managers and the local state. Though managers are torn between their desire for personal gain and autonomy and the need to maintain the crucial official support for reducing transaction costs, the local state is hard pressed by the need to unleash entrepreneurism from managers and by its anxiety over maintaining both control and a proper balance between the conflicting claims on enterprise resources. Consequently, interdependence between the two parties has developed, which is supported by the sanctions available to both parties. The impact of economic reform, or the lack of it, the historical legacy, and the rising influence of managers are all clearly explained in the evaluation.

Chapters 6 and 7, focusing on the implementation of shareholding reform in rural China, further explore the rising role of enterprise managers and the complexity inherent in the redefinition of the state's role in the process of market reform. The interdependence between managers and the local state continues to affect the progress of reform. Chapter 6 provides a general picture of the shareholding reform of enterprises and evaluates its theoretical attractions, and Chapter 7 discusses its implementation. It demonstrates how even a compromise situation – the cooperative shareholding scheme – has been distorted. Local interests have hijacked the whole process and twisted it to suit their needs. State–manager relations remain basically unchanged despite change in the formal organizational structure. This analysis ends with Chapter 8, in which the theoretical issues are re-examined and evaluated. It ends with a discussion of the prospects for the political future of China and how further inquiry can proceed.

2 Transformation in a historical perspective

Rural China has witnessed tremendous changes in its economic and political institutions in the post-Mao period. The collective framework of People's Communes has gone and has been replaced by a new three-tiered administrative structure and a new economic setting dominated by household farms. As discussed in Chapter 1, changes in the institutional setting provided new incentives and opportunities, and the consequent mushrooming of rural enterprises in the countryside is the most forceful evidence supporting this argument. New resources unleashed by the advent of rural reforms and the new incentives inherent in financial decentralization stimulate the local administration to promote the growth of these business ventures. Nonetheless, the preceding discussion has also recognized the importance of history's impact on institutional change. In the case of rural China, although the growing importance of non-farming activities and the new administrative and economic structures represent a departure from the pre-reform rural setting, certain continuities persist. Consequently, the pattern of rural enterprise development exhibits a strong localistic and parochial tendency. This chapter aims to provide a background for understanding the state–managers interaction in the rural context by analyzing the combined effect of these continuities and discontinuities.

The discussion will start with an evaluation of the changes in the economic and political realms in rural China in the aftermath of the demise of the People's Commune. In the economic realm, the discussion will focus on the consequences of the demise of the collective framework of economic management and the introduction of the household responsibility system. On the political side, however, the main concerns will be the implications of the new three-tier administrative structure and the impact of financial decentralization on the local administration. These changes account for the expansion of rural enterprise in post-Mao China. However, as pointed out above, these continuities can only be comprehended by recognizing their connection with the past. The discussion will provide a historical perspective on the development of rural enterprise by presenting a brief review of its development in the pre-reform era. In addition, it will go on to argue for the persistence of certain features of the local political economy. The inheritance of an industrial foundation from

Mao's economy, the intimacy between the local state and local community in the rural context, and the impact of decades of economic planning have all continued to influence the pattern of interaction between state and society, despite the changes. There will then follow a discussion of how the combined effects of the continuities and discontinuities contribute to the concrete context for the development of rural enterprise in the reform era. This chapter will end with a depiction of Zibo's economic landscape on the eve of reform, vividly displaying its tradition of industrial development and the solid foundation of rural industries the prefecture inherited by the mid-1980s.

Changes in the institutional setting

Dissolution of the People's Commune

The People's Commune epitomizes the political ideals of Mao Zedong. His obsession with egalitarianism and self-reliance, and his faith in volunteerism and mobilization, led him to advocate this unique collective framework. For Mao, the establishment of the People's Commune was more than a personal political triumph. It was also an important move in eradicating the problems of socialist China, which was still in its infancy: the inequalities between city and countryside, mental and manual labor, and workers and peasants.[1] The three-tier structure of the People's Commune – the commune level at the top, the production brigade in the middle, and the production team at the bottom – became the administrative framework throughout rural China from 1958 until the advent of economic reform in the post-Mao era.[2] Under the People's Commune system, all aspects of the production and distribution of the rural economy were monopolized by this umbrella collective organization. For Mao, this was the key to achieving an egalitarian society. By subjugating the individual into a larger unit and assigning all means of production to this entity, the inequalities stemming from differences in endowment, skill, or other factors could be eliminated. Within the basic accounting unit, income was distributed according to work points earned, which should theoretically have been in line with the principle of "to each according to his work," and hence a more equitable form of distribution.[3]

However, soon after Mao's death, the People's Commune began to decay. Under the pragmatic leadership of Deng Xiaoping, the improvement of the rural economy was the top priority. The immediate objective of rural economic policy in 1979 was to ensure an increase in agricultural production and to eliminate features of egalitarianism – a fundamental tenet of Mao's rural policy.[4] The new economic philosophy, in essence, stressed the importance of material incentives and producer's autonomy. By 1984, People's Communes, which once numbered as many as 26,000, were reduced to fewer than 250.[5] A new economic and administrative framework had emerged in the countryside.

The return of material incentives

In short, a decentralized regime with the primacy of producers' autonomy and an emphasis on material incentives has emerged in the countryside in the post-Mao era. The introduction of the household responsibility system, the abolition of the state procurement system, and a greater role for the price mechanism are the major tenets of the new economic regime.

It may be misleading to describe the innovation of the household responsibility system as a policy of the Chinese state, for the latter is, and generally has been, passive in this matter. The household responsibility system was, rather, a result of numerous spontaneous efforts by local cadres and peasants across the country, trying to reverse the dire state of agricultural production. As Kate Zhou argues, "throughout the whole process, farmers' action preceded the state's reformist agenda."[6] Peasants all over the countryside who were bordering on the subsistence level took the initiative in addressing the problem of poor agricultural productivity. Despite the variations in actual arrangements, a common theme of relating payment to production as directly as possible was evident. Among these diverse experiments, the household responsibility system appeared to be the most popular option. Because of their success, these experiments gathered momentum throughout the countryside, spreading like wildfire in the early years of the post-Mao period, when signals of political pragmatism were observable. By 1984, they were adopted virtually everywhere in the countryside[7] and finally won the full endorsement of the Party.[8] According to Khan:

> [T]he essence of the responsibility system is the contract that the team – the "owner" of land, major capital equipment and large livestock – enters into with groups, individuals and households. The contract specifies a target output. Arrangements vary with respect to the distribution of output (both target and above target), degree of access to land by contractor and various other features of the contract.[9]

In contrast to the collective framework of the People's Commune, the household responsibility system entitled households to comprehensive access to and control over a given amount of land, and autonomy in the production process. There was no more calculation of work points or rationing of food. After the fulfillment of the target output agreed upon in the contract and the payment of specified levies, households retained the remaining output. Peasants were now free to allocate their incomes and decide their work schedules. They could also choose the most effective mix of household economic activities that they thought would bring about the fullest utilization of their resources. These were all luxuries seldom enjoyed under the previous system.

Another significant change in the late 1970s was the increase in procurement prices for agricultural products. In Mao's China, procurement prices were deliberately held at a low level in order to support the urban sector.

The rural sector was both a supplier of cheap raw materials and foodstuffs and a dumping ground for inferior consumer goods from urban industries. Peasants who were imprisoned in the collective framework had no alternative but to sell their products under this arrangement, as private markets, with few exceptions, had disappeared in rural China. This trend was reversed in the post-Mao period. In addition, as part of the policy package to revitalize agricultural production, state procurement prices for agricultural products also increased sharply during 1978–82. The purchase prices for the principal agricultural products rose by 50–100 percent during this period, and in 1978–80 alone such increases enabled peasants to enjoy an additional net income of forty-six billion yuan.[10]

The financial implications of this price readjustment were significant. Constrained by their concern for maintaining low inflation in the urban area, the central treasury had to bear the full financial burden incurred by the increase in procurement prices of agricultural products. In 1978, the total bill for the financial subsidy on the prices of grain, cotton, and edibles was only 1.1 billion yuan; however, by 1984, the figure had increased to 20.2 billion yuan.[11] This unintended consequence contributed to another major reform in the rural economic order – the abolition of the state procurement system. The state now signs a contract with the individual household that specifies how much the household will sell to the state at an agreed price. In return, the household will be provided with chemical fertilizers and diesel oil at subsidized prices. The disposal of any amount above the target will be at the discretion of the household; it can choose to sell it on the market, a once forbidden activity that is now permitted. A new economic philosophy has emerged in the countryside, as noticed by Walker:

> [U]nlike the production team, the household was inevitably concerned with maximizing profits. Hence costs and prices were now central to decision-making and for the first time peasants had to consider what quality and quantity of different crops could be sold at what price.[12]

Administrative restructuring

As the household responsibility system and the other market-oriented inno-vations mentioned above gathered momentum and became an irreversible trend, the compatibility between the old administrative framework and the new ethos was apparent. The new approach in rural economic management, which stressed economic laws and incentives instead of coercive administrative means, exposed the damaging effects of excessive administrative intervention in production, management, and distribution. The People's Commune system was a multifunctional organization, responsible for local administration, Party affairs, social welfare, public security, militia training, economic planning and management, culture, communications, and investment.[13] The separation of government administration from economic management was now deemed desirable. The central Party leadership endorsed the idea, and the new constitution of the People's Republic of China (PRC), passed in 1982, stipulated the reinstatement of township governments and stripped the communes of all political, administrative, and non-economic powers. Within a few years, People's Communes had almost completely disappeared in the countryside. Consequently, a new rural administrative structure – a township government-centered system aimed at achieving a higher degree of separation between government and economy and endowed with a greater financial independence – developed in rural China.

Township government (*xiangzhen zhengfu*) was re-established with the intention of separating the Party (*dang*), the government (*zheng*), and the economy (*jing*). The People's Commune was replaced by the township Party committee, the township people's government, and the township economic commission (*jingji weiyuanhui*) or economic and trade commission (*jingji maoyi weiyuhui*). At the same time, the production brigade was replaced by the village branch of the township Party committee, the villagers' committee (*cunmin weiyuanhui*), and the village economic co-operative (*cun jingji hezuoshe*). The township government supervised the villagers' committee, and the township economic commission supervised the village economic co-operative. In turn, the township organizations reported to and were supervised by their counterparts at county level. In principle, a clear division of labor was established: Party organizations concentrated on Party and political affairs, government was responsible for civil administration and other social development, and economic organizations were primarily concerned with the management of collectively owned business activities, such as enterprises.[14]

Financial decentralization

Another fundamental change in rural administration was the new element of financial independence instilled into the township administration. This was a dramatic departure from the centralized public finance system practiced in the pre-reform era. Under the old system of "uniform income and outlay," except for some local taxes and a few small income items that could be retained by local governments to offset certain expenditures, all incomes were centralized in the central government. The same applied on the expenditure side: all expenditures of local government had to be included in the budget and had to be approved by and reported to the central government.[15]

The post-Mao Party leadership had a different view on the appropriate financial arrangements between levels of the administration. In essence, financial decentralization was launched, benefiting the township administrations significantly. The responsibility for finance and tax planning and administration was extended to the township level in 1984. Under the new arrangement, township governments were permitted to keep and spend a portion of the total revenues they collected for the county government. The exact amount that could be retained by the township government was determined by another innovation – the fiscal contracting system (*caizheng baogan*). Under the system of fiscal contracting, a contract was signed between different levels of the administration. According to the contract, the former agreed to pay the latter either a fixed percentage of the tax collected or a set amount of tax revenue. In either case, the township government retained all, or at least the bulk of, the remaining tax.[16] This change provided a great incentive and a potential source of revenue for developing the local economy. Not only did this change provide a source of finances necessary for the effective functioning of the local administration, but it also enabled the local government to enjoy a share of the fruits of local economic prosperity, hence providing a greater incentive to promote local economic growth. This remained the dominant practice across the countryside until the extension of tax assignment reform in the late 1990s.

New challenges for rural governance

The changes in the post-Mao period described above confirmed the township administration as a key force in the process of rural governance in China. However, compared with its predecessor, the People's Commune, the township administration faced the much more complicated task of local governance. The emergence of thousands of autonomous producers, the deprivation of conventional policy leverage, and the pressure of financial self-reliance all made the task of rural governance under the reform ethos more difficult. The development of rural enterprises was a logical means for helping the local administrators out of their predicament by utilizing the resources unleashed by the new setting.

One immediate consequence of the changes in rural administration in the post-commune era was the changing composition of the rural polity. For the newly established township government, the target of governance was no longer a handful of production brigades; instead it now faced tens of thousands of rural households with diverse economic interests. According to one estimate, an average commune had 13.5 production brigades,[17] but by 1985 an average township government had to rule over 4,800 rural households.[18] Under the People's Commune system, local economic management was mainly a matter of bargaining and negotiating between communes and brigades; the response of individual households hardly bothered the former. However, in the post-Mao era, the township administration had to make sure that individual households, which had regained their productive autonomy, were moving in line with its vision of local economic development. Households' economic decisions, which were to a large extent independent from that of the township administration, had to be reckoned with in the process of local economic management.

The difficulty of governing was further complicated by the growing diversity of the rural economy in the reform period. This was reflected in the dramatic change in the mix of production activities in the countryside in the post-Mao period. Over the period 1978–87, the percentage of the output value of farming activities in terms of total agricultural output dropped from 76.7 percent to 60.7 percent.[19] An even more fundamental change was the overall decline in the importance of agricultural production in the rural economy. It declined from 68.6 percent in 1978 to 46.1 percent in 1990.[20] Clearly, a more profit-oriented and diversified economy had emerged. For the township administration, it meant that a more sophisticated approach to local economic management would be required. As pointed out by Blecher and Shue, the reform unleashed "spiraling demands of administering, regulating, and planning a swiftly growing economy and a society that was increasingly on the move," and the work of rural administration became "more detailed, intense, specialized, and technically sophisticated and demanding."[21] Worse still, unlike previously, when there had been an array of mobilizing and ideological weapons available, the new ethos and economic setting had rendered a top-down definition of "public interest," the imposition of which was a very difficult task. In short, the new institutional setting deprived the township government of many of the policy instruments its predecessor had enjoyed. Kojima has given a vivid description of the situation:

> In the past the government could move agriculture in the direction it desired by applying direct controls to both production and distribution processes. This was done through issuing command-type directives to the production teams through the two processes. The government, however, could no longer maintain a grip over these processes and had to allow greater freedom in two ways. First, it had to relax controls over the direct production process and to shift controls over distribution of farm produce. Secondly, it had to relax its control over distribution too and allow the rise of a market economy.[22]

Under the new circumstances, cadres at the rural grass roots found it more and more difficult and frustrating to carry out their jobs.[23]

In addition, the new financial system of fiscal contracting, which provided a strengthened connection between the revenues and expenditure of local governments, was a double-edged sword. Under this new financial regime, the simple principle was "the more you collect the more you spend, the less you collect the less you spend" (*duoshou douzhi, xiaoshou xiaozhi*). This created pressure for financial self-sufficiency. By giving local administrations a share of local revenues, the central government hoped that the local administrations at the rural grass-roots level would become more enthusiastic toward tax collection, and that this would improve the financial position of the central treasury. However, for local administrators, "rely on yourself to balance your accounts" (*zilai pingheng*) was the other side of the coin.[24] Local administrations were asked to balance their own budget and, with few exceptions, no extra subsidy would be provided for deficits. Worse still, the central state's intention to minimize its financial burden did not come with a parallel decrease in the responsibilities imposed on local administrations. Local governments at the rural grass-roots level were under pressure to meet the targets of public service provision imposed by the higher tiers of government, but seldom were they provided the necessary funds to achieve these targets. To further the pressure, local administrations were evaluated and judged on the basis of their fulfillment of these targets.[25] Thus, local governments at the lower levels, such as county and township levels, were under great pressure to levy additional fees on the local community to fund the mandates. The regular news reports on the conflicts between peasants and local governments over fiscal predation were clear indicators of the weight of the financial burden on the rural population.[26] In other words, the new financial structure presented a challenge as well as an opportunity for the local state.

In short, the local state in the countryside during the post-Mao period was confronted with a series of new challenges. Its immediate task was to maintain the governability of the local community with its tiny resources. Faced with the growing resourcefulness and autonomy of the local population, and the new challenges inherent in the new financial regime and the advent of market-oriented reform, new resources had to be explored in order to maintain control over the local polity. In the new age of materialism, a new base of economic power would be key. The development of rural enterprise appeared to be the answer. As the following will illustrate, though these challenges provided a push for action, the resources unleashed by the changes mentioned above and the unique budgetary structure of township finance emerged as a strong pull for this development strategy. As a result of the combination of these forces, the development of rural enterprises gathered strong momentum in rural China.

Development of rural enterprises as a response to challenges

As a result of the post-Mao changes, more and more of the resources crucial to the development of rural enterprise became abundant in the countryside. Among these were capital, labor, and land. First, partly because of the increase in procurement prices and partly as a result of the growth of agricultural production, peasants' incomes increased significantly after 1978. From 1978 to 1985, peasants' average per capita income in China increased from 134 yuan to 398 yuan, an increase of 197 percent.[27] There has been phenomenal growth in rural savings in the post-Mao years – a sixty-four-fold increase between 1978 and 1993. The total amount of rural savings increased from less than six billion yuan to 358 billion yuan during this period.[28] Evidently, the availability of surplus capital provided a fertile ground for developing rural industries, and bank loans turned out to be a crucial source of capital for the growth of rural enterprises. For example, in 1994, rural enterprises received more than half of the total loans released by the rural credit co-operative.[29]

Surplus labor unleashed by the household responsibility system also provided a source of cheap labor for rural enterprise development. As land was now contracted to the household, it did not matter whether or not all members were engaged in agricultural production, as long as the target output was met. Peasants could choose to work in a factory nearby if they wanted. However, this also implies that the burden of supporting redundant labor had now shifted back to the individual household. In other words, the issue of hidden unemployment, which had been covered under the collective framework, was now exposed. The implication for peasant households was that unemployed family members had to find a job if the household's standard of living was not to be adversely affected. As a result, employment in rural industries was a convenient option.

Last but not least, the household's resumption of the right to use land was also favorable for rural industrialization. The encouragement of diversification and sideline production triggered a shift of land to industrial use. Peasants who were now no longer interested in engaging in farming activities, or were finding it less rewarding, were tempted to explore alternatives for cashing in on their land use rights. Legal or not, more and more land was transferred to rural enterprises. From 1970 to 1984, about fifty-five million rural residents entered the new sector, which occupied a total of thirty million *mu* of arable land. Arable land was reduced by a further fifteen million *mu*[30] in 1985, more than half of which was taken up by rural enterprises.[31]

The new fiscal contracting system provided the local administration with a share of local revenues, an extra incentive to develop the local economy. More specifically, township government could now enjoy several sources of income through the development of rural enterprises. First, the township government would get a share of all tax revenues paid by enterprises. In the case of collectively owned enterprises, two extra sources of income could be extracted, both of which fell under the category of discretionary revenues in township finances. Township governments were also entitled to a portion of the management fees collected from collective enterprises, a levy imposed on these enterprises for its provision of administrative services. In addition, these enterprises had to submit their profit to their administrative supervisors, the township governments, though the exact amount was negotiable.

The desirability of developing local enterprises was further reinforced by the unique structure of local revenues. The revenue of township government falls into two categories: budgetary and extra-budgetary. The former refers mainly to the township's retained portion of the tax revenues collected in the area. The township government had control over disbursement of this retained portion, but these revenues were part of the state budgetary system, making their use subject to the supervision of the government's fiscal system. These revenues were generally used for specified purposes such as state employees' salaries or administrative expenses. Extra-budgetary revenue, on the other hand, was usually generated by the business operations of township government or by levies imposed on peasants or enterprises. Such funds remained a separate account under the control of the township government. Until further fiscal reforms in the mid-1990s, these revenues were immune from budgetary supervision, so the township government had more freedom of usage.[32]

Consequently, rampant development of rural enterprises was evident in post-Mao China. The dramatic growth is clearly presented in Table 2.1. Within less than two decades, there was tremendous growth in terms of number of enterprises, employment, and output value. Non-agricultural economic activities emerged as an indispensable component of the rural economy. Private initiative played a significant part in this progress, but the contribution of the collective is evident.

For rural administrations, the economic benefits brought by the rapid development of rural enterprises has been enormous. Hundreds of billions of yuan are produced by these new economic ventures every year. Rural enterprises have, in fact, become the most important source of economic value in the rural sector. In 1992, the total value of agricultural output constituted only 35.8 percent of the total rural output value,[33] and, on average, more than fifteen billion yuan of the income generated by these rural enterprises has been used to subsidize local investment in infrastructure, welfare and agricultural production in the rural area every year.[34]

In addition, rural enterprises have also become an important source of employment for local residents. At the national level, this represents a way of diverting the pressure from the urban sector. Locally, it also helps to reduce domestic employment pressure. Since 1984, new rural ventures have made a significant contribution in this direction. By 1994, these business ventures in

Table 2.1 Growth of rural enterprises in China, 1978–98

Year	Number of enterprises (million units)	Number of workers employed (million persons)	Output value (billion yuan)
1978	1.52 (1.52)	28.26 (28.26)	49.31 (49.31)
1980	1.43 (1.43)	30.00 (30.00)	65.69 (65.69)
1984	6.07 (1.86)	52.08 (38.82)	170.10 (146.6)
1986	15.15 (1.73)	79.37 (45.41)	354.09 (251.7)
1987	17.50 (1.58)	88.05 (47.19)	476.43 (323.8)
1988	18.88 (1.59)	95.46 (48.94)	649.57 (436.3)
1989	18.69 (1.54)	93.67 (47.21)	742.84 (485.6)
1990	18.50 (1.45)	92.65 (45.92)	846.16 (542.9)
1991	19.08 (1.44)	96.09 (47.67)	1,162.17 (772.0)
1992	20.79 (1.53)	105.81 (51.50)	1,797.54 (1,210.0)
1993	24.53 (1.69)	123.45 (57.68)	3,154.07 (2,036.1)
1994	24.95 (1.64)	120.18 (58.99)	4,258.85 (2,886.6)
1998	20.04 (1.07)	125.37 (48.27)	9,669.37 (4,329.8)

Sources: *Zhongguo Tongji Nianjian (China's Statistical Yearbook)*, 1995, pp. 363–5; *Zhongguo Xiangzhen Qiye Nianjian (China's Rural Enterprise Yearbook)*, 1999, p. 111.

Note
Information in parentheses indicates the contribution made by TVEs.

the countryside had already absorbed more than 120 million peasants, more than a quarter of the total rural labor force.[35] "Leaving agriculture but not the soil" (*litu bu lixiang*), i.e. the absorption of surplus rural labor into local non-agricultural enterprises in the countryside, is regarded by policy advisers in China as one of the possible options to halt the outflow of the rural population.[36]

Even more important for local administrations is the enormous revenue generated by the rapid growth of rural enterprises; the direct financial contribution of rural enterprises to local administration has also been tremendous. According to Wong *et al.*, rural enterprises are:

> by far the dominant source of revenue in the rural PRC. In 1990, they paid 27.55 billion yuan in taxes, more than three times the total agricultural tax of 8.8 billion yuan. Their 1989 tax payment of 27.55 billion yuan accounted for 37 percent of all fiscal revenues at and below the county level.[37]

In 1993, extra-budgetary income constituted about a quarter of the total revenue available at the township level, of which income extracted from rural enterprises was a major component.[38] In short, wealth generated by rural enterprises has become a crucial supplement for local finance.

The development of rural enterprises provided a new source of resources for the local administration. The pressure of financial self-reliance and the revenue incentive motivated the local state to encourage the development, and the new economic environment and the resources unleashed by the demise of People's Communes presented the opportunity and means. Together, all these factors contributed to the rapid development of rural enterprises in post-Mao China. Rural enterprises are now an indispensable component of the rural economy of China. For local administrators at the rural grass roots in China, the question of how to maintain the vitality of these business ventures, particularly the collective enterprises under its immediate control, is high on the agenda. The enterprise operators, the managers, are key to the process. As will be seen later, their technical skills, knowledge of the industry, managerial experience, and, most important of all, their entrepreneurial drive have made them functionally indispensable to the local economic dynamism and have earned them a strategic position in the local economic and political hierarchy. A new landscape has evolved in the rural economy, which implies a new power configuration and a new pattern of interaction between the local state and social interests.

Institutional legacies of Mao's economy

Nonetheless, notwithstanding the changes, one can only comprehend these departures by recognizing the continuity of the past. That is, despite the dramatic changes in the political and economic order in rural China, the changing state–society relation in the countryside in the reform period is still affected by several enduring features of the Mao era. It is the combination of these new and old elements which contextualizes the changing state–society relations; neither one of them alone can sufficiently account for the new power pattern in rural China in the post-Mao period.

Three features of the rural political economy in the pre-reform period are particularly noteworthy. These are the legacy of Mao's rural industrialization, the impact of economic planning, and the vulnerability of the rural administration to local pressure. These factors are important as they continue to impact economic management in the countryside, and all contribute to one distinct feature which underlies state–enterprise relations in rural China: *the communal nature of rural enterprise development*. This parochial and localistic characteristic has a fundamental impact on the pattern of interaction between the local state and enterprises.

Industrial inheritance from Mao's China

It is important to realize that the tremendous development of rural enterprise in the post-Mao period was built on the substantial foundation established by the rural industrialization effort in the pre-reform period. Mao's guiding principle of developing rural industry by relying on local resources and technology, and by aiming to serve the local community, has had a significant impact on the development of rural enterprise in the post-Mao era. There is a pool of skills and development experience, but the paternalism of the local state and localism in local economic management are also part of the inheritance.

According to one estimate, in the early 1950s, there were about twelve million Chinese in the countryside engaged in small-scale, non-mechanized industrial production, either on a full-time basis or as a sideline.[39] Nevertheless, these non-agricultural activities were all collectivized in the mid-1950s during the first Five Year Plan period. In 1958, they were transformed into commune-brigade enterprises (*shedui qiye*, CBEs) when the new collective framework of People's Communes was in place.[40] The Great Leap Forward (GLF) of 1958–60 provided further momentum for this new sector.

The impetus came from Mao Zedong. Mao's stress on local initiatives in economic development and management, and his belief in the possibility of the simultaneous development of agriculture and industry – the development strategy of "walking on two legs" – provided the momentum for rural industrialization.[41] These newly established CBEs were to be developed according to the principle of self-reliance; communes had to rely on their own resources. They had to use indigenous technology and local raw materials. Moreover, processing, as well as marketing, of the products was to be confined to the local area too. In addition to its primary function of serving agriculture, rural industrial development was also to serve the daily needs of local consumers. Mao hoped that this strategy could reduce the demand for resources by agricultural development and provide an alternative source of consumer goods and, at the same time, contribute to the nation's industrialization program with minimal impact on the urban sector.[42] Consequently, in the face of the powerful drive from the top, the number of rural enterprises increased significantly, though many of these were no more than workshops or sheds.

Whether Mao's economic aims were achieved is debatable,[43] but, in terms of output volume, the development of these industries was significant. By the late 1970s, a huge rural industrial capacity had been developed, which accounted for almost one-third of the total output of steel and iron, two-thirds of cement, and more than half of the nitrogenous and phosphorous fertilizer production in the country.[44] On the eve of rural reform in the post-Mao period, as seen in Table 2.1, there already existed a substantial number of rural enterprises in the countryside. This inheritance has three major implications.

First, it implies that a substantial number of rural residents have been involved in non-farming economic activities, or even industrial management, since the collective era, and by the time that rural enterprises were taking off in the mid-1980s much of the rural population, cadres and non-cadres alike, had already accumulated considerable knowledge and skills in enterprise management. They were better equipped to take on the challenge of managing an enterprise than fellow peasants with no such exposure. As will be seen in Chapter 3, this accounted for the prevalence of enterprise managers with non-cadre backgrounds in the reform era, and it also had a tremendous impact on the relationship between the local state and enterprise managers.

Second, it also contributed to the persistence of local state dominance over enterprise management in the reform era. In theory, the people owned CBEs in the local community; however, in practice, the local state was the owner. It maintained absolute control over the operation, the allocation of resources, and the development of CBEs. The intimacy between local state and enterprises is clearly demonstrated by the financial linkage between the two. In the early 1980s, for China as a whole, incomes generated by CBEs constituted roughly one-third of the total income of all communes.[45] It is hardly surprising to see the persistence of a paternalistic mindset among local administrators in rural China in the reform era, particularly in their handling of the relationship with collective enterprises.

Last but not least, the parochial tendencies of enterprise development inherited from the pre-reform legacy are also noteworthy. Despite the prevalent view that parochialism and an inward-looking orientation is an entrenched trait of the Chinese rural community,[46] it was the momentum unleashed by Mao Zedong's vision of rural development that provided the space for the expression and consolidation of this particular trend in the pre-reform era. Mao's policy of self-sufficiency of enterprise development – feeding on indigenous resources and technology and serving the local market – gave this parochial tradition a new political and economic meaning. More importantly, this idea appealed to local leaders, especially in the post-Cultural Revolution era. According to Donnithorne:

Self-sufficiency gives rise to a clear chain of command with those controlling a local administrative unit being responsible for its economic as well as political stability to a degree that would not be possible if it depended on other administrative units for a large proportion of its raw materials and other supplies. For this reason a policy of local sufficiency might well appeal to the military men who after the Cultural Revolution came to control the administration of many local authorities. It made it easier for them to feel in control of what was happening within their domains. In any case, when the arrival of supplies from other units rests on administrative decisions, it is dangerous to be highly dependent on such supplies, because the other units in time of shortage are apt to put their own needs first.[47]

Consequently, it was logical to find a mushrooming of "small but independent industrial systems" all over China. For Mao, this may have been a triumph of local initiatives and of the principle of mass mobilization, but for the national economy its disintegrating effect is obvious. The stress on self-sufficiency was conducive to the rise of protective measures among local governments, which aimed at blocking the outflow of resources, capital, and even labor:

China forms a Customs Union but not a Common Market. That is to say, the whole country has a common trade barrier against the outside world, but does not have free trade within its national boundaries.[48]

Under these circumstances, the development of an inward-looking orientation among enterprise operators and local cadres seems natural. Unused to extensive connections and linkages with the larger economic context outside the locality, they may have found it a daunting task to adjust to the volatility and intensity of cross-community exchange inherent in the market economy.

Underdevelopment of the market mechanism

A simple but often forgotten fact is that rural reform in China was introduced into an economy that had experienced decades of being planned. The consequence of this heritage was profound; post-Mao reform was confronted by an economic mechanism that was underdeveloped in terms of both the hardware – infrastructure – and software – cognitive skills of economic actors – that are necessary for market operation. Not only did this constrain the progress of market-oriented reform, it also reinforced the localistic tendency of enterprise development.

The underdevelopment of several aspects of the rural economy is particularly relevant to the concerns here: the low level of transportation development, the lack of sophistication in storage capacity, the low degree of standardization of products, and the limited flow of market information. All of these conditions have reinforced the localistic tendency of rural enterprise development, and have thus hindered the growth of an effective market mechanism in rural China.

The public transport system may not have been the least developed sector in Mao's China, but it was designed on the premise of an immobile population and minimal cross-regional flow of goods. The *hukou* system, the household registration system introduced in the 1950s, had effectively reduced the movement of the Chinese. The principle of self-sufficiency also reduced the demand for transportation, as inter-regional commerce was kept to a minimum. The transport system was simply not prepared for the mobility of resources across the countryside that the market setting required.

As the "tails of capitalism," the suppression of commercial activities in the Chinese economy during the pre-reform period is hardly surprisingly. Riskin points out that, by the late 1970s, the share of commerce in terms of net material product of China was below 10 percent.[49] That is, commerce was kept at an insignificant level during the Mao era. Given the low regard for commerce, the neglected of development of storage capacity in Mao's China is not surprising. What may be surprising is the persistence of such a situation even a decade after the introduction of market reform. For instance, in 1994, less than two billion yuan was invested in developing storage facilities – about 1.5 percent of the total amount the national economy pumped into the transportation, storage, postal, and telecommunication sectors in the same year.[50] This was hardly sufficient for a detectable improvement given the vast size of the country and the underdevelopment of facilities inherited from Mao's economy. Consequently, the majority of the storage capacity in rural China remains far from desirable in both quantitative and qualitative terms, and remains in much the same shape as it was during the last years of Mao's era. In many cases, the so-called storage houses were nothing more than sheds.[51]

There is also an inherent tendency toward a low level of standardization of products in a planned economy. According to Kornai, with industrial firms primarily concerned with satisfying administrative quotas of output rather than meeting market demand and, given the nature of the shortage economy under state plans,[52] firms are inevitably engaged in "forced substitution." That is, as the necessary inputs are in most cases not available, the standard input combination is lacking. The result is often a non-standard product.[53] Mao's China was no exception.

A limited flow of market information is another distinct feature of a planned economy. Like public transportation facilities, the development of telecommunications in the pre-reform period was far from satisfactory. For instance, by 1978 there were fewer than four million telephone sets in China serving one billion people scattered over a vast territory. With 80 percent of the population living in the countryside and the rural sector entitled to only about one-third of the capacity, the rural situation was even worse.[54]

The three-decades-long planned economy had also left its mark on the cognitive aspects of economic actors, which in turn made progress to a market economy even more difficult. People were used to a different economic logic in the planned economy, which was in many ways incompatible with the new economic order based on impersonal exchange beyond the locality. Enterprise operators' exposure to market-oriented transactions was particularly circumscribed by two distinct features of Mao's version of the planned economy: minimal use of markets and a low degree of monetization.

There were fluctuations in the role of the market during the Mao period, and there was a constant struggle at the top level over the appropriate extent to which to apply the market mechanism in economic regulation. However, overall, anti-market advocates prevailed in shaping commercial policy in China; distribution channels were largely centralized, private commerce was suppressed, and rationing was put in place. In the rural context, commerce was largely monopolized by the state-controlled supply and marketing co-operatives, and private traders were forced to disappear, even while traditional rural markets were being suppressed. In short, market exchange was, to a large extent, suppressed in the pre-reform period.[55]

A clear indication of the suppression of the market principle in Mao's economy was the limited use of money as the medium of exchange. Administrative means, not prices, were used to maintain the balance between supply and demand, and such a method penetrated all aspects of the economy. In the rural sector, the work point system was in place and remuneration was, in many cases, in kind rather than in cash. Even compulsory procurement of agricultural products or direct agricultural taxation involved materials, not cash.[56] Under such circumstances, economic actors required different survival skills from those necessary for their counterparts in a market economy. Social and negotiation skills, instead of the ability to predict market change and price fluctuations, were more critical in getting the materials that were needed. In addition, the limited availability of cash among the Chinese population further restricted the use of the market in the pre-reform economy. In 1978, the annual per capita consumption value of the Chinese population was only 184 yuan; the figure for the rural population was as low as 138 yuan.[57] In other words, even if people had a demand for consumer goods, they could hardly have expressed it in monetary terms. Thus, the function of price as a signal for production was further diminished. Again, economic actors in Mao's China were deprived of the experience of adjusting to price fluctuations.

The vulnerability to local pressure

Despite the administrative restructuring at the rural grass-roots level, the vulnerability of rural administration to the pressures of the local community – a fundamental aspect of rural politics in China since imperial rule – remained intact. Officials in the countryside continued to act as the bridge between state and local society, and, most significantly, remained exposed to local community pressure.

A peculiar feature of the composition of personnel of the Chinese rural administration was that the majority of them were categorized as local cadres (*difang ganbu*). In rural China, there were two types of cadres (*ganbu*) in the local administration: state cadres (*guojia ganbu*) and local cadres. There were substantial differences between the two in terms of their welfare entitlements, social status, and career prospects. The former were part of the state administrative services and were on the payroll of the state budget. They also had much better career prospects, as they could theoretically move all the way to the apex of the administration and reach the ministerial level through promotion. In most cases, these state cadres would be assigned to different posts across the country throughout their career, and hence have greater social exposure and better job prospects. In terms of benefits, they were also guaranteed the standard welfare payments for state cadres across the country, including a retirement pension and other welfare benefits. In addition, in the rural context, their entitlement to the status of urban resident was particularly important. Although market reform and the growing affluence of peasants may have diminished the value of being an urban resident, the fact that the *hukou* system was still in place, paired with the general prejudice against rural areas, still made this status something special.[58] The benefits enjoyed by local cadres were remarkably different. They were not on the state payroll and their pay and welfare were mainly determined by the financial situation of the local government. In addition, their careers were restricted to the local administration. Unless they managed to get themselves admitted as state cadres at some point in their service, their career was confined to the locality. Equally important, these local cadres retained their peasant status.[59]

In general, cadres at county level or above were mostly state cadres, whereas the situation at the township level was somewhat mixed – those in the most senior positions were likely to be state cadres, but a substantial portion were still local cadres. Even after the re-establishment of township government in the post-Mao period, the personnel composition of local administrations in the countryside remained more or less the same.

The implications of this contrasting categorization go beyond the administrative dimension and personal concerns. The most fundamental contrast between these cadres was their social distance from the local community. Unlike state cadres, local cadres were mostly natives of the local community. Given the general immobility of the rural population in China, they were likely to come from families who had lived in the local area for generations. Their peasant status also kept them in touch with other fellow residents on a regular basis, as they were still allocated land for farming. All these attributes contributed to a unique feature of local cadres; compared with their state cadre colleagues, they were better informed of local customs and values and they shared common experiences. Even their personal benefits, income, and welfare were directly linked with the financial condition of the local administration, which in turn was mostly determined by the prosperity of the local economy.

Most important of all, they were more likely to be regarded as part of the local community by the local population.[60] These close affectionate and functional ties with the local community contributed to a common tendency among these local cadres at the lower levels: they were more vulnerable to local influences, and they also tended to be more willing to indulge in maneuvering to protect local interests while trying to satisfy the demands from above. In this case, where one lived determined where one stood on certain issues.

There were many reasons for the Party's tolerance of such intimacy between the local administration and the local community. Financial concerns were certainly one reason. By excluding a substantial portion of local administrators from the state payroll, the central treasury could relieve itself of a huge burden. The heavy responsibility of financing the gigantic rural administration was now mostly transferred to local governments.

Nee, however, draws attention to the historical connection with the Chinese Revolution. He argues that the Party deliberately created a new type of local leadership, which was loyal to the state but embedded in the local setting – an instrument which best suited its political purposes:

> The Chinese Communist Party won state power through its ability to mobilize the peasantry over the course of a protracted historical process, which gave rise to the state's commitment to maintain a permanent organizational presence in villages. This made possible sustained mobilization extending from the Sino-Japanese War, through the civil war and revolutionary land reform, to the collectivization of agriculture and creation of the people's commune.[61]

Thus, this new local leadership, which acted within a moral order molded by local customs and values and yet remained under the command of the state organization, was the most effective agent in implementing the mass-line policy and campaign mobilization – strategies that had proved to be successful in the past.

Alternatively, Zweig provides a power struggle perspective in explaining the consolidation of rural localism during Mao's era. Focusing on the period of the Cultural Revolution, Zweig argues that the intense power struggle provided space for the rise of this localistic tendency:

> [I]n factional battles in Beijing over who was the apotheosis of the correct line, the only indicator of correctness was whether or not the masses followed the policies derived from that line as their own and implemented them. Whether the policy was useful, enforced through coercion, or implemented only in form were secondary to the central leaders' need to demonstrate to their political rivals widespread implementation. In many ways Pye is correct to refer to mass participation as a "new form of public pretense." As local formalistic behavior was political expedient to both national elites and middle level bureaucrats, they all had little

reason to delve behind the facade of support and prove that evasion was occurring.[62]

In addition, according to Zweig, the intense struggle at the top also led to constant fluctuations in instructions from the top and to ambiguity in the guidelines for policy implementation. This provided room for "formalism" – changing the content of policy by implementing it at only a superficial level. Zweig concludes that, as a result, national policies remained "prisoners of local political economies and rural value systems."[63]

Zibo on the eve of reform

Given the importance of historical legacy to our analysis, a revisit to pre-reform Zibo might be appropriate before proceeding to the evaluation of the dynamics of rural industrialization in the post-Mao years.

Zibo was among the earliest localities in the establishment of communist administrations. It had a revolutionary tradition and witnessed strong political activism during the most turbulent years of modern Chinese history. Locals had made significant contributions to the Boxer Rebellion in the late nineteenth century, Sun Yat-sen's revolutionary movement, and the Northern Expedition against warlords in the 1920s. The first Communist Party organization was founded in Zibo in 1924. Since then, local revolutionaries have played an active role in organizing strikes and military actions against the Nationalists as well as the Japanese. Zibo is also remembered for its glorious involvement in the Civil War. More than 200,000 locals were drafted into the famous Huaihai Battle, one of the three defining battles in the eventual Communist victory in 1949.[64] As might be expected, the pattern of administrative restructuring after 1949 resonated with the national rhythm. The first primary agricultural cooperative, made up of fifteen rural households and seventy-five people, was formed in April 1952.[65] But the scale of collectivization soon escalated in response to Mao's intensified drive to fulfil his socialist dream. The first People's Commune in Zibo was set up in the Zichuan district in September 1958. The acceleration of the pace of collectivization was evident, as the commune was composed of 10,362 households and 45,900 persons. Within two months, all of Zibo's 868 agricultural cooperatives were reorganized into forty-four People's Communes.[66] Mao's death and the conclusion of the Cultural Revolution saw a gradual demise of the collective framework. By May 1985, the subcounty administration had completed its administrative restructuring with the dissolution of all People's Communes and the founding of ninety-six township administrations. People's governments were set up in all these townships and the operation of people's congresses and Party organizations resumed in most of these localities.[67]

Zibo had an average endowment of agricultural resources. Its per capita entitlement of 2.3 *mu* arable land, which was slightly above the national norm, enabled the local population to match the national average of agricultural output.[68] And, like most of the rest of Mao's villages, most land was devoted to grain production. Ninety percent of the land was reserved for growing wheat and corn, but peanut, tobacco, and cotton occupied less than 5 percent of the total arable land area.[69] Huantai county, however, stood out in its agricultural productivity and was later awarded the title of ton-producing farm (*dunliangtian*) by the provincial government in the 1990s, attracting visits from top Party leadership, including Premier Li Peng and Vice-Premier Tian Jiyuan. However, Zibo enjoyed a rich endowment of energy resources. The prefecture benefited from a rich base of iron mines, with its capacity constituting a quarter of the province's total. Zibo was also blessed with enviable reserves of petroleum and coal. The potential of the two oil fields in the region, Gaoqing and Jinjia, was estimated to be in the region of forty-five million metric tons.[70]

Zibo's handicraft industry also had a long history. Zibo's Boshan area was renowned for its china and pottery. The industry prospered in the Ming dynasty, after a rapid recovery from the turbulent years under Mongolian rule. By the mid-Qing period, Boshan had emerged as a major production and sale center for these products in the region, and it won a reputation equal to Jingde town of Jiangxi province. Zibo was also famous for its silk products. The Zhoucun area, with its long tradition of silk production, had attracted investors from all over the country and was the center of silk manufacturing for Shandong province. Unfortunately, these industries were badly damaged by years of German and Japanese aggression in Shandong in the late nineteenth century. The simultaneous influx of synthetic textiles from Britain, Italy, and Japan into the region also imposed severe economic strain on local silk producers. However, although foreign aggression and economic imperialism may have had devastating effects on traditional industries, aggressors also brought to Zibo capital, new technology, and industrial know-how. These inputs in turn transformed the economic structure of the prefecture. After the collapse of Qing rule in 1911, the Republican government had a different economic strategy for utilizing these foreign inputs to revive Shandong's economy. Energy production now became the priority. During the relatively stable period of the early 1930s, a number of local and foreign investors were attracted to the coal and electricity industries in Shandong, and these sectors soon became the pillars of local industry in Zibo. The Communist takeover in 1949 did not change this pattern. In fact, between 1958 and 1965, one-third of the 510 million yuan invested in local industries went to the electricity and coal-related sectors. The energy sector gained another major impetus during the 1960s. A large state-supported petroleum refinery, the Qilu Petrochemicals Company, was set up in Zibo in 1968. The value of petrochemical products soon contributed more than one-third of the local industrial output value.[71] In addition, metal manufacturing was another important sector. This was, however, typical for most localities, as iron and steel production held a sacred place in Mao's industrialization scheme. Consequently, Zibo's industrial mix was dominated by energy-related sectors and the metal industry, as summarized in Table 2.2.

The solid industrial foundation in urban areas and decent agricultural sector performance provided a fertile habitat for breeding rural enterprises. Zibo did accumulate substantial industrial assets in its rural backyard on the eve of reform. Rural industries, mainly agriculture-related sectors (cements, fertilizers, energy, construction materials, etc.) were launched in the Zibo countryside in response to Mao's call for "walking on two legs" and self-sufficiency. Agricultural mechanization was officially set up as a policy goal in 1959, and steel and iron and chemicals manufacturing were the top priorities.[72] The development was interrupted by the radical years of the Cultural Revolution, as these rural sidelines were attacked as "tails of capitalism." But the momentum was soon regained. Between 1970 and 1985, the number of industrial enterprises invested by communes and brigades jumped from 183 to 3,575, dominated by factories specializing in metal manufacturing, energy-related and construction materials (Table 2.3). The number of employees also went beyond 200,000, accounting for more than 10 percent of the rural population of Zibo. Most townships were engaged in the industrialization process. By 1985, one-third of the townships had reached the industrial output value level of five million yuan.[73] The accuracy of the figures is not of concern here; rather, they serve to show the prevalence of the industrialization strategy in rural localities in Zibo. Local leaders remained enthusiastic about rural enterprises during the later part of the collective era, and the slogan of "one hand on grain, one hand on money" (*yishou zhualiang yishou zhuaqian*) was devised by the local propaganda machine to promote the policy of simultaneous development of agriculture and rural industries.[74] Development of rural enterprises continued to take its place on local administrators' agendas after the demise of collective era. An official policy document titled "Tentative Decision on Further

Table 2.2 Industrial composition of Zibo in 1985

Industry	Percentage of total output
Metal manufacturing	8.47
Energy	6.94
Coal and coke	3.48
Petrochemical	30.32
Chemical	9.70
Machinery	16.67
Construction material	5.07
Timber processing	0.80
Food processing	4.56
Textile	8.70
Sewing	0.74
Leather and fur	0.23
Paper manufacturing	0.80
Culture and art	1.15
Other	2.37

Source: *Zibo Shizhi* (*Zibo Gazette*), p. 803.

Table 2.3 Development of rural industrial enterprises in Zibo, 1981–5

	1981	1982	1983	1984	1985
Total enterprises	2,101	2,062	2,532	3,145	3,575
Commune-owned	488	493	590	627	650
Brigade-owned	1,613	1,569	1,942	2,518	2,925
Total employees	95,465	124,801	149,440	181,426	203,113
In commune-owned enterprises	48,403	51,472	58,131	60,912	66,401
In brigade-owned enterprises	57,062	73,329	91,309	120,514	136,712

Source: *Zibo Shizhi (Zibo Gazette)*, p. 1,459.

Development of Rural Enterprise" (*Guanyu Jiakuai Fazhan Xiangzhen Qiye di Jueding Shixing*) was jointly released by the Zibo Party Committee and Zibo People's Government in 1986, highlighting technological upgrade, efficiency improvement, and speeding up of the growth rate as the goals for enterprise development.[75] The official endorsement, together with the solid industrial base in the urban sector of the prefecture – which is likely to be a source of contracts, business contact and information, technical support, and management know-how, and a decent agricultural sector – provide a fertile ground for the further growth of rural industries in the reform era.

In short, on the eve of reform, rural enterprises had already made their presence known in Zibo's local economy; a solid industrial foundation was in place, and a substantial portion of the local population had been involved in industrial production. Among these personnel with earlier exposure to non-farming activities were serious contenders for corporate control, social status, and political recognition decades later. They are the protagonists in this story.

Summary

As seen above, on the eve of rural reform in the post-Mao period, there was a lack, if not a non-existence, of those conditions appropriate for market development. The decades of development along the Maoist principles of local self-sufficiency and economic planning had given an inward-looking character to the rural economy and rural enterprises. This is hardly a desirable starting point for the prospective new economic order, which, in contrast, stresses mobility of resources, material incentives, and expanded linkages beyond the locality.[76]

The localistic and parochial tendency, particularly of rural enterprise development, was further reinforced by the financial incentives and pressures inherent in the new arrangement of fiscal contracting. Rural enterprises were now regarded as an important source of resources for promoting local development and financing the local administration. For this reason, the local state was understandably unwilling to see any leakage of the resources generated by these local business ventures to the outside world. As will be seen in the forthcoming discussion, this mentality did affect the local state's perception of the community obligations of these enterprises, and hence its legitimate intervention in employment, resource allocation, and other matters concerning local enterprises.

The expectations of the local population added further impetus to this localistic tendency of enterprise development. Decades of experiencing a collective economy, especially in Mao's version of egalitarianism, had probably instilled in the local populace a unique perception of its legitimate claim on collective resources. The people were, according to socialist ideals, the owners of these collectively owned enterprises. In reality, they were barred from enterprise management and received little direct monetary benefit from these business ventures. However, as these non-farm activities became more and more important in the rural economy, it is understandable that local people wanted a "fair share" of these collective assets. The combined effect of the small size of most Chinese rural townships (with an average of around 20,000 persons each), the immobility of the population, and, most importantly, the intimacy between the administration and local community imply that their expectations could be translated into concrete pressures on the local state. These pressures are likely to have reinforced the localistic tendency of enterprise development in rural China. In fact, these parochial and localistic tendencies were galvanized into certain forms of local protectionism in China during the reform era. In pursuing their local interests, local governments in China were, according to many observers, "at war" with each other. According to one account, "the current market is one where feudal lords contend, regions put up blockades, trades practice monopolies and the wars are ceaseless."[77] Measures such as discrimination and double standards in law enforcement against outside products were indispensable parts of inter-regional commerce in China.[78] The "commodity war" in the 1980s, which occasionally involved intervention by the local militia, shows clearly how this tension could be expressed in an extreme form.[79] Although it is hardly surprising that local interests were a high priority on the agendas of local governments, the obsession with parochial concerns probably was expressed in its full strength in post-Mao rural China.

The recognition of the contextual continuity of rural China with the Maoist legacy is important. It enables the analysis to transcend the limitation of simply trying to understand the prospective development in rural China by reading the impact of the changes in rural institutions, and hence facilitates a more sophisticated perspective for understanding. The above analysis has hopefully provided a new dimension on the impact of Maoist legacies for comprehending the trajectory of rural transformation in post-Mao China; the historic continuities may manage to dilute and offset, to a certain extent, the momentum unleashed by the changes, and persist to exert their impact on the new order. Together, these new and old elements produced a distinct context for the development of rural enterprise in the reform era, which, in turn, determined the dynamics of interaction between state and society in rural China. The tension between the past and the present is evident; the inward-looking orientation of the rural economy and the habitual paternalism of the local state were now joined with the new outward economic ethos, which stressed expansive external linkages and an entrepreneurial response to profit. The exchanges and interaction between the new and the old occurred at a historical juncture which itself was a product of historical legacy and unprecedented innovations. This set the scene for new state–society relations, and, more relevant for the present concerns, for the interaction between the local state and enterprise managers in the rural context of reforming China.

3 The rise of enterprise managers in rural China

What happened on October 12, 1998 is a vivid reflection of the rise of rural entrepreneurs. Lu Guanqiu, a leading rural entrepreneur in China who within two decades had successfully transformed a small workshop in rural Shandong into a giant industrial conglomerate with asset values of more than two billion yuan and 6,500 staff, was invited by the State Economic and Trade Commission to give a lecture on his experience. In the audience was British Prime Minister, Tony Blair.[1] Lu's phenomenal ascendance to fame and prestige reveals the rising role of enterprise managers in China, and more importantly points to possible links between success in enterprise management and public influence. Yet this is hardly an isolated case. Reports of the activities of rural entrepreneurs have become a regular item in major national newspapers.[2] They have emerged as a new breed of social celebrity in reform-era China. The image of enterprise managers in less prosperous communities, who have yet to parallel Lu's success, may appear relatively modest; however, their contributions are equally valued in their local communities. They easily stand out from other local residents, with their privileged access to a chauffeured sedan, a mobile phone, or a comfortable mansion. But, more importantly, they distinguish themselves in terms of power in economic and political matters within their local communities. They are emerging as the new power elite[3] in rural China.

However, as pointed out in Chapter 1, while there has been considerable academic interest in the background and social origins of managers in private, state, or other sectors, the background of the managers of collective enterprises in rural China remains relatively unexplored. Nonetheless, such knowledge is crucial for understanding the changing state–society relations. I would argue that experience and expertise in enterprise management play a significant role in managerial appointments. Many peasants with no record of service in local administration have accumulated useful experience and knowledge of enterprise management through a long period of apprenticeship in CBEs during Mao's era. Their technocratic credentials enable them to compete against the cadres or ex-cadres, who are likely to be better educated, more experienced in administrative work, and well connected with the bureaucracy, in the scramble for top managerial posts in TVEs in rural China. In short, cadres and ex-cadres do not have a monopoly over the know-how necessary for managing an enterprise. Given the rising role of rural enterprises in the local economy, the pressing concern for the local state is how to tap into this human capital, which is indispensable for the vitality and growth of local TVEs. This is an important dimension of the interdependent relationship between the local state and the manager.

Using the empirical evidence of Zibo, this chapter will focus on three crucial issues concerning TVE managers. First, the economic role of TVE managers will be examined, starting with the formal appointment procedure, followed by a discussion of the possibility of entrepreneurship in the rural collective sector. It is argued here that, because of the unique opportunity structure in the rural context, entrepreneurship is possible, despite the fact that these managers are not the enterprise proprietors. Second, the chapter will examine the social background of TVE managers. It will show that only a minority of these managers had served in the local bureaucracy before they were appointed to their managerial posts, thus defying the argument of the dominance of ex-cadres. Third, this chapter will go on to evaluate the rising political influence of these managers. It will demonstrate a clear connection between managerial success and a manager's position in the local political hierarchy.

TVE managers: entrepreneurs without ownership

As *de facto* owners of collective enterprises, township governments, in theory, have full control over the managerial appointment process in rural China, the formal appointment (*renming*) process being conducted by the township Economic and Trade Commission (ETC, *jingji maoyi weiyuanhui*). However, as seen in the case of Zibo, underlying this formal procedure are diverse paths that rural residents can follow in order to reach the top of the TVE managerial hierarchy. However, no matter which alternative route they take, they are all propelled by the distinctive incentive and punishment mechanism inherent in the rural context, which makes them behave in an entrepreneurial fashion similar to that of their private sector counterparts and, hence, acts as the motor of growth for TVEs.

Different routes to managership

As seen in Zibo, there are several ways in which a rural resident can reach the top managerial position in a TVE: winning the contract to run an enterprise; internal promotion within the enterprise; by the invitation of the township governments; or by transfer from another administrative rank.

The first route to TVE managership usually starts with a call for tender from the township government. The process is open and public, and the conditions of the enterprise concerned and the general terms of the proposed contract are published in the local newspaper. This is mainly a formality, as most interested parties in the local community are quite well informed about the general situation of local enterprises, and the news of a forthcoming opportunity usually spreads before the official announcement. People who are interested can submit their bids and the contract will, in most cases, go to the applicant who puts forward the best bid.

Internal promotion is another possible route, and the recommendation of the outgoing or retiring manager is influential. As will be seen later, this is a major path to managership, and most managers have had a long service record in their enterprises. In a few cases, an election will be held and the full staff will vote on several candidates agreed upon by the township government and senior management of the enterprise. The township government then appoints the candidate with the highest number of votes.

People can also be invited to manage a collective enterprise. This happened mainly during the early years of reform and was confined primarily to smaller-scale enterprises. For instance, manager Yu had served as a village doctor when he was approached by the villagers' committee in 1998 and offered his present job. He had no previous experience or knowledge of enterprise management, but, given his relatively good education, he was invited to head a small village-level factory, founded three years earlier, with fewer than 800,000 yuan in fixed asset value and a tiny staff of thirty people.[4]

Finally, managerial posts can be filled by those transferred directly from the bureaucracy. As will be seen later, this is more likely to occur at the village level. At the township level, the township ETC, an administrative unit that specializes in enterprise management, supplies most of the cadres for this task. This is understandable, as the nature of the work of ETCs is highly relevant to the new task of enterprise management. Equally important, cadres in these posts are obviously, in terms of information and connections, much better placed to seize these business opportunities than are colleagues serving in other administrative units.

Managers as the motor of entrepreneurial activities

In operational terms, managers are the organizers of all the enterprises' economic activities. Their daily routine includes setting objectives, organizing work, motivating and communicating with staff and business partners, measuring the performance of subordinates, developing the human potential of the enterprise, and making relevant decisions concerning all these matters.[5] In short, they are the salesmen, supervisors, accountants, or even technicians, but, most importantly, they are the decision makers in their enterprises. However, enterprises need entrepreneurs, not just managers. As Schumpeter argues:

> [T]he function of entrepreneur is to reform or revolutionize the pattern of production by exploiting an invention or, more generally, an untried technological possibility for producing a new commodity or producing an old one in a new way, by opening up a new source of supply of materials or a new outlet for products, by reorganizing an industry and so on.[6]

Thus, inventive decisions, not just routine managerial decisions, are needed for the survival and growth of an enterprise.

The notion of the entrepreneur under socialism is, however, controversial. Two issues are central to the debate: the red (the ideologue)–expert (the professional manager) problem inherent in the socialist regime and the lack of a motivational mechanism. The new economic setting in the reform era has removed most of the unfavorable conditions for the rise of entrepreneurs. Berliner provides a succinct summary of the red–expert problem in the context of the socialist enterprise:

> [T]he political leadership is always dependent upon persons with a monopoly of professional expertise (physicians, generals, engineers), which gives the latter a certain form of power. Professionals also tend to have a worldview and a set of values and commitments that differ from those of nonprofessionals and which may lead to the vesting of interests in certain institutional arrangements. Some analysts regard this matter as of major political importance, to the point of arguing that the technical managerial elite, in pursuing its own interests and its own brand of rationality, will eventually dig the grave of communism. One need not subscribe to the gravedigger hypothesis, however, to recognize the existence of a certain permanent tension between the state and the entrepreneurs in a socialist economy.[7]

The tension was evident in industrial management in pre-reform China. Shortly after the brief honeymoon period in the early 1950s, when the professional managers still enjoyed an equal status with the Party secretary in the enterprise, hostility toward managers accelerated. Apart from the early 1960s, enterprise managers, together with other professionals and experts, were constantly humiliated and disparaged. During the Cultural Revolution, they were labeled the "stinking ninth category" (*choulaojiu*) – the lowest social stratum in the society. Participation in physical labor was compulsory for managers as a way to ensure that they learned from workers and eradicated their bourgeois mentality. In enterprises, they were no longer in charge, and in most cases their advice was ignored and even scoffed at. More often than not, managers simply kept their heads down for self-protection.[8] However, though this matter may still bother a few ideologues, its significance has definitely been reduced by the prevalence of pragmatism and the anxiety over economic growth in the reform era. The status of professional managers has been reinstated by the new reform leadership, and measures have been introduced to ensure managerial autonomy and to increase the incentives for managers.[9] In short, with the growing de-ideologization of enterprise management and the new market ethos, the issue of the red–expert tension has lost much of its relevance in present-day China. Rather, the entrepreneurship of professional managers is now enshrined by the Party leadership as the key to prosperity and to the socialist modernization program.

Another major question concerning the nurturing of entrepreneurship centers on motivation in the form of incentives and risks. It is argued that the risk of loss and the presence of sufficient incentive are the necessary conditions for entrepreneurial behavior. In a capitalist economy, entrepreneurs are generally also proprietors, and so the risk and incentive mechanism is straightforward. As the owner, the entrepreneur has to bear the full risk of investment and is the residual claimant in his business. He will be punished for any bad business decision. Similarly, sound judgment will be rewarded. The same mechanism is also applicable to private entrepreneurs in rural China. However, for economic managers in the collective sector, who are not principals operating on their own risk and responsibility, but agents employed by a public body, problems may arise. Are they suited to entrepreneurship? The controversy here is what constitutes personal risk and whether the incentive to perform well is sufficient. It is argued that the distinct opportunity structure of rural China and the advent of market reform have, in fact, provided the necessary risk and incentive mechanism for the rise of entrepreneurship in the countryside.

The adoption of various forms of performance-related remuneration methods in collective enterprises in the post-Mao period has strengthened significantly the linkage between a manager's personal losses and business failure.[10] The effect is such that, although managers may not have to invest any personal capital in the enterprise, the threat of losing a potential stream of income is genuine. The most common method of relating performance and pay is, of course, the contract responsibility system. For managers of non-contracted enterprises, the principle of remuneration is basically the same, though the final amount is determined by the outcome of negotiations and bargaining rather than by a legal contract. The extent of target fulfillment serves as the major reference point in determining the bonuses and salary level of the manager concerned. Thus, in both cases, a direct linkage between enterprise performance and the manager's well-being is established. For managers, making a profit is important. Minimum wages are guaranteed, but there exists a huge gap between just getting by and having a comfortable standard of living. As we will see in the following, in a few cases of exceptional success in Zibo the managers concerned take home a bonus of more than 100,000 yuan – an astronomical amount in rural standards, as the average income of a peasant-worker is no more than 5,000 yuan a year.[11]

Defining risk

Those who claim that socialism and entrepreneurship are incompatible may be right, if risk implies only the loss of personal capital invested in the enterprise.[12] However, several unique features and developments in rural China render this narrow definition of risk inappropriate.

In rural China, the implications of managerial failure go beyond the loss of tangible capital; it can be a constant source of embarrassment and stigma.

The extent of such social pressure is likely to be magnified in the small communities in which most rural enterprises are located. The story of manager Zhang Chengyu, who is in charge of a township food-manufacturing factory, is a good illustration. Founded in 1991, the factory was once one of the largest food-manufacturing firms in the prefecture, in terms of fixed asset value, profit, and tax. At one time, its total assets were valued at more than sixteen million yuan, and the total tax and profit payment was as high as seven million yuan. However, the business started to deteriorate, and in 1994 Zhang was assigned to reverse its decline. Unfortunately, his efforts were futile. By the time this author visited the factory, production had already stopped. Zhang refused to disclose the current financial details of the company, but according to township government statistics the factory had failed to meet its modest profit target of 100,000 yuan in 1994.[13] It may be unfair to blame Zhang for the company's misfortune, because the downward trend had been in place before his arrival. Still, there seems to be a general feeling in the community that Zhang should be held responsible. Fellow managers in other enterprises expressed contempt whenever his name was brought up in conversation, and some even regarded him as a "loser." In this small township of about 40,000 people, with about 20 percent of the labor force employed in the fifteen township-level collective enterprises, and with the typical immobility of the Chinese rural population, such gossip and character attacks can be truly damaging to one's reputation. Zhang's failure to gain a seat on the township people's congress says everything about his disgrace. It is not known whether he lost in a contest or simply could not win the Party-controlled nomination; either way, it confirms the view that he is seen as a person who does not deserve the honor of being admitted into the ranks of local dignitaries, whether in the eyes of his peers or those of the Party organization.[14]

The misfortune for people like Zhang is more than psychological. His long-term career, in either business or administration, will be significantly jeopardized too. In rural China, a "loser" has little chance of resuming a managerial career. The unique community nature of TVEs means that managerial posts are unlikely to be open to outsiders, reducing the possibility of being given a second chance elsewhere. Worse still, as economic development is gaining importance in the performance appraisal of local cadres, failure to manage an enterprise will surely have an adverse effect on the administrative career of someone desiring to join the bureaucracy. Whereas in Mao's time performance appraisals for cadres were highly politicized, in the reform era greater weight is placed on individual ability and achievement.[15] Economic management ability has become an important variable in determining the career prospects of cadres. In Zibo, most township administrations have adopted a detailed scale for evaluating the performance of cadres involved in industrial management. A 1,000-point scheme (*qianfenzhi*) is used, which assigns the cadre concerned certain scores according to his position and the performance of rural enterprises.[16] The findings of Edin, who conducted in-depth research on the implementation of the cadre responsibility system in the area, also points out that economic targets such as tax revenues, sales incomes, and profits of local enterprises are always categorized as hard targets (*ying zhibiao*) specified in the performance contract for evaluating township officials.[17] In other words, the better the development of the local enterprises, the higher the score, and those in a senior position earn more points as a result of their greater responsibility. Thus, with his poor track record, Zhang's prospects of rescuing his career by returning to administration are poor.

In short, although TVE managers do not have any formal ownership rights over the enterprise they operate, they cannot simply walk away from a loss-making enterprise without any cost. Managers of TVEs in rural China have much at stake in the company's fortunes.[18] This analysis is confirmed by the observations in Zibo. Managers are actively involved in exploring new product mixes and new markets, experimenting with new technologies and equipment, and initiating new business projects. They are fully aware of the pressure for performance. The local state, as will be seen in Chapters 4 and 5, is also involved in the process. However, local state involvement, in many cases, is confined to a gate-keeping role; it retains its veto power, while the managers play an active role in market research, analysis, and persuasion. In short, even before the intensification of shareholding reform in the second half of the 1990s, despite their non-owner status, TVE managers were motivated and capable of performing the entrepreneurial function – a role crucial to the success and dynamism of rural enterprises in China.

The importance of human capital

A changing economy also implies obsolescence of some skills and knowledge and increased demand for knowledge of how to exploit the new economic opportunities. In this process, some succeed while others fail. This section will focus on the winners – those who succeed in reaching the top TVE managerial posts, a new career alternative offered by the change in economic institutions. Based on the case of Zibo, this section argues that, despite the persistence of bureaucratic influence over the local economy, human capital has become the major determinant of the allocation of TVE managerial posts. That is, TVE managership is not monopolized by cadres or ex-cadres. Instead, the Zibo case shows that those who possess managerial know-how (knowledge of the industry, and experience and skills in enterprise operation) are far more successful in the scramble for the top TVE posts. The local state, which is keen to maintain the competitiveness and growth of local enterprises, views managerial competence as the top priority in the selection process.

There are two contrasting views on who will succeed in taking advantage of opportunities unleashed by institutional changes during the process of socialist transformation. The gist of the debate focuses on whether the communist cadres can maintain their dominant position in the face of the new challenge. In the terminology used by Rona-Tas, the two views are the changing elite thesis and the surviving elite thesis.[19]

The changing elite argument proposes that there will be a significant change in the composition of economic elites as a result of the socialist transformation. New faces emerge and cadres are the main losers in the process. It argues that the advent of market reform will simply erode the influence of the political capital[20] possessed by cadres and hence will diminish their dominance and privileges. Nee, one of the major advocates of this view, asserts that "the more complete the shift to market coordination, the less likely that economic transactions will be embedded in networks dominated by cadres, and the more likely power – control over resources – will be located in market institutions and in social networks . . . of private buyers and sellers."[21] Cadres, according to Nee, are not necessarily better equipped than others in terms of the experience and orientation required for entrepreneurial activities. Szelenyi goes further, elaborating on who will be better prepared for the economic contest. Analyzing the background of Hungarian entrepreneurs in the newly emerged second economy, Szelenyi claims that those who have managed to exploit the business opportunities offered by the new reform initiatives are those who had previous entrepreneurial experience. And "during the years of the command economy and forced collectivization, people with entrepreneurial aspirations could resist the pressure to become fully proletarian or the temptation to become a cadre. Thus, they preserved the will and the capacity to reenter the embourgeoisement trajectory when opportunities reopened."[22]

The alternative view, the surviving elite thesis, is that the cadres are the primary beneficiaries of market reform. It is based on two major arguments, the power conversion argument and the technocratic continuity argument. The former holds that the personal connections accumulated in their official capacities enable the cadres to excel in the transitional economy. These connections provide valuable access to key resources such as business information, credit, and other bureaucratic services, and are extremely useful in exploiting the uncertainty inherent in the market transition process. The technocratic continuity argument is more focused on the acquired expertise of cadres. It holds that cadre-ship is strongly tied to education under socialism and claims that "there is a common meritocratic–technocratic character of both Party and entrepreneurial recruitment that is the main source of continuity . . . as a whole, people with more education will do better in the newly forming market sector than those with less, and thus cadres will be in an advantageous position."[23]

Rural China: lingering of cadres' influence?

The generally low level of literacy in rural China and the partial market reform of the Chinese economy appear to support the surviving elite thesis. Despite the interrupting effect of the Cultural Revolution, cadres, even in the rural administration, are generally still educated to a higher level that non-cadres.[24] In addition, administrative experience gives cadres improved skills in the areas of communication, mobilization, and organization and coordination of tasks.

Furthermore, the relative immobility of the rural population may enhance the relative competence of local cadres in the rural context. Although most peasants are have little experience of the world outside their immediate locale,[25] rural cadres have greater exposure to the outside world. The constant influx of information from the higher levels of the bureaucracy, the chance to interact with colleagues from other parts of China, and the opportunity to travel around the country in an official capacity may all help to expand the vision and horizon of these cadres. All these attributes are undoubtedly important ingredients in the making of a competent business administrator.

The present stage of market reform in rural China may also work in the cadres' favor. Oi's notion of local state corporatism, which argues for the continued dominance of local cadres in rural China during the reform era, provides the most comprehensive theoretical view on the subject.[26] Many other works on the political economy of reforming China share a similar view of the persistence of bureaucratic influence.[27] As will be argued in Chapters 4 and 5, the local state does continue to play a significant role in the local economy in rural China and remains valuable for reducing transaction costs in business transactions.

Certainly, in terms of individual caliber, cadres excel in administrative and social skills, which gives them a competitive edge in the contest for top managerial posts. However, whether these are sufficient to produce a good enterprise manager is debatable. Their experience in the bureaucracy, can, in a way, hinder cadres' prospects in the business sector too. The communist bureaucracy is the antithesis of the market-oriented enterprise. The two represent contrasting philosophies in management. Administrative bureaucracy, particularly that of socialist China, is characterized by job security – "iron rice bowl" (*tiefanwan*) – and egalitarian rewards that are determined mainly by an administrative grade-based system and seniority. Within this organization, the Party is the core of everything. Efficiency can be measured only in terms of the technical or political yardsticks laid down by a superior administrative body. Managing a market-oriented enterprise, such as a TVE, however, requires a completely different mentality. Achievement of profit is the primary objective of these business ventures. This requires a different personnel management policy, which rests on labor mobility and a meritocratic and performance-based reward system. The manager, who has a strong sense of allocative efficiency and profit maximization, and who is endowed with professional skills, is the one running the show, not the Party. Prior experience in the bureaucracy may not be very useful in the enterprise.[28] Worse still, it may even prolong the readjustment process for those who move from bureaucracy to enterprise.[29]

In addition, two crucial ingredients required in a good manager are obviously not part of the cadre-training program: technical production skills and a knowledge of the industry and enterprise concerned. While the former includes basic book-keeping and accounting skills and specific knowledge of the technical aspects of the production process concerned, the latter involves an understanding of the operation and the market conditions of the specific industry, an awareness of the prospects and constraints of the industry, and a comprehension of the strengths and limits of the existing staff of the enterprise. These are not accessible to someone who has no actual experience of working in the industry or the enterprise concerned, and are definitely not available to those cadres who work in their office and monitor progress from a distance. However, these forms of knowledge are crucial for performing the entrepreneurial role of manager. Without this knowledge, a manager cannot make innovations contributing to the more efficient use of the enterprise's resources. They may also fail to detect the market potential of their products and hence may miss lucrative business opportunities. The inability to make these important decisions hinders the chance of survival of the enterprise in tense market competition. Such knowledge can, of course, be acquired over time, but the expense of the learning process is a matter of concern.

These reasons may account for the fact that those who have no record of serving in the local bureaucracy, but have accumulated considerable experience in enterprise work, can appear as the major contenders for the TVE manager posts. Here, Szelenyi's theory of interrupted embourgeoisiement is revealing. A parallel between the Hungarian and Chinese cases provides historical continuity. While the formative years of the Hungarians' entrepreneurial aspirations can be traced back to 150 years of Turkish occupation and the pre-Communist era, many Chinese peasants learned their trade during the Mao period. Many of them had their first exposure to the new organizational life of business when they worked in CBEs set up during the collective era. It is worth recalling that, as seen in Table 2.1, by 1978, the year that rural reform officially commenced, the Chinese countryside had already accumulated 1.52 million enterprises employing more than twenty-eight million peasants. In other words, a huge pool of experience and skills in enterprise management was already available on the eve of rural reform. As in Hungary, when a new opening emerged, those who were equipped with the right skills and aspirations were among the most successful in grasping the full benefits, with or without the assistance of political capital.

Several empirical surveys of the background of enterprise managers also provide support for this argument. Though focused on enterprises with different ownership systems, a common finding is that prior experience in enterprise work, rather than ex-cadre experience, is the common professional background of enterprise managers in public enterprises.[30] It seems that in the scramble for the gains offered by the new business opportunities in rural China during the reform era, "there are many ways to get to the top," as argued by Yunxiang Yan.[31]

The case of Zibo

In this section, the validity of these contrasting arguments will be evaluated by analyzing various sets of data on managerial background in Zibo. The focus is deliberately confined to a single township, Tangshan – the township with one of the highest levels of TVE development in the prefecture – in the belief that such a focused study will provide a clearer picture.

Tangshan township is one of the leading town administrations in Zibo, which has a considerable degree of industrialization and a dominant collective sector. It is regarded as among the top twenty-five townships in Zibo prefecture. Its position in the upper echelons of local administration, in terms of the number of rural enterprises and economic development, provides a good case for analyzing the origins of enterprise managers in the collective sector. There are fifteen township-level enterprises and 141 village-level enterprises in the collective sector in this area. Thirty-one managers were interviewed, and all but four of the township-level managers are the chief executive managers of the enterprises concerned, and the four exceptions are all senior managers. The sample covers a wide range of enterprises in terms of size and profitability. All enterprises are industrial firms with two exceptions from the construction sector. These construction firms are included because of their economic importance in their communities.

These data (hereafter, Tangshan data), however, will also be contrasted, when appropriate, with two other sets of data on the background of enterprise managers in the collective sector: (1) data on the background of fifty candidates in the national contest for outstanding rural entrepreneurs of 1987 (hereafter, national data)[32] and (2) data on the background of sixty-eight outstanding rural entrepreneurs in the Zibo prefecture in 1994 (hereafter, Zibo data).[33] These data sets were produced on the basis of Chinese materials published in national newspapers and local gazettes. Cross-examination of these different sets of data allows us to argue with greater confidence that, despite the limited size of the present samples, the conclusions drawn may still have a certain degree of generality and relevance for other localities in rural China. Political capital[34] alone can hardly explain all managerial appointments, and prior experience in enterprise work, a chance to acquire managerial know-how, appears to be more important.

Certainly, these data have limitations. First, the managers included in the national and Zibo data sets are outstanding entrepreneurs; thus, in some respects, the findings for such managers may be different from those for average managers. This should warn us not to take the findings, especially the exact figures or percentages for certain types of origin, at face value. However, if the claims for political capital are to be persuasive, its influence should be even more apparent in these two cases, as these enterprises are mostly companies with sound economic foundations and strong profit potential. Thus, if cadres do exploit their political capital for personal gain, we should expect them to show even greater domination in these enterprises. Second, the definition of political capital here mainly refers to the previous or present occupation of leading positions in local Party or state organizations. The major problem with this positional analysis[35] is that it can only identify a subset of political capital.

Informal connections such as a cadre's position in a patron–client network, indirect influence, and, most important, family ties will not be reflected. Notwithstanding these constraints, as analyses of the background of managers in the collective sector are few and far between, the findings of the present exercise may serve as a good starting point. Thus, far from aiming to be the definitive account of the background of TVE managers in China, the present effort is better perceived as an attempt to evaluate the prevailing arguments about managers' background in a somewhat systematic manner.

Cadre experience tells only half the story

In the case of Tangshan, Table 3.1 shows that a minority of enterprise managers interviewed (39 percent) had served as cadres in the Party-state administration before they started their business careers. Of these, two were village Party secretaries, one was a deputy village Party secretary, one was a production team leader (the equivalent of villagers' committee leader in the post-collective period), and four had served on the villagers' committee. The other four had served in township administration; two of them had served in the Agricultural Management Station, a functional division under the leadership of the Ministry of Agriculture, and the other two were cadres in the township ETC.

Furthermore, outstanding managers are not much more likely to have prior political capital than managers generally. The national data reveal a very similar figure of 40 percent, but a surprisingly much lower figure of 18 percent is recorded in the Zibo data. This raises doubts about the validity of the claims for political capital as the primary explanation of managers' appointments. A logical deduction from such claims is that those managers who are running the most important enterprises in their communities must have substantial political credentials before their appointment to the enterprise. However, this is not confirmed by the data. Even if the unexpectedly low figure among these exceptional managers in these two data sets is set aside, the fact that at least two-thirds of the managers who reach the top of their enterprises are without previous political connections needs to be explained. Something else must account for their appointment.

Table 3.1 Previous cadre experience of enterprise managers in Tangshan township

	Total	*Number with cadre experience at*	
		Village level	*Township level*
Number of managers interviewed who previously served as cadres in Party/state administration	12 (39%)	8 (26%)	4 (13%)

Source: author's fieldwork.

Note
Figures in parentheses denote percentage of the thirty-one enterprise managers interviewed.

Enterprise experience as an important credential

A closer examination of the background of Tangshan managers is revealing. Prior management experience is common among managers in TVEs. As shown in Table 3.2, twenty-one of the thirty-one managers interviewed in Tangshan had various kinds of experience in enterprises before they were appointed to their present positions.[36] Several points are noteworthy. First, the number of managers who had spent their entire career as bureaucrats before their managerial appointment is low. Only six out of the thirty-one (19 percent) fall into this category. The other six managers who had also accumulated political capital prior to their appointment had worked in enterprises in different capacities. In other words, even in the case of cadres-turned-managers, a close look at their background may reveal that political capital alone cannot fully account for their appointment in the business sector. Second, experience in business is even more important for those who do not have any political capital before their appointment. Fifteen of the nineteen who are disadvantaged in this respect had a taste of work in enterprises before their appointment to their present managerial posts. Seven started as ordinary workers or technicians and gradually expanded their experience from production to other activities. Another eight began their careers in business in various management posts at a lower level, including a salesman, an accountant, and a divisional chief. Wang Bing, the manager in charge of one of the largest collective enterprises in Tangshan, who started his career as an ordinary worker in a commune-brigade factory more than twenty years ago, claimed, "I earned my managerial post through a long period of apprenticeship and hard work, not political favor."[37] This may, of course, be an exaggeration. As we will see in the next two chapters, local government is not completely absent in enterprise operation and expansion. But Wang's perception of himself as a self-made success and his faith in meritocracy is still relevant. It is this perception of self-importance that forms the basis of the changing pattern of interaction between managers and local state. Third, another four managers started with no particular

Table 3.2 Previous business sector experience of managers in Tangshan township

	Number of managers
Managers with previous political capital	12 (39%)
Without any previous experience in enterprise management	6
With previous experience in enterprise management	6
Managers without political capital	19 (61%)
With previous experience in enterprise management	15
Started as technicians or workers	7
Started in junior management posts	8
Without previous experience in enterprise management	4
Total	31 (100%)

Source: author's fieldwork.

business experience or any record in administration. One used to be a village doctor and was invited to run a village collective enterprise; he believed that his relatively good education was the reason for this. The other three were peasants who won the contract to run a village enterprise.

In short, experience in business appears to be a common credential among managers in the collective sector. Two-thirds of the managers had some experience of business prior to their present appointment; those who relied purely on political capital, on the other hand, constitute only a minority.

Limits of political capital

The issue of the relative importance of political and human capital can be further probed by finding where political capital matters most. A consistent pattern for the location of successful cases of cadres-turned-managers can be observed in our three data sets. The majority are confined to collective enterprises at village level. Political capital seems to matter most in the clamber for managerships at this lower level, and its competitive advantage diminishes in the contest at the higher level. Several features of the village context may explain this phenomenon: the comparative competence of cadres, the relative simplicity of the management role, and the limited opportunities available (Table 3.3).

Given that the average population of Chinese villages is around 1,000, and that many local communities still suffer from a shortage of talent and general illiteracy, village cadres, with their administrative skills and experience, and most important of all their social exposure and connections, are understandably in a better position to win management posts. Such attributes are less likely to be useful to cadres at the township level, where the community is usually more socially exposed and resourceful and at least ten times larger.

Village enterprises also exhibit a smaller scale of production. In Huantai, one of the most industrialized counties in Zibo, a village enterprise employs only twenty-nine workers on average, which is about 30 percent of the average labor force of a township enterprise. In terms of fixed assets and output values, the former is also much smaller than the latter. A village enterprise in Huantai, on average, has a fixed asset value of only about 6 percent of that of a township enterprise, and produces less than 20 percent of the output

Table 3.3 Level of enterprise where managerships are held by ex-cadres

	Tangshan data	*Zibo data*	*National data*
Village enterprise	8 (67%)	11 (91%)	15 (75%)
Township enterprise	4 (33%)	1 (9%)	5 (25%)
Total	12 (100%)	12 (100%)	20 (100%)

Source: refer to notes 32 and 33.

value of the township counterpart.[38] It is reasonable to expect that, compared with enterprises at township level, the operation of these village enterprises is relatively primitive and simple. The experience and skills learned from administrative work in the bureaucracy alone may be sufficient to meet the requirements of the management role at this level. However, the inadequacy of such managers may soon be exposed when confronted with the greater complexity and sophistication of the operation of larger enterprises at a higher level.

Another major difference between the village and township levels is the number of enterprises. In general, a village administration has far fewer enterprises under its command than its counterpart at the higher level. In Huantai, there are on average 2.3 enterprises per village, whereas there are, on average, nine township-level enterprises in each township.[39] In addition, in rural China it is very unlikely that a village cadre will be appointed to manage an enterprise outside the local community. Thus, the village administration has very few job opportunities at its disposal with which to satisfy everyone's demands for a chance in the business sector. There is little scope for the village administration to consider candidates from outside the administration who are no less competent than the contenders with a cadre background. In fact, as shown above, most managerial jobs at the village level are taken by the secretaries or deputy secretaries of the village branch of the Party. In contrast, the township authority is in a relatively relaxed position when it comes to choosing the right person for an enterprise. Not only does the authority at township level have more enterprises under its immediate supervision, but its superiority to the village administration implies that the appointment of managers at this level is also within its jurisdiction. Thus, the township administration has more room for maneuver in satisfying cadres who are keen to obtain a job in business and, more importantly, more resources at its disposal to balance the conflicting concerns of local economic prosperity, political reliability, favoritism, and the cadre's self-interest.

This analysis shows that human capital – managerial experience and skills – is most crucial in explaining managerial appointments in TVEs. Administrative experience provides people with certain resources that can enhance their competitiveness in the contest for management posts. This explains why people with previous cadre experience manage to take a significant share of the top management posts in the countryside. However, such interpersonal skills and connections are not restricted to people with an ex-cadre background. These attributes can be gained through other work experience. In addition, the task of enterprise management may require other knowledge and know-how that may not be on the list of requirements for a competent cadre. Rather, the long apprenticeship in CBEs during Mao's era provided a chance for many non-cadres to equip themselves with the valuable human capital required for the manager's job. And, as reflected in the analysis above, this category does extremely well in the scramble for managerial posts, and surpasses the groups who have only political capital. The local state is theoretically in a commanding position in deciding who gets what in the contest for posts. Yet the inadequacy of cadre experience of enterprise management and a concern for enterprise performance have tied its hands. Like it or not, non-cadres have to be appointed.

TVE managers on the road to political power

The discussion on the origin of enterprise managers sheds more light on the impact of economic reform on rural society. Economic reform has advanced the transformation of China's social and economic order from one based mainly on principles of social revolution into one in which legitimacy and success is gauged according to economic and material progress. Entrepreneurial skill has emerged as an important factor in determining one's life chance in the new order. However, the story does not stop here. Not only is entrepreneurial skill now an effective and legitimate tool with which to compete for a better life chance, but it can also provide access to political power. It is argued here that enterprise managership is not merely a commanding role in the management of an economic organization; it is a position of strategic importance, which can potentially convert economic success into public power. Command over leading enterprise entails control of life opportunities for the local population (employment, access to better income opportunities, and non-farming activities) and the allocation of resources. The rising autonomy of managers in enterprise operation will be elaborated on in Chapters 4 and 5, and we will also see how managerial brilliance can be cashed in via the intensification of shareholding reforms in Chapters 6 and 7. But, as seen in the case of Zibo, there is a also strong functional necessity to co-opt TVE managers, particularly the successful ones, into the local political hierarchy. Performance in the managerial realm, in other words, can also be a license to public power.

Co-opting managers

The Zibo case shows that the political co-option of TVE managers into the local political hierarchy is an attempt by the local state to enhance its own capability in local economic management and its legitimacy in general governance. The process goes beyond the conventional practice of granting social celebrities fame and recognition – a move in which the state has great discretion and in which the titles granted are mostly of little real political significance (e.g. "model manager," "socialist worker"). In a growing number of cases involving successful managers, the situation is different; more is at stake and the awards are not just nominal political titles but leading positions in the Party-state administration. In addition, managers are more assertive in the process. This does not mean that they are confrontational or provocative in their claims for political power; instead, they make their voices heard by playing an indispensable role in local economic management. The local state still has the final say in the distribution of political capital, yet again the demands of political and economic reality have limited its freedom. The functional requirements of the new economic order necessitate the accommodation of the claims of those managers with proven talent and success.

The rising importance to the local economy of rural enterprises can be attributed mainly to their growing contribution to local finance. Take Huantai county as an example. Local finance benefits substantially from this development. As can be seen from Table 3.4, non-agricultural activities have already replaced agricultural activities as the major source of revenue. Among the former, about half of the local budgetary income collected by the county government is from value-added tax, sale tax, and income tax, and enterprises are the major contributors of these taxes. They are also the

Table 3.4 Income of Huantai county government, 1998

Income source	Income provided
Value-added tax	24.56
Business tax	16.10
Enterprise income tax	10.50
Foreign enterprise income tax	0.52
Personal income tax	9.49
Fixed-asset investment orientation tax	3.01
Urban construction and maintenance tax	5.26
Real-estate tax	5.43
Stamp tax	0.59
Urban land-use tax	0.83
Vehicle utilization tax	0.12
Animal slaughter tax	0.11
Agricultural tax	59.60
Special agricultural product tax	0.66
Farm land-use tax	0.86
Contract tax	0.20
Administrative charges	3.00
Fines	4.22
Earmarked incomes	7.51
Other incomes	5.16
Earmarked subsidies and other transfers from municipal government	57.02
Total	175.62
Extra-budgetary income	15.77

Source: *Shandong Huantaixian Guomin Jingjin Tongji Jiliu* (*Economic Statistics of Huantai County*), 1998 p. 216, and *Huantaixian Zhengfu Gongzuo Baogao* (*Huantai County Government Report*), 1999, p. 6.

Note
Units: million yuan.

major suppliers of extra-budgetary incomes through profit remittance and other forms of financial contributions to local governments. In other words, even a conservative estimate reveals that the overall financial contribution of rural enterprises in Huantai is in the region of one-third of total revenue. Nevertheless, three other functional requirements may also help to account for the ascendancy of rural enterprises.

A new form of coordination

One of the major implications of de-collectivization for rural administration is the demise of the framework of centralized coordination. Under the previous framework, during Mao's period, matters of political, economic, and social management were all administered by one institution – the People's Commune – and coordination could be easily achieved. With the advent of reform, new principles of political order are in place. Particularly noteworthy is the advocacy of the separation of politics and economic management. Local administrations are under pressure from the higher levels to distance themselves from direct involvement in enterprise operation. However, driven by their concern for local prosperity and by the residual effect of the paternalism of the collective era, they are eager to find means of maintaining coordination. Enterprises, with their growing influence over the well-being of the local population and the life opportunities available, can be a good vehicle for enlisting compliance and reducing administrative costs. On the other hand, managers, endowed with independent expertise and effective management skills, simply cannot be pushed around by the local administration. An arrangement that can help to maintain better economic coordination without antagonizing enterprise managers or violating the new reform requirements would be most welcome. The co-option of managers into the decision-making process appears to be one option.

For rural cadres, the pressure of managing a booming non-farm sector in the countryside is immense. Non-farm economic activities have replaced agricultural production as the core of economic life in the countryside, raising doubts as to the adequacy of the administrative skills and experience of rural cadres for their new economic role. Their task is unprecedented, not only because of the size and pace of expansion of the local economy but also because of the range of businesses and the new skills required. An examination of the profiles of the Party secretaries and mayors of the twenty-five most developed townships in Zibo prefecture reinforces these doubts. It is true that these cadres all have remarkable educational qualifications.[40] However, only one-fifth of these officials had ever been involved in economic management. Moreover, most of this experience was confined to service in administrative posts in taxation, finance, or commercial bureau of local government. Only three of the forty-nine cadres examined here had previously been in charge of enterprises.[41] It is doubtful whether these bureaucrats could fully comprehend the complexity and the different operational logic of the business sector. The co-optation of managerial talents can be a solution to such limitations.

The co-option of managers also has extra political relevance in the rural context. It is in line with the general philosophy of rural administration in Communist China: rule by non-native and open administration. In rural areas, it is almost a rule that leading officials above village level will not come from the local communities. This is a strategy intended to minimize parochialism and to ensure better control over cadres at the lower tiers of administration.[42] The rural administration in present-day Zibo prefecture reveals the same pattern. All but two of the leading officials in the twenty-five of the prefecture's most developed townships are outsiders in their communities.[43] Nevertheless, this "avoidance principle" has to be supplemented with other measures if bonding with the local population is not to be affected. As mentioned in Chapter 2, a certain degree of intimacy between the administration and the local community has to be maintained. A sense of being ruled by outsiders or a feeling of emotional detachment is undoubtedly detrimental to the legitimacy of the local state. The comment made by a TVE manager is a good illustration. This manager in Tangshan complained that the township government did not provide appropriate assistance. He attributed this to the fact that the deputy mayor in charge of industrial development was an outsider. He thought that, as an outsider, this cadre did not understand the local situation and perhaps did not even care about local development. Against the background of such general perceptions, some form of intermediation is needed to maintain harmony with the local community. As pointed out in Chapter 2, in Communist China this role is played by those cadres who are locally recruited (*difang ganbu*). Beneath the apex of power in most township administrations, posts are mostly filled by cadres who are natives of the community. In the case of Zibo prefecture, out of the total of 7,246 cadres serving at the township levels, half of them are local cadres (*difang* cadres).[44] Most of them spend most of their lives in the community and will not be transferred elsewhere unless they manage to break into the ranks of state cadres. Local people regard them as the embodiment of local trust and values.[45] Their presence helps to enhance the local authority's respectability and familiarity. They are the friends and life-long acquaintances of most of their fellow peasants. Managers-turned-leaders can serve a similar function. There may be a certain degree of tension in the workplace or of jealousy toward managers among peasant-workers. However, the ability of the managers is, in general, well admired. They are usually regarded as "*nengren*," which literally means "a man of competence." Many workers believe that an enterprise is a meritorious institution in which talent excels. The success stories of many workers-turned-managers have instilled a faith in the possibility of upward mobility in the workplace among workers. For them, it seems to be a natural development to see these capable persons included in the local leadership. There is a sense of pride when a fellow villager manages to reach the top of the local administrative hierarchy.[46] For the local state, this co-option will hopefully lead to an automatic transfer of trust and respect for authority.

Enterprise as a stepping stone to political power

Table 3.5 provides a summary of the political capital possessed by enterprise managers. In the case of Tangshan, the majority of enterprise managers interviewed (61 percent) have been granted political capital of various kinds. This provides the managers with access to the policy process in differing degrees. Particularly noteworthy of this group are those who are concurrently serving in leading positions in Party-state institutions (36 percent). Three of them have been made deputy mayors of the township administration and the other eight serve as the secretary or deputy secretary in the village Party branch. In addition, another eight managers (26 percent), who have failed to break into these ranks, have been granted some consolation prize, such as membership of the people's congress and the people's political consultative conference. As shown in the case of Tangshan, it seems that enterprises have provided not only an avenue for the pursuit of economic success but also a path to political power.

Success in enterprise management appears to be the major determinant of the distribution of political capital. A clearer picture emerges when the

Table 3.5 Present political capital of enterprise managers

		Tangshan data	Zibo data
(a)	Managers concurrently holding official posts in Party/state organization	11 (36%)	29 (43%)
	As Party secretary/deputy secretary at township level	0 (0%)	7 (10%)
	As mayor/deputy mayor/chairman/deputy chairman of township Economic and Trade Commission	3 (10%)	9 (13%)
	As secretary/deputy secretary of village Party committee	8 (26%)	13 (19%)
(b)	Managers holding seats in the People's Congress or Political Consultative Conference only	8 (26%)	12 (18%)
(a) + (b)		19 (61%)	41 (60%)
(c)	Managers with none of the above titles	12 (39%)	27 (40%)
(a) + (b) + (c)		31 (100%)	68 (100%)

Source: author's fieldwork.

Notes
For managers holding more than one post, only the most important title in the analysis is counted; see note 34.
Figures in parentheses denote percentage of the total number of enterprise managers.

Tangshan data are contrasted with the Zibo data. The distinguishing characteristic of the latter is the generally higher level of managers' performance. Thus, a higher concentration of political capital is expected if the proposition that there is a correlation between economic success and political capital is to be confirmed. At first glance, the validity of the argument appears doubtful. Table 3.4 shows that in Zibo the percentage of managers with political capital is only 60 percent, lower than Tangshan. However, if the analysis is confined to the distribution of political capital of greater importance (i.e. leading positions in the Party-state administration), the contrast is clearer. Of Zibo's managers, 43 percent fall into this category, whereas in Tangshan the figure is only 36 percent. An even greater discrepancy can be detected when we further narrow the focus to the township level. The Zibo data reveal that 23 percent of managers concurrently hold leading positions in the Party-state administration at township level, whereas only 10 percent of managers in Tangshan hold posts at the same level, and none of these is a leading Party official.

Managerial elites who are concurrently holding deputy headships in Huantai show a similar correlation between business success and political power. As shown in Table 3.6, the nine managers who are appointed as deputy heads at township levels are all running leading enterprises in local communities. In terms of employment and revenue contributions, their economic significance is evident.

The connection becomes even more vivid if the analysis is narrowed to the distribution of political capital among managers of the fifteen township-level collective enterprises in Tangshan. The parallel between success in enterprise

Table 3.6 Profile of enterprises run by managers holding deputy township headship in Huantai county

Manager	Staff employed	Total asset value (million yuan)	Tax submitted in 1998 (million yuan)
Jing Jie	583	136	3.5
Zhang Jian	590	130	6.3
Zhang Ying	1,088	85	4.5
Zhou Cai	210	119	4.8
Xun Li	820	182	3.7
Li An	NA	NA	4.0
Wang Li	5,000	280	4.0
Wang Bing	514	NA	3.0
Ma Zhen	200	50	4.5

Source: author's fieldwork.

Notes
The average amount of total tax revenues generated by all TVEs in a township in Huantai is in the region of ten million yuan every year. In other words, these enterprises alone are responsible for at least one-third of the total revenues captured by their township.
NA = not applicable.

management and the possession of political capital is obvious in Tangshan, as shown in Table 3.7. Profitability is probably the most important yardstick of a manager's competence, and there appears to be a strong correlation between this variable and the level of political capital. The most important post – the deputy township mayor in this context – has been granted to the managers of the three most profitable enterprises in Tangshan (cases 1, 2, and 3). Together these earned more than eight million yuan in after-tax profit in 1994, i.e. more than 90 percent of the total after-tax profits earned by all town-level collective enterprises in Tangshan that year. They also occupy a similarly dominant position in terms of employment and fixed asset value.

It appears to be the norm to include enterprise managers in the local people's congress in Tangshan. Membership of the people's congress is highly valued by these managers. It is a sign of recognition and approval and can also be a stepping stone to a higher level in the hierarchy of power. Most manager-members think that they deserve such political status because of their contribution to the local economy.[47] In 1995, the township government collected about five million yuan in taxes and profit extraction from TVEs, which accounted for at least a quarter of its total annual income. Further, managers believe that their contribution is even more obvious if one considers

Table 3.7   Distribution of political capital of managers of township-level collective enterprises in Tangshan township

Manager	Enterprise statistics			Political title of the manager
	Number of workers	Fixed assets (10,000 yuan)	Profits after tax and management fees (10,000 yuan)	
1 Wang Li	4,000	1,700	400	DTM
2 Zhang Jian	432	1,157	349	DTM
3 Wang Bing	600	1,383	261	DTM
4 Rong Yao	185	220	25	CPC
5 Zhang Bing	90	200	15	TPC
6 Zhang Jin	50	62	Nil	TPC
7 Zhang Ping	30	500	Nil	TPC
8 Xu Cheng	130	195	Nil	TPC
9 Hu Zheng	40	52	Nil	TPC
10 Shi Guang	390	284	Nil	TPC
11 Gong Zi	140	574	−30	TPC
12 Zhang Yue	70	300	20	None
13 Chen Hang	11	30	5	None
14 Zhang Chengyu	280	1,686	Nil	None
15 Rong Wen	90	97	−20	None

Source: author's fieldwork. All figures are for the year 1994.

Note
DTM, deputy township mayor; CPC, County People's Congress member; TPC, Township People's Congress member.

the employment opportunities and industrial value that they create. Local officials concurred with this view.[48]

The high regard in which political titles are held is also connected with the consequences of being excluded. This is perceived as embarrassing or even humiliating. Managers regard it as a deliberate act by the local state. There are only five managers from the fifteen township-level enterprises in Tangshan who are not members of the township congress. The top three managers are all members. The manager who came in a distant fourth (case 4 in Table 3.7) has been elected to the county level congress, the people's congress one level higher than the town congress. Thus, for his better than average performance, he was recommended for a higher political status. Of the remaining four cases, Zhang Yue (case 12) has yet to establish his credentials as a competent manager in spite of the good performance of his enterprise. He had just been appointed to his present post when he was interviewed in January 1996. Thus, he can hardly claim credit for this success. The case of Zhang Chengyue (case 14), as discussed before, is a warning for all managers. Zhang's exclusion is generally perceived as a punishment for his failure to deliver.

The remaining two cases (cases 13 and 15) are more unusual. Although all the other collective enterprises under investigation are owned by the township government, these two enterprises belong ultimately to the Ministry of Agriculture. They used to be service units under the technical assistance program provided by the Agricultural Machinery Station in Tangshan, a technical division of the Ministry. In the early 1980s, the Ministry decided to lessen its financial burden by turning these units into profit-oriented companies. They are classified as collective enterprises, but, unlike the other thirteen enterprises, they are subject to control from both the vertical and horizontal line of command. Horizontally (*kuai*), they are under the supervision of the township government; vertically (*tiao*), they are under the leadership of their administrative superior at a higher level, which can stretch all the way up to the Ministry of Agriculture at the center. Like other collective enterprises, they are liable for management fees and other relevant local and state taxes, but, in terms of control over personnel, finance, and resources, they are independent from the township government. Most importantly, this means that possible after-tax profits from these enterprises will not be enjoyed by the local state. Their unique status and mediocre performance may together explain why the local state has excluded their managers from political influence.

Further analysis of the correlation between economic success and political capital can be carried out by looking at the previous political experience of managers. It is hardly convincing to argue that managers who are now in major posts in the local power hierarchy owe their positions purely to their managerial credentials, if these same people had already accumulated a substantial amount of political capital before they started their current managerial careers. An examination of the best and worst performers in Table 3.7 is consistent with the original claim made earlier in this chapter. The top three managers (cases 1–3) had no cadre service record, while the bottom four, who have no political capital at present (cases 12–15), came, ironically enough, directly from the administration. A brief account of the career trajectories of the top three managers may be useful here.

The career trajectories of the three most successful managers in Tangshan are consistent with this pattern.

Case 1:   Wang Li, now 45, joined the Township Construction Company in 1975, three years after its foundation. The company is now the biggest employer in the township and is also one of the most profitable ventures in the county. He started as a worker and has spent his entire career in this company. He was promoted to the posts of division accountant, technician, and division leader, and eventually reached the post of general manager in 1993. In the same year, he was invited to be the deputy township head.[49]

Case 2:   Wang Bing, 55, started his career as a technician in a village factory in 1967. He spent ten years in this factory, was awarded the title of "advanced worker," and was also classified as an engineer owing to his technical competence. His outstanding performance in this factory, as well as his relatively high level of educational attainment (a senior high qualification), paved the way for his appointment in 1977 to his present post of general manager of the Township Metal Factory. Under Wang's leadership, the factory has developed from a small factory with fewer than fifty staff and primitive technology into a leading local business with a total staff of more than 500 and an annual tax contribution in the region of three million yuan. In 1993, he too became a deputy township head.[50]

Case 3:   Zhang Jian represents a new generation of enterprise managers. At 37, he is in charge of the Township Chemical Factory, the most profitable enterprise in the township, which brings in an annual profit of more than six million yuan. The firm is also regarded as a successful model of local development and has been chosen as a showcase for entertaining high-level visitors, including Premier Li Peng and National People's Congress chairman, Wan Li. After spending a few years in the army, Zhang returned to his village and worked as a teacher for two years. He started his career in enterprise management as the head of the production division in a brigade-level chemical factory in the mid-1980s. The technical knowledge of mechanics and engineering that he accumulated during his military training and his relatively high level of literacy probably contributed to his ascent. He was invited to be the manager of the enterprise when it was reorganized into a new chemical factory in 1987. His good performance was recognized, and he was awarded the title of "outstanding enterprise manager" by the prefecture government in 1990 and 1992. In 1993, when the factory was restructured, he retained his managership and also became a deputy township head.[51]

Several common factors exist in the career trajectories of these three managers. First, they all started at a junior rank and climbed their way up to the top managerial post over the years as a result of their outstanding performance. More importantly, none of them served in the administration before they started their careers in enterprise management. Instead, they have spent most of their careers in their enterprises. Political capital only came after they had demonstrated excellence in enterprise management.

A few words can also be said about the losers. Zhang Yue (case 12) and Zhang Chengyu (case 14) were both ex-cadres from the township ETC and were directly transferred from the bureaucracy. It is premature to pass any judgment on the former, but the latter has proved to be a failure. Similarly, Chen Hang (case 13) and Rong Wen (case 15), who had both worked as leading officials in the township Agricultural Machinery Station, are not performing particularly well. The rise of the former in the local political hierarchy may be hindered by the remote link between his enterprise and the township government, but the latter has one of the worst records for delivering profit. This shows that previous political connections alone cannot guarantee success in enterprise management and, similarly, occupation of a managerial post will not automatically bring political glory. Failure to deliver the economic goods can block anyone from access to political capital and status, which are reserved for competent enterprise managers. Or put it in another way, managerial success breeds political status and honor.

Summary

The analysis has demonstrated the growing functional indispensability of managers to the local economy of rural China. Their phenomenal rise has several important implications for the political economy of rural China. First, as shown in the analysis, the public ownership of TVEs does not hinder the emergence of entrepreneurialism among managers. TVE managers are more than just organizers and coordinators of business activities. The unique rural social and opportunity structure and the close connection between personal income and enterprise performance have exerted a distinct motivational effect on managers. Consequently, they are a source of entrepreneurial drive and dynamism in the rural sector and function as the engine of local economic growth.

Second, this case also illustrates the linkage between success in enterprise management and the accumulation of political capital by managers. A TVE, in other words, can be more than just an economic organization. It can also be a platform from which local talents can rise not only to strategic management positions with control over valuable economic resources, but also to the ranks of the elites in the local hierarchy of power. This chapter shows that most outstanding managers are rewarded with a taste of power. This may partly explain the aforementioned misconception about the dominant influence of political capital in the selection of enterprise managers. The problem with this view is that it neglects the timing of their attainment of this political capital. As shown in the analysis above, in most cases political capital is a consequence of, rather than the cause of, managers' success. Awards come only after managers have demonstrated their competence at the job, and vary according to the extent of the success achieved. The stories of the three workers-turned-mayors in Tangshan show that an alternative path to power is possible. The unique features of the rural administration and the importance of economic success in the new economic order have paved the way for the breakthrough of such managerial talent.

Third, the Zibo story also points out that there are many ways to get to the top of the enterprise hierarchy, and political capital can only account for a minority of those who succeed. As shown in the case of Zibo, only about one-third of enterprise managers in the collective sector had previously served in the Party-state administration. Experience and connections accumulated in previous administrative service may be sufficient for the task of organizing a small enterprise at the village level, but the more demanding and compli-cated job of enterprise management in large-scale business organizations may require more professional knowledge. Management skills and experience are required to assist the rapid growth of rural enterprises, and such attributes appear to be the most common credentials among managers. This case shows that the majority of managers had a long period of apprenticeship in enterprise management before they reached the pinnacle of their firms. The local state, which is caught between the self-interest of cadres, instructions and orders from the higher level, and the interests of the local community, has to maintain a delicate balance between professional competence and political credentials in the choice of managers. The development of these TVEs requires the effec-tive utilization of entrepreneurial talent and a tactful combination of political capital. In other words, a synergy unleashed by the encounter between the old bureaucratic coordinated order and the new market-oriented regime in the post-Mao years is the key to rural economic development. This enables us to transcend the dichotomy of the changing elite thesis and the surviving elite thesis mentioned earlier in this discussion. What we see in Zibo is a symbiosis of human and political capital, which is not only crucial in the fight for success, but is also important in the aftermath of proven managerial pedigree. An observation on the new ruling elites in Eastern Europe by Eyal, Szelenyi, and Townsley is revealing for us here. They argue:

> [E]ach individual possesses a portfolio of "stocks" of different forms of capital, and when they confront social change they try to reshuffle this portfolio to get rid of forms of capital which are losing value, and convert them into forms of capital which are more valuable.[52]

This chapter has demonstrated the rise in the rural economy of a group of individuals with entrepreneurial initiative. They earn themselves economic and political power simply by making themselves functionally indispensable to the local economic development. The local state depends on their contribution to maintain effective governance of the local economy and of the community in general. This is, however, only half of the equation of the changing pattern of interaction between state and society in rural China. Managers still need the blessing of the local state in the present institutional setting in rural China. The discussion in Chapters 4 and 5, which evaluate the interaction between managers and the local state in terms of external business linkages and internal enterprise management respectively, will provide a clearer picture of the interdependence of the two parties. In this process, managers, like the new ruling elites in Eastern Europe, are also reshuffling their portfolio of human and political stocks to advance their career interests.

4 Where local government still matters

While academics may dispute the extent of enterprises' dependence on state support, few could argue that the imperfect market mechanism developed in China has yet to uproot the bureaucratic influence on the economy.[1] This analysis, however, cautions against a lack of specificity in defining enterprises' dependence, and warns against the tendency to exaggerate or overgeneralize the dominance of the local government. Huang Yasheng, for example, has attributed enterprises' dependence to three types of policy resources enjoyed by the local state:

> First, they control the allocation of physical inputs – especially scarcity inputs such as energy and raw materials – or at least have the ability to arrange input supplies. Secondly, they invariably have some measure of discretionary authority, arising from either the inherent ambiguity in the central policy directives or their authorized decision-making power. Thirdly, they are in charge of enforcing policy directives and monitoring their compliance by enterprise under their jurisdiction.[2]

These resources are important, but are not the only aspects of the economic activity of rural enterprises; conclusions based only on these encounters can be misleading. Although there is little alternative to the local authorities when it comes to obtaining bureaucratic services such as business licenses or various certification forms (these are the domain of governmental authority and marketization is unlikely to be adopted), more options may be available for other aspects of enterprise external linkages. The major problem, this study argues, is that this statist perspective hinders the recognition of two important dimensions of the relationship between the local state and TVE managers: its dynamic nature and its particularistic pattern. Enterprise's dependence on the local government is dynamic because its extent is determined by the availability of alternatives, which is, in turn, affected by the ongoing process of marketization and its own growth. As we will see in the forthcoming discussion, the pattern of state–enterprise interaction in the 1990s was undoubtedly different from the scenario during the early years of rural industrialization. The relationship is also particularistic, as it is very much determined by the resources under the command of the enterprise concerned and hence its valuation of the potential assistance of the local officials; in fact, there appears to be two worlds of managers operating enterprises of different scale and with different levels of success. In other words, a static view overemphasizing the extent of enterprise dependence can obscure the picture of the state–enterprise relationship. This in turn hinders the analysis of the interaction between TVE managers and the local administration.

On the basis of the experience of Zibo, this chapter will evaluate enterprise's dependence on local government, by focusing on two major areas of business operation: securing capital supply and business networking.[3] The fundamental question in this chapter is: how dependent on the local government are these TVEs and on what basis? This study argues that the availability of alternatives is the key to answering these questions. There are substantial variations in the degree of dependence across the three areas of business operation and between enterprises of different strength. Whereas Chapter 3 demonstrated the local government's dependence on entrepreneurial talents to develop the local economy, this chapter shows that managers also find the support of the local government useful for their business operations. Interdependence between the two parties is evident. The synergy unleashed by their collaboration is the key to local enterprise development.

The following discussion will start with a recapitulation of the macro-environment in which rural enterprises are located, as discussed in Chapter 2. The environment is characterized by a restricted flow of business across the country. Two outstanding features are noteworthy: localism and under-developed market mechanisms. The lack of a desirable legal environment in China further reinforces the trend. This will be followed by an analysis of the specific context in which rural enterprises operate – an empirical analysis of development with respect to capital supply and business networking.

The parochialism of TVE development

This research argues that TVEs are developing in an environment that discourages extensive external linkages among enterprises. Two distinct features of the economy account for this: localism among local governments and the underdevelopment of market mechanisms. The former represents the general tendency among local governments to protect local interests by setting up selective administrative barriers against competition; the latter implies the limited availability of market alternatives, which hinders external linkages indiscriminately. Together, they restrict the free flow of resources and business transactions across communities, and limit space for the growth and survival of rural enterprises. Consequently, linkages with business contacts outside the local community are hard to make and this, in turn, inflates the importance of local state assistance. As argued in Chapter 2, these features are products of the past and the present. The legacy of Mao's developmental strategy of self-sufficiency, the impact of the planned economy, and the incentive of fiscal contracting all contribute to this parochial tendency on the part of TVEs.

An effective legal framework is an important basis for the development of market mechanisms. Theoretically, it can greatly reduce the risks involved in exchange, as a sanction is guaranteed for any breach of agreement or contract. The identity of the parties involved is irrelevant, as punishment will be meted out in any case of non-compliance. This corresponds to the "ideal" market transaction: goods traded anonymously on an impersonal basis according to mutually agreed terms. Certainly, there has been an enormous increase in the number of laws during the reform period. According to one account, there has been a "legislative explosion" in China, and "since 1979 whole areas of law have been embraced by new codes and status."[4] The economic realm appears to be the major beneficiary of this progress. Between 1979 and 1990, the National People's Congress approved fifty-six economic laws and the State Council issued and approved another 860 state administrative regulations and directives on economic matters.[5] However, the number of laws alone cannot be taken as a measure of the rule of law in China: implementation and enforcement of the laws is crucial. The Chinese legal system is plagued by a worryingly low rate of implementation of court decisions. In his 1988 report to the National People's Congress, the Supreme People's Court president, Zheng Tianxiang, admitted that in 1985 and 1986 20 percent of court decisions in economic cases were not enforced, and the figure went up to 30 percent in the following year.[6] According to another account, 50–60 percent of the newly passed economic laws were either "poorly implemented" or "not implemented at all."[7] This is probably a result of the lack of a tradition of judicial independence and of the excessive emphasis on politics in Communist China.

Government intervention is still a major contributor to contract non-performance.[8] However, the progress of the rule of law is hindered not only by the abuse of governmental power and the weakness of the court, but also by the mindset of the economic actors, inherited from the pre-reform economy. A fixed contract is a tool that can provide an extra degree of predictability for a particular transaction, yet its operation also relies on the ability of the parties involved to forecast market change accurately. The development of such cognitive ability requires experience, skill, and information. The suppression of the market in the pre-reform era deprived Chinese economic actors – bureaucrats and enterprise operators – of the chance to nurture the first two attributes, and the poor infrastructure at present limits the supply of the last. It takes time for economic actors to acquire such mental tools, which are required in order to survive in the new business environment.

Ambitious TVE managers are thus in a predicament; the local market can no longer fully satisfy these fledgling firms, in terms of either input-supply or absorption of products, and there are obstacles to the flow of goods and inputs, and to business transactions, across regions. For instance, rural consumption remained at the level of about 300–500 billion yuan per year during the first half of the 1990s, whereas the total rural industrial output had already reached the level of 1,700 billion yuan by 1993.[9] There are several alternative channels that enterprises can go through in order to overcome this dilemma. First, they can fully utilize existing market channels; though far from perfect, the market still has a role to play in the rural economy. Second, the local government can be a reliable source of resources which can facilitate business transactions. Lastly, the TVEs can rely on their own personal connections; relational contracting can be a useful supplement to the other two channels. According to Williamson, a high degree of uncertainty in the transactions and the limited availability of alternative trading relationships make relational contracting necessary. Thus, the limited choice available and the risk involved in doing business with strangers is likely to impel Williamson to develop a recurring business relationship with the people he knows well.[10] This setting is, in a way, similar to the business environment in rural China. The choice of business partner is limited by the underdeveloped market mechanisms and the protective measures imposed by the local government, and the impoverished legal system and ignorance of the market situation impose a high risk in conducting business with strangers. Relational contracting is likely to be an alternative business strategy, supplementing the bureaucratic and market options. The relative importance of these three channels for TVEs will determine the degree of dependence on local government, and thus defines the relationship between TVE managers and local government. In the following section, the situation in Zibo will be examined on the basis of this framework.

The important aspects of the business operation of TVEs, securing the supply of capital and building business networks, will now be examined. While the former ensures the continual growth of enterprise, the latter entails important activities, such as purchasing raw materials, marketing products, and expanding business contacts, which are crucial to the survival of enterprises. More importantly, interaction between managers and the local government in these domains illustrates the challenges confronted by TVE managers in the process of market transformation, as well as their dynamism in the face of these challenges. Motivated by concern about their own careers and incomes, managers are driven to seek the support of the local government, as it remains an effective means of reducing transaction costs in the two areas. However, the Zibo case shows that managers are not simply puppets, content with the paternalism of the local government. They have, in fact, demonstrated their entrepreneurial spirit. They take the initiative in breaking the constraints imposed on them by the environment, and there is ample evidence of their enthusiasm in strengthening the competitiveness of their enterprises. By doing so, they are, intentionally or unintentionally, minimizing reliance on the local government and asserting their own independence. Their entrepreneurism and dynamism are important facets defining the interdependence between these managers and the local government.

General infrastructural support of local government

Local governments in Zibo do a good job of maintaining steady improvement in basic infrastructure, hence providing a favorable habitat for the development of rural enterprises in the prefecture. Two areas are particularly noteworthy: human resources and logistics. Tables 4.1 and 4.2 show sustained growth in education and health facilities in the prefecture over the last two decades. In both areas, 20–30 percent improvement is recorded in most indicators of the conditions of intellectual and physical attributes of the local population. A healthier and better educated labor force certainly benefits the booming business sectors in Zibo. A more astonishing achievement can be seen in logistic facilities (see Table 4.3). Although the volume of freight transport tripled

Table 4.1 Educational development in Zibo

Year	Number of students in ordinary high school	Number of students in technical high school
1980	22.96	0.30
1985	23.03	0.57
1990	20.09	0.78
1995	24.29	1.58
2000	29.13	1.77

Source: *Zibo Tongji Nianjian* (*Zibo Statistical Yearbook*), 2001, p. 368.

Note
Unit: 10,000 persons.

Table 4.2 Development of health facilities in Zibo

Year	Number of health personnel	Number of beds available
1980	11,816	9,667
1985	13,645	10,770
1990	15,693	13,001
1995	17,559	14,771
2000	17,476	14,812

Source: *Zibo Tongji Nianjian* (*Zibo Statistical Yearbook*), 2001, p. 372.

Table 4.3 Volume of transport in Zibo

Year	Volume of passenger transport (10,000 persons)	Volume of freight transport (10,000 tons)	Length of paved roads (kilometers)
1986	1,056	1,634	NA
1990	1,007	2,252	NA
1995	950	3,441	2,629
2000	12,022	3,861	3,112

Source: *Zibo Tongji Nianjian* (*Zibo Statistical Yearbook*), 2001, pp. 196 and 199.

Note
NA = not applicable.

during the last two decades, passenger transport increased tenfold during the same period. Development in the telecommunications sector was phenomenal (Table 4.4). The number of fixed facilities increased 100-fold between 1986 and 2000, while the number of mobile phones, which were non-existent in 1990, surpassed the number of fixed phones within ten years. Certainly, local governments at various levels play a key role in investing, financing, permitting, or promoting the development of all these infrastructures, which are important requirements to enable local rural enterprise to grow and prosper.

Securing capital supply

A steady supply of capital is crucial for the smooth operation of an enterprise. Empirically, external loans, especially those from rural financial institutions – mainly the Agricultural Bank of China (ABC) and the Rural Credit Cooperatives (RCC) – are the major source of capital supply for rural enterprises across China. Several features of the prevalent financial structure of TVEs are illustrative of this general pattern.

First, there is, in general, a high loan–asset ratio among rural enterprises. According to a State Council Development Research Center's survey, on average, almost half the total assets possessed by rural enterprises are loans,[12] and bank loans are an important component of these liabilities. Second, there is a close correlation between growth of the credit supply and expansion of the scale of operation of rural enterprises. As of 1984, banks were allowed to provide loans for rural enterprises, and this proved to be an important impetus for the growth of this sector. Between 1984 and 1987, credit supply experienced an average annual growth of 50 percent, and asset accumulation by rural enterprises also reached a new height of about 30 percent of annual growth during the same period.[13] Third, bank loans are particularly important as a source of working capital for rural enterprises. According to the aforementioned national survey, rural enterprises' working capital is made up mostly of stocks of products and income receivable in the account book.[14] In other words, most rural enterprises are short of cash in their operations and bank loans appear to be an important supplement for them.

Table 4.4 Development of postal and phone communication in Zibo

Year	Total postal transactions (10,000 yuan)	Number of telephone sets of which are	
		Fixed	Mobile
1986	2,000	3,465	NA
1990	4,762	6,017	NA
1995	39,657	47,591	13,407
2000	133,494	347,906	373,771

Source: *Zibo Tongji Nianjian* (*Zibo Statistical Yearbook*), 2001, p. 201.

Note
NA = not applicable.

The situation in Zibo is no different from the national pattern. Loans from financial institutions, mainly the ABC and RCC, are crucial for the operation and development of rural enterprises. About 60 percent of the TVE managers interviewed ranked the steady supply of capital as their major concern for enterprise development and regarded banks as the usual place to turn to for loans. Fortunately, the local branches of ABC and RCC are supportive of their development. About three-quarters of their new loans every year, estimated to be 150–200 million yuan, are awarded to rural enterprises.[15]

The dependence on bank loans is further illustrated when the focus is narrowed to the asset composition of collective enterprises at the township level in Tangshan. Unfortunately, we do not have reliable statistics on the total asset value of the studied enterprises. However, if we assume that the national ratio of fixed and total asset value of TVEs of 1:2, as stated in the State Council Development Research Center's report mentioned above, is applicable in our case here, then an estimate of the loan–asset ratio should be in the region of 40 percent for these enterprises. Even if we ignore these guesses, the level of fixed asset investment appears to be closely related to the level of credit supply. The fifteen enterprises invested a total of about twenty-seven million yuan in fixed assets in 1994; during the same period, they received about twelve million yuan in new loans from ABC and RCC.[16] The contribution of the banking sector has again proved to be substantial (see Table 4.5).

To what extent is the assistance of the local government indispensable to rural enterprises in obtaining bank loans? The operation of the ABC and RCC is, strictly speaking, independent of the township government. Their independence is based on the mandatory credit plan imposed from higher-level banking institutions and the separate line of command.

Hierarchical control of credit

The credit supply of the ABC and RCC is under the strict control of the People's Bank of China. The credit plan is compiled jointly each year by the Ministry of Finance, the People's Bank of China, and the State Planning Commission. This plan is subordinate to the state plan for economic growth and to the state budget. The ABC and RCC can voice their demands during the drafting process. However, once the final decision is made, mandatory credit quotas will be set and then these institutions have to allocate quotas to their branches, down to the lowest level. The system is known as the "pyramid allocation system."[17] Such a credit quota serves as an upper limit on the amount of money that can be loaned within a specific community. Banks in this area cannot release loans exceeding this limit even if there are greater demands or if it has sufficient deposits to support these loans.

ABC and RCC personnel are also independent of local government's control. The local branches of the ABC are under the ultimate control of its central office in Beijing. Each branch is supervised by the office at the next level up. A manager in a county branch disclosed that the local office is independent

Table 4.5 Year-end value of the total assets and outstanding bank loans of township-level
collective enterprises in Tangshan, 1994

Name of enterprise	Fixed-asset value (10,000 yuan)	Outstanding bank loans (10,000 yuan)
Tangshan Construction	1,700	1,200
Romu Metallic	1,383	1,146
Dongyue Chemical	1,157	1,000
Renren Textiles	220	122
Huantai Meter	52	42
Antenna-Manufacturing	62	43
Charcoal	500	400
Tali Furniture	200	NA
Huantai Food Processing	1,686	1,506
No. 2 Manufacturing	195	NA
Automobile Repair	97	90
Silk Manufacturing	284	755
Automobile Accessories	30	15
No. 3 Chemical	574	746
Huantai Metal Equipment	300	NA

Source: author's fieldwork.

Notes
Bank loans here refer to loans from ABC, RCC and other banks.
NA = not applicable.

of the township government in terms of control over three crucial matters
– personnel, budget, and resources (*ren cai wu*) – the major indicators of
administrative control in the bureaucracy.[18] In other words, these matters
are beyond the jurisdiction of township government. A similar system operates
in Huantai RCC.[19]

Despite these administrative barriers, the local government can still influence the credit decisions of local banks for the following reasons. In recent
years, financial reform in China has instilled a greater emphasis on commercialization in the operation of banks. Consequently, the creditworthiness of the
loan applicant has become an important issue in a credit decision. The Huantai
ABC has developed a standard procedure for loan approval based on a scale
of risk index. The index is calculated on the basis of four factors: the credit
history of the applicant, the amount of loan requested, the reliability of the
guaranty arrangement, and the performance and reputation of the applicant.[20]
Requests for loans that exceed a specific index level will be rejected.

This seemingly scientific practice, unexpectedly, provides a chance for
the local government to intervene. As will be seen in Chapter 5, the township government receives a regular update on the operation of TVEs, and
this provides it with a monopoly on information about enterprises. This, in
turn, enables the local government to exert a significant influence over loan
decisions. As a standard company search facility has yet to be developed in

rural China, the township government is an important source of information concerning the performance of an enterprise, making it an indispensable party in the credit process. Banks also respect the township government's view, because of its impact on the repayment ability of an enterprise in the long term and the arrangements in the event of an enterprise's bankruptcy. Township government can directly affect the development of an enterprise in two ways: by allocating enterprise profit and by approving new projects. Although details of how township government can exert its influence on these matters will be elaborated on in Chapter 5, it is important to realize at this juncture that both matters will affect the development of the enterprise and, hence, its repayment ability.

In addition, although the control of bank officials is basically within the jurisdiction of the higher-level branch, this does not mean that these officials are completely immune from local influence. The role of the local Party official can be illustrated by the process of appointing leading RCC officials at the county level. The branch of the ABC in Zibo prefecture is the supervising unit of the county RCC, and any appointment to a senior post in the latter is controlled by the former. The process usually starts with an investigation into the background and performance of the candidates. Their personal files are important documents. Although keeping written records is one of the basic traits of any bureaucracy, the comprehensive scope and political nature of the information stored in each file in the Chinese personnel system is striking. It contains not only records of the life history and an evaluation of the professional competence of the individual concerned, but also political assessments.[21] The Party organization of the unit plays a crucial role in the assessment process, especially for those candidates who are Party members. In turn, the leading bank officials, who are mostly Party members, are subject to the influence of the local Party organization, which acts as the command center for all Party organizations in the community. And, thus, the career prospects of bank officials, despite the independent line of command of the banking system, can still be affected by the local Party organization. Market reform may have diluted the force of this political variable, but the view of the local Party organization is still relevant. In fact, the prefecture ABC always seeks to consult the county government and the Party organization when a promotion investigation occurs.[22] This, together with the other two factors mentioned above, provides possible openings for local influence. This also occurs in the appointment process of bank officials at township level.

Local influence on enterprises' access to the credit supply is also increased by the fact that cross-community flow of bank credit is rare, though not impossible, in rural China.[23] It is very difficult for enterprises to obtain loans from banks in another township, and bank officials even claim that this practice is forbidden.[24] Local banks are also, in general, reluctant to approve such transactions for two reasons. First, there is a higher risk involved, as the knowledge of the performance and financial condition of an applicant from another community is very limited. The local government is certainly willing to provide the necessary information, but as the political leverage enjoyed by these administrations in other communities has little immediate effect on the local bankers, they are less likely to compromise over an unjustified application under such circumstances. Second, there is pressure on the local banks to reserve scarce financial resources for local use. The credit quota controls the volume of credit, yet it also has to be financed by the savings absorbed locally. Within the credit limit, loans are possible only if an equivalent level of bank deposits is available. It is always argued that local banks should minimize the outflow of local resources and make sure that local rural enterprises – the engine of local economic development – can enjoy a large slice of these resources.[25] Local banks, to some extent, share this view, as one of their roles is to facilitate local economic development.[26] In effect, this increases the dependence of TVEs on local banks, which in turn strengthens the local state's position.

The last leverage of local government in influencing local banks' credit decisions is its role in securing guarantee for bank loans. As mentioned above, guarantee is now mandatory for release of a loan, and local government can help enterprises in several possible ways. First, local government can lobby other enterprises to provide a guarantee on behalf of the applicant. Enterprises of more solid financial condition are generally approached by local officials to support other smaller enterprises in loan applications. Nevertheless, as a manager of bigger enterprises reiterates, the financial condition or, more specifically, the repayment ability, of the enterprise concerned, rather than the involvement of local government, is the major determinant in their collaboration. In most cases, enterprises negotiate directly, without the intermediation of officials. As a last resort, local government can provide a guarantee itself. Although the government, as an administrative unit, is forbidden to provide such backing, its subsidiary can bypass the legal restriction. Townships with collectively owned industrial corporations (*gongye zonggonghi*) replacing the administrative ETC as the overseer of collective asset management have this advantage. Though usually staffed with cadres and closely monitored by its administrative supervisors, these companies also enjoy legal economic status, and thus are eligible to provide guarantee for bank loans. However, in Zibo, most local governments are reluctant to get involved in these pursuits and prefer to employ the first strategy. This is probably because of the general reservation of local bankers.[27]

Restrictions on alternative sources of capital

The position of the local government is further reinforced by the limited alternative sources of capital supply in the community and by local government's influence on those alternatives.

Share-issuing can be a means of raising capital for enterprise development. In 1991–6, about 180 million yuan of new capital was raised as a result of share-issuing in Huantai.[28] This is obviously an important supplement to bank loans, which amounted to less than 200 million yuan a year for the county. However, this device is confined to enterprises with a sound economic foundation. Otherwise it is difficult to interest the staff in buying shares. In addition, the capital-mobilizing effect is limited by the underdevelopment of secondary markets.[29] More importantly, as will be seen in Chapters 6 and 7, the local government's influence on every aspect of the shareholding transformation is evident. Initiation and recommendation of the change, asset valuation, and determination of share allocation are all within the jurisdiction of local government.

Enterprises can also raise extra capital through various forms of internal borrowing. Borrowing from workers is a common practice in enterprises in Zibo. Usually a few hundred yuan is borrowed from each worker at an interest rate higher than the current bank rate and these loans are repaid within a short period, usually less than a year. Another common practice is to exact an "admission charge" of one month's salary from new recruits (*yizidailao*) when offering them a job. The usefulness of these loans is, however, generally limited. The amount of capital raised is usually small and it has to be repaid within a short period. In addition, this practice is not possible without the tacit consent of the local government, as it is forbidden by state financial and taxation regulations. Central government is anxious to suppress this practice as it may divert financial resources from the banking sector, thus weakening its ability to maintain a macro-control over the credit supply. It may also affect its financial strength, as the payment by enterprises at greater than the bank interest rate implies a smaller tax base.[30]

Friends or other enterprises are another possible source of capital. In recent years, unofficial lending activities have been expanding fast in rural China. According to one survey, there is fifty to seventy billion yuan circulating in this booming private credit market in rural China, almost double that provided by the formal financial institutions.[31] These activities are particularly prevalent in the coastal region and in rural economies with a dominant private sector, although there is little evidence that a similar development is taking place in Zibo. Neither enterprise managers nor local bank officials are aware of any significant development in this respect. In those few instances mentioned by managers, the amount involved was only a few thousand yuan. On the other hand, inter-firm credit is far more common in Huantai. However, this usually implies a postponement of payment rather than a supply of extra cash. Thus, its contribution is limited.

Rural cooperative funds (*nongcun hezuo jijinhui*) are one of the latest developments in rural finance. There are variations in the organizational structure of these funds, but the dominant form is a kind of credit cooperative; rural residents buy shares in the fund and, as shareholders, they are entitled to borrow money from it. The idea has spread rapidly in the countryside since the late 1970s. By 1994, such organizations could be found in 17,800 townships (37.1 percent of all townships in China) and 125,000 villages (15.6 percent of all villages in China).[32] By the end of 1992, these organizations had already absorbed more than sixteen billion yuan from the rural population and constituted a useful supplementary capital supply for rural enterprises.[33]

Similar organizations can be found in Zibo. Huantai county is among the pioneers that introduced this experiment. Its first fund appeared in 1988,[34] and by 1996 at least four of the thirteen townships had established such an institution. The total amount of deposits received is around ten to fifteen million yuan, and the average deposit in each fund is about 3–3.5 million yuan. Loans from these sources appear to be a useful supplement for local enterprises. However, there are several constraints. First, there is a similar reluctance to allow cross-community flow of loans. Second, most of the loans are short-term, usually three to six months, and the amount involved is relatively small. None of the funds interviewed has released a single loan of more than half a million yuan. Third, the future of these institutions is uncertain. The central government has reservations about this local initiative, as it may disturb the rural financial order. Possible bad debts, high-interest loans, and, most important of all, competition with the local banks are the major concerns. Local bank officials in Huantai show a similar distaste for this development. In 1995, the central government tightened its control over these local institutions by introducing a standard procedure for their establishment and stricter guidelines for their area of business.[35]

A striking feature of the operation of these organizations in Huantai is the strong involvement of township government. Table 4.6 provides a summary of the township administration officials' dominance in running rural cooperative funds in Tinzhuang, Zhoujiazhen, and Qifeng, three of the four funds in Huantai county . All these funds were initiated by the township administration, which is also where all the staff came from. The personnel of these funds all used to work in the township administration and have some experience with financial and economic management. They remain township cadres despite their transfer to a new unit, which means that their personal benefits and career prospects are still under the direct control of the township government. In two cases, Tinzhuang and Zhoujiazhen, a board of directors has been established, yet the involvement of the officials remains strong. The county Bureau of Agriculture is officially the supervising unit of the funds as required by the national regulation. Yet, its control is nominal. Day-to-day operation is firmly under the command of the township government, and control over the resources, personnel, and finance of the funds remains in its hands. Most important of all, township governments are heavily involved in making credit decisions. In Qifeng and Zhoujiazhen, the fund has little autonomy in approving loans, whereas the Tinzhuang fund seemingly enjoys greater freedom. Yet the dominance of officials on its board of directors may offset much of its independence.

Commercialization of Chinese banks

Despite the array of leverage enjoyed by the local government, there are opposing forces. The trend of growing commercialization of banks may, in the future, further dilute the importance of the local government.

Table 4.6 Organizational structure of rural cooperative funds (RCFs) in Huantai
county

	Tinzhuang RCF	*Qifeng RCF*	*Zhoujiazhen RCF*
Initiation of the fund	By the township ETC	By the township government	By the township government
Appointment of the fund manager	By the board of directors of the fund	By the township government	By the township government
Source of staff	Transferred from the township government and remain as cadres	Same as Tinzhuang	Same as Tinzhuang
Composition of the board of directors	Nine members: the manager and two assistant managers of the fund; the township mayor and his three deputies; the chairman of the township ETC; a village Party secretary	No board has been established	Nine members: the mayor of the township as the government chair and eight other major shareholders
Supervising units	The township ETC and the county Bureau of Agriculture	Same as Tinzhuang	Same as Tinzhuang
Loan decisions	By the fund	Loans of more than 50,000 yuan have to be approved by the township government	Jointly by the fund and the township government

Source: author's fieldwork.

More of a commercial flavor has been introduced into the banking sector
in China since the early days of reform. In recent years, central government
action in this direction has shifted up a gear. Major developments include the
establishment of policy banks, such as the Agricultural Development Bank
in 1995, with the aim of separating the policy function from existing banks
like the ABC. It is hoped that, by doing so, the operation of the latter can be
regulated to a greater extent by commercial rather than administrative logic.[36]
Financial discipline has also been strengthened by the introduction of new
prudential ratios for the asset management of banks. Lardy argues that the
introduction of various laws and regulations concerning commercialization of
state banks in the 1990s was specifically intended to "insulate banks at the local
level from political interference in lending decision."[37] In sum, local banks are
under significant pressure to adopt a cautious approach to credit supply.[38]

Rural banks experience the same pressure. Avoidance of bad debts is one of the primary concerns of local bankers because it is not only in the bank's own interest but also in the staff's personal interest to do so. Whereas under the previous system there was no clear link between branch operational profits and staff earnings,[39] this link has been strengthened in recent years. Staff can now earn a substantial bonus if there is good balance of assets at the end of the year. Alternatively, some banks, such as the Huantai RCC, adopt a collective penalty system. Each month 40 percent is deducted from staff's basic salary, and this sum is returned, with interest, at the end of the financial year only if the financial targets are met.[40] The pressure can also be seen in the intense competition between local banks. Various innovative services have been provided. For instance, the Huantai RCC proudly summarizes its service with a gimmicky phrase, "36578," which means that its offices operate 365 days a year and from 7am to 8pm every day. In addition, door-to-door banking services are provided.[41] Local banks' decision to reject administrative units as eligible guarantors for bank loans in 1993 further tied the hands of the local government in this matter.[42] This is a move consistent with the greater emphasis on the debt repayment ability in credit decisions and the increasing awareness of the danger of bad debt. Now, only economic entities can provide a guarantee for bank loans.

Local officials in charge of local economic management were candid in revealing their sense of powerlessness. A deputy director of a township economic and trade commission admitted:

> At present, we can no longer be 100 percent sure that our intervention can secure a loan for enterprise as in the past. We are, of course, still in a position to lobby and pressure local bankers, but they have the final word. Our views matter only when the conditions of our case and the other applicant's are exactly the same. An enterprise's financial strength and repayment ability are the key factors of consideration for banks now.[43]

The development of rural credit funds, he admitted, is, in fact, a reflection the growing frustration of local government. By establishing its own financial institutions, the local government hopes that a more steady supply of credit can be provided for local enterprises. A substantial proportion of enterprise managers share this concern. Only about one-third of the TVE managers interviewed believe that the assistance of the local government is beneficial in obtaining a bank loan. Not surprisingly, they are all managers from enterprises in a poor condition. As the emphasis on applicants' ability to repay increases, it is more likely that enterprises in good financial condition will attract bank support. This is confirmed by the more selective credit allocation policy of local banks. In 1995, the Huantai RCC released twelve million yuan of new loans in Tangshan. The money was shared by the three most successful enterprises in the township: Romu, Dongyue, and Tangshan Construction.[44] The same principle of selective support for core enterprises (*gugan qiye*), enterprises with sound financial strength and prospects, has been adopted by all the banks in the county.[45] The implication is that the performance of enterprises, not just political factors, is now important when bankers make a loan decision. This trend, if it continues, will further dilute the role of local government.

Business networking

Locating raw materials

A distinctive characteristic of TVE development is that it is outside the state plan. This means that TVEs do not enjoy a steady supply of raw materials at subsidized prices or secured procurement of their products. In other words, when compared with their state-sector counterparts, such enterprises are more exposed to volatile market conditions. Whiting, however, supplementing this view with her insight into the role of the state in TVE development, observes, "[C]ontrary to the commonly accepted official rhetoric of 'self-reliance,' the areas in which rural industries were most successful under Mao, were, in many ways, the least self-reliant."[46]

Wong's study of five small industries in the collective era also echoes Whiting's view by demonstrating that state budgetary grants had provided more than half of the total investment in farm machinery between 1966 and 1978.[47] This was, however, not the case for Zibo. Commune-brigade enterprises in Zibo, the basis upon which TVEs in the post-Mao era prospered, remained mostly out of plan in the collective era. Between the 1950s and the early 1970s, with the exception of a small number of plants manufacturing medium- and small-scale agricultural tools, all CBEs in Zibo were excluded from the state plan. Although it is true that many of these rural enterprises were tempted by the security inherent in economic planning, and had fought to be included in provincial, prefectural, or county plans in the late 1970s, few had succeeded. Even in the case of the few exceptions, raw material supplies were not guaranteed.[48] In other words, rural enterprises in Zibo have been accustomed to outside plan transaction.

This section will evaluate how TVEs in Zibo perform in business networking, i.e. identifying suppliers and buyers and expanding business contacts. In short, as a buyer's market is gradually taking shape in rural China, input purchases do not pose a serious problem; the involvement of the local government is the exception rather than the rule. However, marketing of products proves to be a greater challenge. Lack of outside contact and information drives enterprise managers to be more dependent on the local government. Nonetheless, managers can still demonstrate their dynamism and initiative in expanding their own business connections without the support of the local government.

Two features of the purchasing activities of TVEs in Huantai county are noteworthy. First, local suppliers appear to be the major source for the inputs needed for TVE production. According to the information obtained from the twenty township-level industrial enterprises studied, the pattern is clear. The findings are summarized in Table 4.7. Forty percent of the materials needed are bought within Zibo prefecture, and another 35 percent come from other areas of Shandong province. The county Rural Enterprise Administration (REA) (*Xiangzhen Qiye Guanliju*) confirms that this is, in fact, a general pattern for TVEs in this area.[49]

This is probably a legacy of Mao's principle of self-sufficiency in rural industrialization. However, it is also a cost-saving strategy for enterprises. Purchasing from nearby areas can greatly reduce the transaction cost. Long-distance trading definitely involves more transport and research expenses too. Lack of information and understanding of distant suppliers also reinforces the enterprises' preference for someone local. As one manager half-jokingly said, it would certainly cost less to track down your neighbor when he ran away with your money than a supplier in another province. This risk element also concerns the suppliers. In some cases, pre-payment for orders is required lest the contract is terminated unilaterally.[50] In other words, extra-locality transactions may incur extra expense and pressure on the limited cash flow. For those enterprises surviving on a shoestring budget, such money-saving tactics are not trivial.

Second, most of the raw materials are purchased through the market. Most managers claim that they can choose between different suppliers and regard price as the dominant determinant. No administrative permission is needed for these transactions. Thus, the local government does not have much role to play in this matter. These managers claim that they do not need any special personal connection to get these materials either. Apparently, for these enterprises, a buyer's market is emerging.

However, assistance by the local government is not completely absent. Its role depends on the nature of the materials needed. Two enterprises visited still rely on local government support to secure a steady supply of inputs. The first one is a silk factory. Silk is one of China's major exports, and a state plan is still applied to this industry in order to maintain the state monopoly. Thus,

Table 4.7 Location of the dominant source of input supply and the major market of collectively owned industrial enterprises at the township level in Huantai county

	Zibo	Shandong province	Outside Shandong province	Mixed
As a major source of raw materials	40% (8)	35% (7)	10% (2)	15% (3)
As a major market	30% (6)	25% (5)	40% (8)	5% (1)

Source: author's interview.

Note
Numbers in parentheses are number of enterprises.

despite its collective ownership, the silk factory in Huantai is still subject to the mandatory quota of the economic plan. However, only some of the necessary materials will be provided; this guaranteed amount is only sufficient to produce the mandatory quota required by the plan. Nevertheless, the factory also has to sell its product in the market in order to earn extra profit for its survival. At present, 30 percent of its products are sold in the market. Township government plays an important role in obtaining the extra raw materials necessary for market production. As this material is still tightly controlled in China, the involvement of the local government is crucial in bypassing all kinds of bureaucratic obstacles.[51] The second case involves a charcoal factory. Again, the necessary raw material – a petroleum derivative – is covered by the state plan, and it is difficult for the factory to gain access to it. This collective factory, in the first place, is not within the economic plan. A secondary market for this material exists, as plants supplied with this material will sell their surplus in the market, but the demand is great. The manager refused to give the details, but disclosed that he has to resort to "all kinds of tricks" to obtain this material. Nevertheless, he admitted that most of this material is bought with the assistance of the township government,[52] which, as a local government, is better informed of the material's availability in other regions and in a better position to bargain with the suppliers.

The assistance of the local government is, of course, still necessary in securing supplies such as electricity and water. The ultimate control of these utilities lies outside the immediate jurisdiction of the township or county governments, as they are mostly regulated by administrative bureaus subject to separate control from a higher level. However, local governments have significant influence in determining local priority in distribution. For instance, Huantai, like other rural communities, faces electricity shortages and periodic power cuts are necessary. The township government can lobby the county electricity bureau on behalf of local enterprises to arrange cuts at times which cause the least interruption and loss for local industries.[53] In a less dramatic fashion, the support of the local government is also necessary in order to secure an increase in supply. However, the TVEs interviewed seem to have little trouble in securing these services. The steady supply is taken for granted and no manager mentioned any difficulty. Given the financial intimacy between collective enterprises and local government, this is understandable.

Marketing of products is a more challenging task. The local proverb "one person for production, two persons for purchasing and three persons for marketing" (*yiren shengchan laingren caigou sanren tuixiao*) may exaggerate the complexity of purchasing, but it shows succinctly the importance of marketing for rural enterprises. Most enterprises have put substantial effort into selling their products, even setting up specialized marketing departments. In one case, the marketing department has a staff of sixty, while the average size is about 5 percent of the total manpower.[54] According to one salesman, these marketing personnel have to "run all over the country, using every possible method and form of persuasion" (*qianshan wanshui qianyan wanyu qianfang baiji*) to sell their products.

The concern about marketing is reflected in the generous remuneration packages for sales personnel. Salespeople are usually among the best paid in rural enterprises. For example, in a Xinzheng township collective, the top salesman earned 40,000 yuan in 1995, whereas the manager claimed to take home only 25,000 yuan in the same year.[55] On average, the income of marketing personnel is at least double that of ordinary workers. In most cases, a strong link between performance and income has been established for these personnel. Two methods are commonly adopted. First, a system of internal contract responsibility is used. For example, in the Lufeng Metal Rolls Factory in Xinzheng township, a contract is signed between the factory and the individual salesman that, most importantly, lays down a specific sales quota. The latter is paid eight yuan a day as a fixed wage, but on top of that, he can earn a bonus determined by two factors: fulfillment of the quota and the payment period. If the money is collected when the business is concluded, he is entitled to 3.6 percent of the sale value; the longer payment takes, the smaller his percentage. The bonus is also affected by the extent of the quota fulfillment. Failure to meet 85 percent of the assigned target means that the salesman loses the bonus. On the other hand, if he exceeds his quota, he is entitled not only to this bonus, but also to a further reward.[56] The second method is more straightforward. Zibo No. 3 Chemical Factory, for example, provides no basic salary for its salesmen. But, for every successful transaction, they are entitled to 0.52 percent of the sale value. In 1995, a relatively poor year for the factory, its total sales income was about eleven million yuan. In other words, the six salesmen were each entitled to about 10,000 yuan that year, approximately three times the average annual income of a factory worker.[57]

During the early 1990s, as shown in Table 4.7, 60 percent of enterprises this author visited were still confined to local or provincial markets. Several factors are responsible for this. First, confinement to the local market is, to a large extent, determined by the limited resources of the enterprises concerned. The constraint imposed by limited resources exacerbated the TVEs' shortage of market information and business contacts. Primarily dependent on a locally based marketing team, their knowledge of and connection with the larger business community was very restricted. Worse still, the personal connections of these sales personnel – mostly ex-salesmen of state-owned enterprises in the prefecture or ex-cadres in local rural supply and marketing cooperative – and even those of the enterprise management, were also restricted to nearby areas. Their commercial exposure during the pre-reform era was mostly confined to bureaucratic units within a short distance. For them, marketing was a brand-new concept, and the task of promoting products to anonymous customers beyond the locality was a huge challenge.

With limited resources, in-house market research, which is a common source of market information for their capitalist counterparts, is also out of the question in most cases. Instead, many TVEs subscribe to a monthly bulletin of market information, *Zibo Jiage Xinxi (Zibo Price Information)*. Published by the Prefecture Price Information Center in Zibo – a research institute attached to the Economic Research Center of the prefectural government – this publication contains a general profile of the latest policy developments and details of the supply and demand of products, which are, in fact, advertisements put out by other enterprises. Only a crude description of the quantity and price of products required or offered, together with a contact, is provided. It is doubtful how useful this information is, yet its popularity shows the desperation of enterprises or the paucity of market knowledge.

Second, the general lack of an established reputation hinders the expansion of most rural enterprises; most enterprises remain unknown to the outside world. The underdevelopment of quality control and product standardization in this area does not help the image-boosting effort of the local enterprises either. Efforts have been made by the prefectural government in recent years. Since 1988, one technical officer has been assigned to each township administration, whose job is to supervise the standardization of measurements and to enforce the relevant laws and regulations concerning quality standards of industrial products. County governments have also introduced a number of local regulations on product specifications.[58] However, these efforts have failed to inspire the confidence of potential buyers. In the first place, these exercises lack credibility. Given the intimate connections between local industries and government, it is difficult to convince others of the objectivity of these quality tests. One county official also admitted that local governments simply cannot be too rigorous in these exercises, or most of the products will fail. And worst of all, despite the highly public nature of these efforts and the possible intervention of local governments, the pass rate of local products in the quality tests conducted by the county technology supervision bureau – an administrative body under the direct supervision of its superiors at prefectural level – remains unsatisfactory. One-third of the local products tested failed to pass the test.[59]

Third, the risk involved in the non-performance of contracts with business partners also contributes to the sluggish progress in exploring the market beyond the provincial boundary. Most managers interviewed had reservations about the effectiveness of the legal system. Formal contracts, they believe, do not really provide extra protection for their interests. A number of them had suffered bad experiences with their business partners, despite the existence of a formal written contract. The effectiveness of legal remedies is further diluted if the culprit is far away. The case of Li Gongqin, a local private entrepreneur, is revealing. In 1993, he received an order from another private enterprise in Henan province. A contract was signed between the two parties in August 1993 and Li, as required by the document, delivered goods of 23,000 yuan in value to the buyer three months later. However, the buyer refused to pay after receiving the cargo. Li tried in vain to recoup the money. Eventually, Li decided to take the case to the court. The court decision was in his favor. The offender was ordered to clear the remaining payment and pay extra compensation of

10,000 yuan to Li within ten days. He was also required to pay all the legal expenses involved in this case, which were about 3,500 yuan. However, six months later, Li had still not received anything from the Henan buyer. In fact, Li had no idea where the offender was, as the latter did not even bother to show up in court when the case was being heard.[60]

Local government as a source of business contact

While most rural enterprises face many limitations in expanding their businesses into a larger market, the extensive bureaucratic links of the local government can serve some important commercial purposes as a source of market-related information and business contacts and an active promoter of local trade.

The township government can provide access to two types of information useful in developing marketing strategies. First, its bureaucratic status entitles it to timely information about forthcoming policy changes. As a state agency, the township government constantly receives numerous directives and documents from the higher level, updating the latest policy developments. The majority of these materials, though administrative in nature, contain useful information for marketing purposes. For instance, a forthcoming tightening of control over the market and an increase in taxation of specific commodities implies that immediate hoarding of these materials could be rewarding. On the other hand, information about new requirements in terms of product specification may give enterprises more time to make adjustments in production. In an administration in which official secrecy is a guiding principle, the local administration is the only source that enterprises can turn to for this information.

In addition, the township government can also provide access to information on market conditions in other localities. The operation of the market in China is still, to some extent, subject to administrative control. Fluctuations in the prices of certain products remain under the supervision of the Price Bureau, and the running of the market place is within the jurisdiction of the Industry and Commerce Administration (ICA). Administrative units like these keep a large pool of market information concerning the price and availability of commodities. Exchange of this information between bureaucratic units is frequent.[61] The township government is also generous in sharing this information with enterprise managers. This is, in fact, the highlight of the monthly meeting with TVE managers, and updating this information usually uses up half of the meeting time.[62]

The township government can help enterprises to establish several channels to the larger community, including regional business organizations and political institutions. These expand the enterprises' business contacts with the outside market and help them to explore the nationwide market.

As documented by White and Shue, there has been considerable growth of social organizations "from below" throughout the country during the reform era.[63] Among these is the growing number of business organizations at the local level. A similar development can be found in Zibo. There are three different business organizations in the area: the Individual Laborers' Association (ILA) (*geti laodongzhe xiehui*), the Federation of Industry and Commerce (FIC) (*gongshang lianghehui*), and the Entrepreneurs' Association (EA) (*qiyejia xiehui*). The first two are business organizations catering to the needs of the private sector in the area, and the last is mainly a regional chamber for collective enterprises in the county. However, the FIC in Zibo has also extended its reach into the collective sector in recent years, and hence is also relevant to our analysis here.

The FIC has a nationwide organizational network. The organization was established in 1953 when a substantial private sector still existed in China. After the Cultural Revolution, the Federation was revived in 1979 and continued to serve as a bridge between government and the non-state sector. The Huantai branch was set up in 1988. Officials in the FIC claim that it has more than 500 members.[64] The local organization has an elaborate organization network with branches extending to each of the thirteen townships in Huantai. In addition, thirty-three member enterprises are also designated as contact points, through which other members can communicate with the organization at the county level. The subcounty networks function as a vital part of the business network among members. A meeting is held every three months at the township level, and these gatherings provide opportunities for managers who are eager to make connections or to network.

The county Entrepreneurs' Association (EA) is, however, a more elitist body, with only sixty-one members and with its only office located in the county seat, Suozhen township. Founded in 1994 as an initiative of the Economic Commission of the county government, it is, strictly speaking, an association not confined to TVEs but open to all "successful enterprises" in the county. This stringent admission requirement is clearly driven by the Party's aversion to social organizations with a large base. As most large enterprises in the area are collectively owned, TVE managers naturally constitute the majority. At present there are only three members from the private sector. The township government's recommendation is crucial for admission into the Association. The Association demands the support of the enterprise's administrative superior as a prerequisite to membership application. For township collective enterprises, this means that the recommendation of the township ETC is indispensable. The recommendation will be examined by the county Party committee's organization department, which will give its "advice" to the Association.

The county government's close control over the Association is, ironically, the major attraction for managers. Although the president and eight vice-presidents of the Association are managers elected by other members at the annual general meeting, the daily operation of the Association is administered by a secretariat staffed by cadres from various government departments. Of the eight members of the secretariat, three come from the county Economic

Commission, one comes from the county Finance Commission, and one comes from the county REA. This provides a chance for managers at township level to extend their linkage with county-level officials, which can, in turn, increase their access to information and contacts with the larger community. Encounters with officials from even higher levels are possible too, as occasionally officials from prefectural or provincial levels are invited by the Association to explain the latest policy changes. The county Party chief, the mayor, as well as the presidents of the County People's Congress and the People's Political Consultative Conference are honorary presidents of the EA. Members benefit most from the regular social gatherings organized by the Association. The invitation of major businessmen in the area provides them with numerous opportunities to exchange market information and make contacts crucial for business expansion. The chance to maintain personal contacts with important figures on a regular basis is particularly welcome; the general managers of all five local banks, the chief of the county government, and the county Party secretary are all members of the Association. Aware of the importance of these social gatherings, the Association decided to build its own clubhouse and regarded it as the top priority for the coming year.[65] The FIC provides a similar business–officials network at the subcounty level, with the Party chief and the mayors of all thirteen townships secured as honorary presidents for its local branches.[66]

The township government can also assist local enterprises with connection building by recommending them to the Rural Entrepreneurs' Association at the prefectural level. The major difference from its county counterpart is the higher profile of its members. Of its 150 members, one-third have been granted provincial status or above – a status granted on the basis of the scale of operations and asset value of the enterprise. The minimum asset requirement for a provincial-rank enterprise is thirty million yuan, whereas the ministry or state ranks require 100 million yuan. In other words, membership implies even greater exposure to a much larger business community.[67]

There are, however, several factors offsetting the networking effect of these business organization groups. First, the tension between the supervising departments behind these associations may make horizontal connections difficult. Like other social organizations in China, all these business bodies are monitored by different administrative units. Whereas the ILA is under the leadership of the Industry and Commerce Administration, the FIC is subject to the management of the county Party's United Front Department. Similarly, the county Economic Commission extends its command over the EA. Overlapping jurisdiction and competition for recognition and resources contribute to the uneasiness between these bureaucratic units and, understandably, they have little incentive to organize joint efforts among these business organizations. The same logic can also be applied to cross-border interaction. However, as we will discuss later, the diversity among enterprises may appear to be an even more crucial factor in hindering communication between enterprises. The difference in resources and endowment may point to different strategies and possibilities in advancing enterprises' interests among managers.

Political organization membership surprisingly has a certain commercial value too. Meetings of the Local People's Congress and People's Political Consultative Congress provide occasions at which enterprise managers can meet managers from other major enterprises and officials from the relevant administrative units in the locality. Certainly, the higher the level they reach, the greater the exposure and social connections can be. One manager called the annual meeting of the People's Congress "a major trade fair" – manager-members spend most of their time rushing between hotel rooms to exchange business cards and make deals. Needless to say, the local government has the major influence in controlling access to these organizations.

The township government can also take various direct actions to expand the reach of local businesses beyond local confines. For instance, the county government is entitled to send a trade delegation to major trade fairs held in the region, such as the annual events held in Qingdao and Harbin, the most important business events in eastern China every year. Participants include not only enterprises from Shandong, but also tens of thousands of interested parties from all over the country and overseas. The county government will assign a certain quota for each township administration, which can, in turn, nominate local managers to join the delegation. Such an opportunity is highly valued by enterprise managers as it is a great chance to expand their business contacts in the larger market. In addition, the township government also makes its own efforts to promote local products. The Tangshan ETC, for instance, organized trade delegations to a number of cities in Shandong and other provinces nearby. Official sponsorship of these trips is crucial, not only in terms of financial support, but also for logistical convenience. The presence of senior local officials can always secure an official reception from the host administration. With the generally low degree of horizontal connections among businessmen in China, official coordination is essential for these activities.

Under exceptional circumstances, the township government can also come to the assistance of an enterprise by becoming directly involved in negotiations. In one case, a deputy director of a township economic commission was invited to accompany a manager to Nanjing for business negotiations. The factory was on the verge of bankruptcy and failure to win the deal would certainly have marked the end of the business. The enterprise in Nanjing was satisfied with the quality of its products, yet still could not be confident about the deal because of the huge amount of money at stake. When the collapse was imminent, as the last resort, the manager approached the township ETC for help. The presence of a local official helped to increase the Nanjing partner's confidence and saved the enterprise from immediate crisis.[68]

A different universe for key enterprises

The value of the bureaucratic services listed above is a function of enterprise resourcefulness. Bureaucratic representation can also be an effective substitute for reputation and credibility, particularly for an enterprise in its infancy, when resources are limited and it is not yet known outside the local community. Small enterprises with shoestring budgets might also find official assistance valuable in expanding their connections with the outside world. However, enterprises with more resources do have more alternatives for linking with the larger business world. Dongyue Chemicals, one of the giant chemical factories in the area, for example, has its own extensive business network. It has representative offices in fifteen major cities including Beijing, Shanghai, Jinan, and Qingdao. In fact, the reputation of Dongyue Chemicals' products is a magnet for business collaboration. Recently, Qinghua University, China's most prestigious university in science and technology, collaborated with this factory to convert its latest research findings in air-conditioning technology for the market. Local officials admitted that they played no part in forging this collaboration.[69]

The external linkages of the Romu Metal Factory, another local giant, are no less astonishing. By 1995, the factory had already established formal agreements for cooperation with more than forty prominent enterprises across the country – located in Shandong, Tianjin, and Beijing, as well as Xinjiang. Among the partners are large state-owned enterprises such as Qilu Petrochemical, one of the largest industrial firms in China. Such agreements guarantee a secure business relationship with these partners, which means a steady supply of raw materials and purchase orders. In addition, the factory manages to establish regular exchanges with research institutions, and there are collaborations with academic institutions, such as Qinghua University and Shandong Industry University, and departmental research units such as the Shandong Construction Materials Research Institute, a research unit under the Construction Commission of the provincial government. The quality of the factory's product and its reputation are the major reasons for these successes. In fact, its outstanding performance also attracted the attention of central government units; the factory was invited to participate in several research projects commissioned by the central departments.[70]

Tangshan Construction Company goes one step further by inviting prominent figures to serve on its management board. On the company's board of directors, company senior management personnel hold five seats. Of the remaining two places, one is occupied by the director of the Planning Institute of the Ministry of Chemical Industry, a central-level administrative unit, and the other is taken by a senior manager of the Shandong Construction Company, the largest construction company in the province. Both are paid directors of the company. The company is proud of these connections and stresses that they are the result of its own efforts; the local government has nothing to do with it.[71]

In other words, large enterprises with more resources under their command are enjoying alternatives to bureaucratic support. These managers are distinguishable not only in terms of income, lifestyle, status, and social respect, but they also have different views of the role of local government. Mediocre managers still rely on the support of local officials and are highly grateful for it. They are not hesitant to ask for officials' help whenever problems arise. Their limited resources deprive them of the alternatives enjoyed by their larger counterparts, and the local government's blessing is the only support they have when a situation arises that they cannot handle themselves. As one manager puts it:

> Enterprise still cannot live without government support. From dispute settlement to business negotiation, from raw materials to bank loans, we all need local officials' help to sort these out. It is true that local officials are keeping a close watch on our operation. I have no resentment of it and I think it is a reflection of their concern.[72]

However, those managers who are running leading enterprises in the local community are more confident of their own ability and regard the services of local officials as unnecessary. One manager claimed:

> We are very independent these days and basically government interference and support are not necessary. Problems like the supply of raw materials, market and capital can be solved by the market or our own efforts. I cannot recall any major incident which I could not solve without government's intervention.[73]

These may be exaggerations, but local officials seem to share a similar view. The chairman of a township Economic Commission concurred, "We should restrain from interfering in the operation of big enterprises. In fact, they don't need much help from us, and I think this is good for their development too." Another local official was less diplomatic in elaborating on the different attitudes among managers:

> For leading enterprises (*gugan qiye*), their managers don't bother to talk to us. Most of them are arrogant bastards! They treat us like their poor relatives who come to beg for money and don't show much respect. But for other smaller enterprises, it is the opposite. You just have to hide away from their managers' sight as they will come to the office frequently to ask for all sorts of assistance and favor.[74]

In other words, there exist two worlds of enterprise managers. They are distinguished not only by the size of the enterprise they manage and the social recognition, income, and lifestyle they enjoy, but also by their attitude to local government. And this psychology, as we will see in Chapters 6 and 7, is a key force behind the shareholding reforms in the 1990s. Confidence grows with the rising concentration of local business, and innovation in reward methods and economic organization is needed to accommodate these managerial elites.

Summary

Without local government assistance, life can be difficult for enterprise managers. Either because of the structural constraints of underdeveloped markets and an imperfect legal framework or as a result of the enterprise's own limitations, horizontal linkage between enterprises is discouraged, and the flow of resources and business transactions beyond the locality is costly. The impact of the past is clear. The economy inherited from the Mao era continues to haunt reform-era development; it poses obstacles, in infrastructure and cognitive terms, to the progress of market development, and shapes the landscape in which business takes place. This, in turn, reinforces managers' reliance on the local government. Consequently, the involvement of the local government is, in general, regarded by managers as a viable option for overcoming these constraints, and this contributes to their dependence on local government. Together with the functional indispensability of managers revealed in Chapter 3, interdependence between enterprise managers and the local government has emerged in the countryside during the reform era. The collaboration between the two parties unleashes synergy for rural development. The combination of the creativity inherent in the managers' entrepreneurialism and the value of the local government's bureaucratic influence in reducing transaction costs and expanding business access is the recipe for TVE development.

However, the above analysis also demonstrates the complexity inherent in this interdependence. In short, there are different degrees of enterprise dependence in different areas of business operation, and the pattern of dependency remains particularistic. As stated at the very beginning of the discussion, when claiming that enterprises depend on the local government, one has to be specific. From the above analysis, one should realize that the question is not just *how* (to what extent), but also by *whom* (by which type of enterprise) and *when* (under what circumstances) the bureaucratic assistance is mostly needed. The foregoing analysis has hopefully provided tentative answers to these questions. The importance of the local government's support varies, and so does the pattern of dependency. Variation also exists among enterprises with a different scale of operation. Two factors stand out in accounting for these variations: availability of alternatives and the resources of enterprises. Larger firms are less reliant on local government support, and most managers do not solicit the government's support as a knee-jerk response whenever a problem arises. More established firms have more resources at their disposal with which to solve their own problems. Even in the above case of direct solicitation of official intervention, it is regarded by the enterprises concerned as a last resort.

Managers' spontaneous search for business alternatives also draws attention to the dynamic nature of this dependent relationship. Intentionally or unintentionally, managers' innovations, such as recruiting social celebrities into enterprise management, have minimized the importance of bureaucratic assistance, and hence the degree of the enterprises' dependence. Two trends that may further devalue the role of the local government are conceivable: the intensification of marketization and the growth of TVEs. As demonstrated above, enterprises' dependence on local government is inversely proportional to the availability of alternatives. Both processes are likely to act against the dominance of bureaucratic channels. It is, of course, hard to predict the prospects for these two processes; however, what is important here is that these possibilities raise concerns about the analytical inadequacy of the statist view of bureaucratic dominance. This analysis argues that enterprise dependence, or enterprise–government interdependence, has to be comprehended within the historical context of economic reform. This is a historical juncture in which the impetus for change and innovation is gathering strength and empowered social interests are asserting their presence. The energy and spontaneity of the Zibo managers confirms this view.

Thus, in the age of reform, the challenge facing the local state is enormous. Its interdependence with enterprise managers requires it to maintain a delicate balance between conflicting concerns in regulating the local economy. The reconciliation of the fundamental tensions between control and managerial autonomy, material incentives, and egalitarianism, and local interest and compliance with central directives is the core of the local governance. Defining the appropriate role and involvement in the internal management of TVEs is central to this challenge, and analysis of this process can provide for further elaboration of how interdependence affects the interaction between managers and the local state. This is the subject of Chapter 5.

5 Accommodating managers' autonomy

Chapters 3 and 4 have demonstrated the interdependence of managers and the local administration in the reform era. This condition implies compromises and collaboration; give-and-take is the key to maintaining it. This chapter will further explore this pattern of reciprocity and self-constraint on the part of managers and the local government in the internal management of TVEs. Although concurring with the general concept of local government presence in enterprise management at the micro level,[1] this chapter challenges this view for its tendency to exaggerate the local government's role and to give insufficient attention to the dilemma that is faced in defining the appropriate level of involvement in rural enterprise management. That is, how is it possible to maintain a hands-on approach without dampening the entrepreneurial initiative of managers? This analysis argues that the local government is, in fact, subject to conflicting forces in regard to its involvement in enterprise operation. On the one hand, the local government is obliged to improve the general welfare of the local community, but, on the other hand, it is anxious to maintain and enhance the growth of local enterprises. These two imperatives are not inherently contradictory, but the profit-oriented activities of the local enterprises, as well as the personal financial concerns of managers, are not always consistent with community goals, especially as the latter may occasionally involve non-economic considerations such as redundant workers. For local governments, the task of economic management is further complicated by their concern for the entrepreneurial drive of managers. The foregoing evaluation of the managers' appointment process clearly reflects the officials' awareness of their own limitations in managing economic ventures, and thus partnership with managerial talent is regarded as the key to local prosperity. Only when managers' business judgments are fully respected can managers really be utilized as the motors for growth and expansion. However, this is the very antithesis of the ethos of administrative intervention. Thus, more attention must be paid to the local officials' balancing act when assessing its role in the operation of rural enterprises. This chapter suggests that somewhere between the conventional wisdom of active intervention typical of planned economies, and a laissez-faire approach, the local government in rural China is trying to strike a balance. However, the profit imperative has enabled managers to become more and more autonomous in enterprise operation.

This chapter will examine this issue by evaluating the role of the local government in three important aspects of the internal management of TVEs in Zibo: setting and implementing economic targets, personnel management, and the allocation of enterprise resources. The discussion will show that, before the further intensification of ownership rights in the late 1990s, the local government still played a considerable role in all these aspects. In some areas, its intervention was robust and left managers little room to maneuver. However, in general, bargaining and negotiation were the major factors shaping its relationship with managers. Concern for enterprise performance acted as the major brake for local government involvement, and this was the foundation on which managers could negotiate for a greater say in enterprise management. The economic and financial importance of the enterprise concerned and a manager's proven record appear to be crucial determinants of the managers' autonomy and freedom from the influence of the local state. The relationship, in short, remains particularistic; the involvement of the local government varies according to the relative strength of the enterprise and the manager's competence. Again, the two-world scenario between mediocre and outstanding managers is evident.

The following discussion will start with a brief evaluation of the reason for the general tendency of the local government to maintain its presence in TVE management. In addition to the ownership structure and economic reasons mentioned previously, the legacy of egalitarianism in the countryside is noteworthy. This factor is particularly important for comprehending the local officials' dilemma in adjusting their role in enterprise management; socialist legacy, at the cognitive level in this case, is evident. The discussion will conclude with an evaluation of the general principle of collective enterprise management in Zibo. Its unpleasant experience with the trials of the contract responsibility system in enterprise management accounts for the general dissatisfaction with this approach in Zibo, and for the fact that more direct control is preferred.

Motivating the involvement of local government

As pointed out in Chapter 1, a TVE is, theoretically, owned collectively by the local residents; however, in practice these nominal owners do not enjoy any significant control over their asset. Instead, the local government is entrusted with management of the TVEs. Whereas in a capitalist firm managerial control derives from the voluntary delegation of rights by the owners, and mechanisms are available for retrieving the power delegated if the performance of the manager falls below the expected level, the local government's control over a TVE derives from state power. Because there is no mechanism for local residents to take control back from the local government, the latter's control over TVEs is unconditional and complete. In theory, the local government can do whatever it likes with the enterprise.[2]

In reality, local government perceives TVEs as a new resource for policy purposes. TVEs are a source of income for the local administration and provide other economic benefits, particularly the creation of jobs for the local community. Both contributions are important supplements for local governments, which are under pressure to be financially self-sufficient, and no longer have the conventional leverage of policy implementation in the reform era. These considerations account for the eagerness of the local government to develop rural enterprises.[3] Given their strategic importance for the local community, the local government is understandably, inclined to become involved in steering these business ventures in order to ensure their healthy development.

The local government is, however, not motivated merely by its financial concern; the claims on TVEs by the local population, who believe that they should be given a fair share of these resources, also affects local government's involvement in the management of these collective enterprises. Findings of several studies are consistent with this assertion. For instance, James Kung's study of Wuxi county in southern Jiangsu found that workers in collective enterprises perceived themselves not only as employees but also as stakeholders by virtue of their status as villagers.[4] Similar sentiments can also be found at the township level, as observed by Liu Shiding and his collaborators in their studies in Shandong.[5] In other words, members of the local community believe that they have justified claims on the resources of these collectively owned ventures. For them, these collective enterprises, which are feeding on local resources – technology, labor, land and even capital – are obliged to cater to their interests, especially in terms of employment and income.

The experience of the collective era of people's communes is arguably a root of this way of thinking. Mao's egalitarianism, which aimed at eradicating income inequality, was the primary principle of distribution under the People's Commune. Remuneration was community-based, instead of individual-based, under the famous Dazhai work-points system adopted in the collective era. According to Richard Madsen:

> [U]nder the Dazhai system, workers were paid according to a collective judgment of the overall quality of their contribution to their production team. These judgments were made by one's production team peers in regular appraisal meetings. At these meetings, each worker was given a work-point ranking that determined how many work points he or she would be entitled to for a full day's work... under the Dazhai system the differentials between the highest and the lowest paid workers were much smaller than those under the piece-rating system.[6]

The aim of this collective-based remuneration system is to narrow the income discrepancy among the local population.[7] The demise of People's Communes in the post-Mao period has scarcely uprooted this egalitarianism in the countryside. For instance, during the implementation of the household responsibility system, land was distributed on a per capita basis, with great emphasis on individual need. Every effort was made to avoid inequality in distribution; periodic readjustments of household entitlement occurred when the size of the household concerned changes, as a means of avoiding unfairness. The principle of equal entitlement to collective resources is well respected even in the era of reform.[8]

Certainly, post-Mao reforms have instilled new elements into the peasants' perception of fairness of distribution. The emergence of the "10,000-yuan household" (*wanyuanhu*), i.e. a rural household with an annual income of more than 10,000 yuan, and the official policy of "letting some people get rich first" may have diluted the egalitarian ethos in rural society.[9] However, this does not mean that the collective memory of the "good old days" is gone. The social pressure faced by private entrepreneurs – largely a result of their fellow peasants' uneasiness with their successes – reveals the persistence of this old mentality.[10] The "inequality" in employment opportunities and income, related to collective enterprises, is even more difficult to swallow. This bitterness is further fueled by the rising importance of the income earned from employment in these economic activities. According to national statistics, non-agricultural income constituted at least one-third of the average per capita annual income in the countryside by 2000,[1] and such income was also the main source of the growth of peasants' income in the reform era.[12] One in four rural laborers are now participating in rural enterprise production. The welfare of almost every rural household is thus affected by its members' opportunities to work in these enterprises. In some areas in which the local government does not have sufficient capital to launch a new business venture on its own, local residents are even required to donate money for the investment (*lingdao tanpao*).[13] This arrangement only reinforces the validity of the local population's claim on TVEs.

As argued earlier, several unique features of China's rural administration may help to amplify this normative pressure: the small size of rural communities, the limited mobility of the rural population, and the dominance of indigenous people in the administration. In other words, the accountability and responsiveness of the local administrations is not guaranteed by a democratic electoral system, but is a result of the sociological fundamentals of rural governance. The local government is driven, not only by its own paternalistic intentions but also by popular expectations of the TVEs economic obligations to the local community, to intervene in enterprise operation.

The Township Economic and Trade Commission (ETC) (*zhen jingyi maoyi weiyuanhui*), an administrative unit under the direct leadership of the township government, is responsible for the management of TVEs at the subcounty level. At the professional level, it is also under the guidance of the Rural Enterprise Administration (REA) (*xiangzhen qiye guanliju*) at the county level. The REA, which is the administrative unit specializing in the general management of rural enterprises in China is, in turn, under the vertical command of the central government's Ministry of Agriculture. Central policies and directives concerning rural enterprise management are usually passed from the REA to the ETC for implementation. As the REA does not extend its reach below the county level, it entrusts the ETC with the task of managing TVEs. In other words, the ETC is, in principle, under dual leadership, though in reality its relationship with the REA remains nominal and minimal. It is mainly accountable to the township government. It is the township government, rather than the REA, which maintains control over matters concerning the personnel, finance and resource allocation of the ETC. In most cases in Zibo, the ETC is chaired by a deputy Party secretary of the township, one of the most important figures in the local administrative hierarchy. At the village level, collective enterprises are regulated by the village economic cooperative (*cun jingji hezuoshe*), which is accountable to the township ETC.

In most cases, the control over TVEs is delegated to managers through a contract, officially known as the "management responsibility contract." This stipulates the basic duties and privileges of the management and includes an agreement on the method of remuneration. However, it should not be confused with the contract responsibility system, which basically contracts out the enterprise concerned. After its initial success as an alternative to the traditional approach to enterprise management through a planned economy, the validity of the contract responsibility system has been queried by economists as well as officials in China.[14] Local officials involved in economic management in Zibo take a similar view. After a few years of unsuccessful experimentation, they believe that such a contracting-out system, which basically leaves the collective assets in an individual's hands for a fixed period in return for a fixed income, is not in the best interests of the local community. As one local official recalls:

> [T]he major danger is that contract responsibility system always left "the monk getting rich while the temple staying bankrupt" (*fuliaoheshang qiongliaomiao*). Managers only cared about their financial rewards during the contract period and they would never think about the long term development of the company. We couldn't blame them because they couldn't be sure whether their contract would be renewed after its expiry. They are not the owners after all.

More direct control of collective enterprises is preferred, and the essence of this alternative approach is well summarized by a deputy director of a county REA:

> Administrative intervention is beneficial for enterprises and separation of politics and economics is not necessarily a good thing. Certainly, this does not mean that we should, as in the past, substitute politics for economics; but on the other hand, the argument that a limited role for the government can always strengthen the vitality of rural enterprises does not sound too convincing for me. Administrative measures are sometimes indispensable for enterprise management.[15]

In short, there is a clear preference for an intimate relationship between enterprises and local officials in this area. This, however, should not lead us to jump to the conclusion that there is complete local government control over TVEs. As will be seen below, the need to maintain the right balance between different claims on the enterprises' resources requires the local administrators to show self-restraint and tolerance of autonomy.

Benchmarking enterprise performance

As in the state sector, the imposition of production targets on TVEs is a key component of the township ETC's regulation of local collective enterprises. The kinds of targets found in rural enterprises are similar to the standard requirements imposed on their counterparts in the state sector. Although there may be variations between different enterprises, Table 5.1 provides a general summary. These targets are measured on a yearly basis and each enterprise is expected to meet these requirements by the end of each financial year. They can be revised annually or every three years; the arrangement differs among enterprises.

It should be noted, however, that unlike the state sector, the economic targets applied in TVEs are market-oriented. That is, the imposition of targets does not imply either a guaranteed market for their output or a supply of subsidized raw materials. The local government's lack of resources to enforce a more restrictive plan means that these targets are mostly for guidance, and

Table 5.1 A list of the major economic targets for TVEs in Zibo

Output value
   Total value
   Per capita value

Gross profit
   Total value
   Per capita value

Income
   Sales income
   Other operational income

Profit remittance and other fees
   Amount of profit remittance
   Management fee
   Education support fee
   Agricultural support fee
   Other fees

Tax payment
   Guaranteed level
   Target level

mainly reflect its expectations of the performance of the TVE concerned. These enterprises, after all, have to respond to the market to regulate their production plans. These targets mainly serve as a benchmark for evaluation of enterprises' performance and as a framework for bargaining and negotiation.

Setting the targets

The interactive nature of the relationship between the local government and enterprises is well reflected in the process of setting these economic targets. The township ETC is responsible for assigning targets for the enterprise concerned. The process involves extensive bargaining and negotiation with managers, and a delicate balancing of the different interests.

First, the economic targets imposed by the higher tier of government affect the targets of enterprises. The township government is subject to an economic plan imposed by the county government. Two components are particularly noteworthy: production targets, such as output value, the volume of turnover, or growth rates; and financial targets, especially tax payments. The performance of local officials and of the administration will be evaluated on the basis of its fulfillment of these targets, and the career prospects of the former are closely linked with the assessment result. According to Maria Edin, who undertook her empirical study on the implementation of cadre performance evaluation methods in rural Shandong, these economic targets, particularly tax revenue targets, are invariably categorized as hard targets (*ying zhibiao*) in the cadre performance appraisal;[16] leading cadres who fail to fulfill these hard targets must expect a poor appraisal by their supervising authority. Naturally, such pressure trickles down to the enterprise level and constitutes an important variable affecting the setting of enterprise targets. Second, the financial needs of the township administration are important. A bigger bill for administration, or a more ambitious welfare program in the coming year, certainly requires more intensive financial extraction from enterprises.

Although these two factors may determine the general level of financial and economic demands on TVEs, it is the performance of the enterprise concerned which affects the specific target levels most. Two factors are particularly important: the track record of target fulfillment and the financial strength of the enterprise. Both affect the assessment of the enterprise's ability to meet a higher target. There is no standard formula for renewing economic targets, and, as a rule, better-performing enterprises usually have to take a greater increase in target level, whereas those which have failed to fulfil their quotas in the past are given targets close to their previous level. In a sense, this is a disincentive for managers and also sounds unfair for successful enterprises. However, as will be seen below, this tension is very much offset by the possibility of getting a better deal with a more desirable mix of economic targets. The concern for managers' enthusiasm explains the readiness of the local government to compromise.

Negotiating the targets

TVEs are subject to a number of financial extractions: tax payments, management fees, profit remittance, and other administrative surcharges. However, the township government's entitlement to each of these varies. This implies different incentives for collection and enforcement. Even more importantly, it allows the possibility of the local government to lower the enterprise's burden without jeopardizing its own share. The administration at the higher level is, in most cases, the unfortunate victim of the compromise between local interests.

In 1993, China announced a comprehensive reform of the fiscal and taxation system and one of the major innovations was the introduction of the tax-sharing system (*fenshuizhi*). Under the new system, taxes would be divided into three categories: central tax, local tax and shared tax. As a response to the central initiative, county administrations in Zibo adopted the system in 1994, and the new financial arrangement was extended into the township level by 1997. The existing tax bureaus were split into national and local tax offices. The former is responsible for collecting the central and shared taxes, whereas the latter mainly concerns itself with local taxes.[17]

TVEs are subject to all three types of taxes. Central taxes include mainly consumption tax and tariffs, whereas capital gains tax on land and property sales, income tax, and business tax all fall under the category of local tax. The major type of shared tax is the value-added tax (VAT). For the township administration, as summarized in Table 5.2, each category provides a different rate of return.

In principle, all central taxes collected from local TVEs are enjoyed solely by the central government. This is, in fact, the rationale of the reform, which aims at giving the central treasury a greater slice of the fruits of economic growth. However, in order to gain local support, the new tax-sharing scheme is supplemented by a transitional tax rebate system, which guarantees that the income of local governments will not be affected.[18] Under this system, 1993 was fixed as the "base year" on which to calculate the rebate. The difference between the total revenue enjoyed by the local administration after adoption of the new scheme and its total revenue in 1993 will be the amount of the rebate made by the central government. For instance, in 1995, a total of sixty-four million yuan in central taxes was collected in Huantai, of which forty-one million yuan was returned as a rebate. This rebate was then distributed among the townships.[19]

A fixed proportion, 25 percent, of shared taxes (VAT in particular) has been allocated for the local government. In 1995, Huantai county was given three million yuan for the thirteen million yuan in VAT it collected. Again, this was redistributed among the subordinate administrations.[20] There is, however, a built-in disincentive for the township government to be as enthusiastic about collecting these revenues as it is for collecting other levies. The township administrations resent the method used for redistribution of the returns

Table 5.2   Destinations of different financial submissions of subcounty-level collective
enterprises

Type of levy	Entitlement of the township government
Central taxes	In principle, all taxes will be enjoyed solely by the central treasury, but in practice a tax rebate will be given. The rebate will be redistributed throughout the township but contribution is not the only criterion of redistribution
Shared taxes	The county government is entitled to 25 percent of the taxes collected in the area; the amount will be shared by the thirteen township administrations. Again, contribution is not the only consideration in distribution
Local taxes	Shared between county and township governments according to a predetermined formula
Management fees	Shared between township government and county REA
Profit remittance of collective enterprises	Enjoyed solely by the township government and immune from budgetary control from above
Other administrative fees	Enjoyed solely by the township government and immune from budgetary control from above

Source: author's fieldwork.

from the central treasury, as it is the county administration that determines
the allocation of these revenues. More often than not, contribution is not
the sole criterion for distribution, and need is always a major concern of the
county government when redistributing funds among the thirteen township
administrations. The county government, which is more concerned about the
general development of the territories, believes that this is the appropriate
approach. Tangshan, for example, ranks second in the county in terms of revenue contribution, but only received an average tax return in recent years.[21]

Local taxes are mainly shared by the township and county governments
according to a set sharing scheme. The two parties agree on a certain amount
of tax revenue, which the township government has to submit to the county
finances every year. Once the quota is fixed, it is effective for three years. The
first year of this agreement is the "base year," upon which a fixed growth rate
of tax submission will be measured.[22] As an incentive, if the total of submitted
revenue exceeds the quota, the extra amount will be shared between the two
parties on a 30:70 basis, with the township getting the larger share.[23]

In the case of local taxes, there is a more direct link between contribution and return than with central or shared taxes, and this is preferable in
the eyes of township administrations. Here, a loophole can be exploited for
local interests. Pressure from enterprise managers, complaining about their
enterprises' heavy financial burden, can be accommodated simply by selective
enforcement of the tax laws. Understandably, it is the first two tax categories
that most flexible; whereas for the local tax category, which is closely linked
with local finance, law enforcement appears to be more rigid.[24] A mix of tax

targets that maintains the same level of extraction from TVEs, but with a higher level of payment stipulated for the local tax category and a lower level for central and shared taxes, will serve the interests both of the TVE concerned and the local government.

TVEs are required to pay management fees to the township ETC for its administrative services. In principle, the collection of management fees is calculated on the basis of a formula specified by state regulation. Fees should be charged at a rate of 0.6 percent of the sales income of the TVE concerned. However, in practice, the collection is arbitrarily implemented. For instance, the total sales income generated by all TVEs in one township was about 600 million yuan in 1994, which means that the total management fees collected should be about 3.6 million yuan. However, the director of one ETC in this township disclosed that the total amount of profit remittance and manage-ment fees collected in this year was less than two million yuan. The levied amount is obviously below the legal requirement. A possible explanation for the irregularity is that, despite their off-budgetary nature, the management fees collected still have to be shared between the township ETC and the REA at the county level. This arrangement implies that the financial loss of the township government is somehow less than expected if, for some reason, it chooses to collect less than the stipulated amount.

The common characteristic of other administrative fees and profit remit-tances is that they both fall under the category of off-budgetary income in the township finances. The most important financial implication is that such income, unlike the other financial payments mentioned above, will be enjoyed mostly by the township government. In addition, at least until the mid-1990s, use of these revenues was immune to budgetary control from the higher level; thus the township government has greater freedom in deploying these resources. The incentive for collection is obviously greater than that in the case of tax payments.

In short, variations in the returns from different sources of revenue, and in the string attached, are conducive to a specific strategy in determining the level and mix of financial targets imposed on TVEs. The existing arrangements provide the township government with a way to maximize its gains without increasing its level of extraction from enterprises. This can be achieved by readjusting its mix of extraction – by waiving or reducing those financial obligations with the least financial return to the township government and increasing those which yield the greatest return. The key to the strategy is that the five major targets listed in Table 5.1 do not have to move in the same direction or at the same pace. The same enterprise may find an upward adjustment in two of its targets while the other three go down.[25] Although he declined to give details of the negotiations, Wang Bing, the managing direc-tor of Romu Metal, one of the largest enterprises in Zibo, disclosed that he accepted less than a 5 percent increase in the targets for management fees and other surcharges after the township ETC had agreed to decrease tax pay-ments.[26] Such flexibility provides both parties with more room to maneuver when negotiating the target level.[27]

Monitoring target fulfillment

Another crucial aspect of implementing these economic targets is the regular monitoring of enterprise operations, through the monthly report system and regular managers' meetings. This provides the township government with a constant flow of up-to-date information on the performance of the enterprise concerned; it can intervene if there is the risk of an enterprise failing to meet its targets.

Collective enterprises are required to submit three separate reports to the township ETC every month. These are reports on the asset-liability account, the profit and loss account, and the financial balance account. These reports provide the most up-to-date information on the financial and operational details of the enterprises concerned. Within the first week of each month, each enterprise has to fill in the three standard forms provided by the township ETC, which report on the details of the previous month's operation. A total of 239 items have to be provided, with sixty included in the profit and loss report, 124 in the asset–liability report, and fifty-five in the financial balance report.[28] The ETC officials are empowered to conduct on-site investigations of the enterprise's accounts and to request extra information if they are doubtful of the authenticity of the data submitted.

Every month, managers from all township-level collective enterprises are summoned to attend a meeting chaired by the director of the township ETC. The chairman usually spends half of the time briefing the managers on the latest developments in laws and regulations concerning production, safety, and other aspects of their operations. He also updates them with the market intelligence he has gathered from other administrative units. Managers then take turns reporting on their operations. Usually, these verbal reports are short – around five to ten minutes each in most cases – and financial details are seldom given, as managers are reluctant to reveal their financial situations to others. However, they do provide information on the major events concerning their operations, such as prospective deals and investment information. ETC officials also hold separate meetings with individual managers from time to time. In general, enterprise managers are in frequent personal contact with ETC officials.

Allocating enterprise resources

The power to decide how enterprise resources should be utilized is another important aspect of enterprise management. It is the area about which the local government cares most, as the fulfillment of community goals is, to a certain extent, determined by the amount extractable from enterprises. Enterprise managers are, on the other hand, keen to establish their influence in this area. For them, it is not only a matter of personal income, but also a decisive management power, without which they cannot be sure that the future development of their enterprises will proceed in the right direction. The extent of the local government's intervention and interaction with managers in three areas – financial, staff remuneration, and investment decisions, require a delicate balancing act to accommodate both community goals and the managers' enthusiasm. In short, the financial concerns of the local administration and the distributive norm of egalitarianism appear to exert a significant impact on the process, though managers, on the whole, still preserve their influence over these matters.

Remuneration of staff

The township government's control over total expenditures on wages and bonuses is crude but effective. Every year, the enterprise management proposes an amount for total wages and bonuses expenditures. The proposal is examined by the ETC, which has the final word. The enterprise's performance in meeting its economic targets is a crucial factor in the decision. Satisfactory performance in this respect usually guarantees lenient treatment, and above-quota achievement is always rewarded with a larger wage budget. However, the request is always balanced by the other uses of the enterprise's resources, of which investment is another major concern. An extraordinarily large wage bill may also arouse the concern of other administrative units, particularly the tax bureau. These factors compel the ETC to act with prudence in assessing the managers' proposals, but the ETC still retains firm control over the upper limits to this expenditure.

Managers, however, enjoy substantial freedom in deciding who gets what within the limit. A sophisticated wage system is observable among most TVEs in Zibo. Under this system, all staff are classified into different categories: ordinary workers, clerical workers, technical and engineering staff, and management staff. This order represents the hierarchy within the enterprise, and there are ranks within each category. Each category's wage level is composed of fixed and floating components. The former is the basic salary, which is determined by the rank and category of the staff concerned, whereas the latter is largely determined by the participation rate, which consists mainly of overtime payments and a full-attendance bonus.

The enterprise manager is empowered to revise the wage structure, as long as this does not incur expenditures exceeding the total permitted by the ETC, though he has to inform the ETC for the record. However, the wage discrepancy between categories remains small. In general, ordinary workers are at the bottom of the spectrum. Respectively, the wages of clerical staff, technical and engineering staff, and management personnel are about 150 percent, 200 percent, and 250–300 percent of those of ordinary workers.[29] There seems to be an agreement among managers to maintain a narrow wage differential within the enterprises. This is also the official position of the township government. Despite an exemption from the Ministry of Labor guidelines, which suggest that managers in state-owned enterprises should not, in principle, be paid more than three times the wages of ordinary workers,[30] local officials are anxious to maintain this egalitarian wage structure. As one official stresses, "We have to consider the response and feeling of fellow peasants and we have to maintain the right balance between equality and incentives in fixing wages."[31]

However, the position is not as rigid as it seems, especially when the managers concerned come from the major enterprises in the community. In one township, for instance, though the annual wage of most managers is between 8,000 and 10,000 yuan, the managers from leading enterprises earn about 20,000 yuan per annum.[32] The size of the financial contributions made by these enterprises certainly provides these managers with much greater bargaining power and requires a more pragmatic approach by the ETC. However, it is important to realize that, though the wage gap may have been double the norm in these cases, the discrepancy remains relatively narrow. The pressure for egalitarianism is not completely ignored.

Bonuses are another major component of staff income. There are three different parts to the total bonus enjoyed by a TVE: the target fulfillment bonus, the profit bonus and the above-target achievement bonus. The first reflects the extent to which the enterprise fulfills the economic targets imposed by the ETC. The second is awarded when a net profit is achieved, and the last is released when the enterprise exceeds its target level. Each staff member then shares the total bonus approved by the ETC, according to a pre-determined formula that basically reflects the rank of each staff category. Managers enjoy complete freedom in making individual adjustments; they have the final word in deciding who gets what in their enterprise.

Managers have a dominant say in allocating bonuses to their subordinates, but their personal bonuses are subject to the close scrutiny of the ETC. The bonuses are determined by two factors: the fulfillment of economic targets and the result of the ETC's performance assessment. As for the subordinate staff, the manager's bonus varies with the extent to which the targets are fulfilled. For any above-target achievement, the manager is, in principle, entitled to 5 percent of the amount of tax payments and remitted profit in excess of the assigned quota. This explains why the setting of the economic targets is a major area of contention between the managers and the ETC; the lower the target, the greater their personal bonus.

However, the final allocation is also determined by the ETC's performance assessment, which uses a 1,000-point scale (*qianfenzhi*). The manager's performance is evaluated in six areas: Party work, implementation of government policies, maintenance of industrial safety, accountability to the ETC, industrial production, and fulfillment of financial obligations.[33] It is interesting to see that, despite the economic nature of their posts, managers are expected to perform certain political functions. They are expected to contribute to "construction on the ideological front" (*sixiangjianshe*), which implies mostly development of Party membership and providing logistical support for Party activities. They are also responsible for the implementation of certain state policies, most notably the enforcement of the birth control policy. "A manager is responsible for persuading his staff to follow the one-child policy and imposes necessary measures, like deduction of wages or other monetary penalty to ensure compliance," stressed one local official.[34] In a way, the growing importance for rural households of wages earned from rural enterprise makes managers effective agents for securing the obedience of the rural population. In addition, managers are evaluated on their performance in enforcing regulations concerning industrial safety and security. However, the overall result of the manager's assessment is largely determined by his economic performance. About two-thirds of the total possible score is related to the last two areas mentioned above, i.e. the manager's ability to meet the assigned targets. Any manager who can score 900 points will be awarded the full 5 percent entitlement; the smaller the score, the smaller the bonus.

Although most managers interviewed refused to disclose details of their bonuses, the make-up of their income differs from that of other staff. For non-management personnel, the bonus usually constitutes the minority of one's total income. However, for managers, wage income may make up a quarter or less of their total annual income. In other words, the income discrepancy among staff is greatly widened when the bonuses component is taken into account. Local officials admit that they are reluctant to suppress the size of bonuses for managers, though they claim that the final arrangements are always within reason, and that they pay due respect to the issue of equality.[35] Their leniency in this matter is a result of their concern about maintaining the enthusiasm of enterprise managers. They believe that, without a satisfactory bonus, the narrow income differential between ordinary workers and managers is insufficient to motivate the latter. At this juncture, concerns about managers' enthusiasm seems to prevail over the normative pressure of egalitarianism, although, as will be pointed out in the forthcoming discussion, the local government tries to compensate through other redistributive measures. However, the need to strike a balance between egalitarian concerns and managers' demands for greater rewards continues to be a daunting task for the local government. In fact, even with the substantial bonus, grievances appear to be common among managers, who think they are underpaid for the huge responsibility put on their shoulders. The rising expectations of these managers and the normative and financial constraints imposed on the local state in meeting this demand is the impetus for change. The discussion of the experiment in shareholding reforms in Chapters 6 and 7 will further evaluate the impact of this issue on the rural political economy.

Investment decisions

Investment is another major use of enterprise resources, and is also the means by which managers can implement their business judgment in the form of concrete actions to steer the enterprises' development. Two areas of investment decisions are crucial: initiation of new projects and investment in fixed assets.

In brief, decisions concerning the initiation of new business projects are jointly made by the manager and the local government, whereas the latter maintain monopolistic control over decisions about investment in fixed assets.

Enterprise managers play a significant role in initiating new business projects. As a result of their business insight or knowledge of emerging opportunities, managers appear to be the driving force behind new business ideas in the county. Most of the new projects started with proposals by managers. The standard procedure requires managers to submit a full feasibility study to the township ETC. A detailed financial analysis of the proposed project is needed, and an estimate of the prospective flow of income and expenditures, the asset composition, a production forecast, and the source of financing must be included in the report. The ETC reserves the ultimate right of approval. For any project involving more than one million yuan, the township government has to be informed and its approval is necessary.[36]

Nevertheless, the extent of the local government's involvement varies between enterprises and in some cases such approval power is no more than a formality. It depends on the local officials' confidence in the manager's professional ability to make an accurate financial analysis and the enterprise's financial capacity to sustain the project. These factors affect the attitude of managers toward the local government's involvement too. Managers from modest enterprises, particularly those making losses or village-level enterprises, are in fact, glad to see the local officials involved in making decisions. They are, in the first place, not capable of financing their own projects without substantial backing from local banks, and officials' involvement can certainly persuade the local government to lobby the banks on their behalf. By committing the local officials in the preliminary stages of a feasibility study, these managers are, in fact, also insuring themselves. If the project goes wrong in the future, the ETC has to share the responsibility, as its approval has been given. Moreover, managers also believe that the ETC, with its administrative status and better contacts, may have more information concerning the prospects of the proposed project. For these managers, they genuinely believe that involvement of local officials can help to improve the quality of the risk assessment exercise.[37] Thus, it is not surprising that the managers of small enterprises do not always resent the intervention of the local government in investment decisions. Sometimes, practical concerns prevail over the issue of autonomy.

However, managers of large enterprises take a quite different attitude. Manager Wang of Romu Metal, for instance, regards the role of the township ETC as "advisory." By this, Wang means that he is the decision maker, though the ETC's advice "will be taken into account." Despite the potential tension, there has not been any direct confrontation between the two parties so far. According to Wang, none of his proposals has been rejected, and occasionally, official approval was obtained only after the project had already commenced.[38] ETC officials, surprisingly, did not show any bitterness in this situation. A township ETC director argues:

[B]ig enterprises which have sufficient financial strength and business experience should be encouraged to take more initiative. This is good for the community. The ETC should not pose an obstacle to their entrepreneurial drive.[39]

The presence of the local government is, however, stronger in the are of fixed asset investment. Its control is exerted in two respects: total amount of investment and approval of specific investment. The ETC assigns each enterprise a portion of its retained net profit for investment in fixed assets. This is usually in the region of 50 percent. It is set at a relatively high level, as the township government wants to be sure that the majority of the retained profit is used for reinvestment purposes – buying new equipment or upgrading the technological level of production – rather than wages or other welfare purposes. Approval for specific investment is needed too. Usually the purchase of materials costing less than a certain amount does not require prior approval and retrospective notification is sufficient. Beyond this level, prior approval is needed before any purchase can be made. In addition, the specification of the order has to be endorsed by the ETC. The threshold, however, varies between enterprises. The degree of control appears to be dependent on the reputation of the manager concerned, but mostly on the financial strength of the enterprise. On average, the threshold is in the region of 5,000 yuan, though in one extreme case approval is needed for any transaction of more than 300 yuan.[40] Again, the big enterprises are treated more leniently in this respect. Like other collective enterprises, they are subject to lump-sum control, but they are exempted from requesting approval for specific investments.

The control is obviously extensive and tedious. One manager complained that he couldn't even decide the brand name, model or even the color of his new company car. However, there seems to be a justification for this excessive intervention. Relaxation of control is likely to end up with most of these allotted resources spent on luxurious consumer goods instead of new machinery or equipment for production purposes. Although their total income – wages plus bonuses – is much higher than that of ordinary workers, managers are generally discontented over incomes. Their frustration is reflected in the tendency for managers to use the company's money to provide themselves with free sedans with chauffeurs, well furnished apartments, "business trips" to major tourist destinations at home and abroad and, of course, free banquets and limitless expenses for wining and dining guests. The ETC is not unaware of the situation. However, it regards a reasonable amount of such expenses as a form of "hidden compensation" for managers, and hence acceptable.[41] At the same time, the ETC is afraid that a further relaxation of financial control over fixed asset investment is likely to provoke a dramatic upsurge in such consumption. For local officials, it is not simply a matter of misappropriation of fund or wastage; a shameless display of extravagance among managers is likely to intensify class tension too. Again, the issue of equality matters.

Financial obligations to the local community

Financial submissions imposed by the local government represent the main outflow of resources from TVEs, and understandably this is another area of contention between the local government and enterprise manager. Concern for the general welfare of the local community appears to be an important determinant of the local government's position on this matter. To put it another way, TVEs are regarded as the major source of resources that can be used for improving the general living standard of the local population, and as a means for raising extra funding for public projects. TVEs are, in a way, taking over part of the financial burdens that used to be shouldered directly by local citizens. Resentment is understandable. Again, these grievances are appeased by lax enforcement of state policies, and local interests are satisfied at the expense of the central state.

Whereas various forms of mandatory submission – taxes, management fees and profit remittance – were examined in the foregoing discussion, this section will focus on various forms of petty extortion (*tanpai*) and the numerous administrative surcharges imposed on TVEs. Unlike those financial obligations specified in the enterprise's list of economic targets, which are more predictable – they are paid at a specific time and the rate of extraction is predetermined, at least in principle – many of these extra surcharges and extractions are arbitrarily imposed at any time and the amount involved is unpredictable.

TVEs are commonly approached for welfare donations. With the existing financial arrangement between the levels of administration, which basically leaves responsibility for financing welfare services to the local community, the financial pressure is substantial. Community projects such as the expansion of local schools, the building of new bridges and roads, or the organization of local traditional celebrations and festivals are among the items for which sponsorship is requested. The amount involved on these occasions may be relatively small, but the frequency of these requests imposes a considerable strain on enterprise resources. Tangshan Construction, for example, usually spends about 200,000 yuan a year for this purpose. The average amount is in the region of 20,000 yuan a year, which is quite a burden for enterprises not making significant profits.[42]

Although most managers regard welfare donations as one of their responsibilities to the community, they are bitter about the frequent petty extortion (*tanpai*) by different bureaucratic units. The experience of Shi Guang, director of the Silk Factory, is representative. Every year, Shi is reminded to renew his enterprise's subscription for forty copies of *Huantai News* (*Huantaibao*). This local newspaper is published by the county Party Committee, which has been suffering from financial difficulty in recent years. Understandably, it is eager to keep subscribers like Shi's enterprise, which contributes more than 3,000 yuan a year to its ailing finances. According to Shi, he and his workers are hardly interested in reading the paper, but there is little option but to comply. Sometimes, these petty extractions operate in a more indirect way.

For instance, calendars are a popular social gift in China and it is common for people to send friends or colleagues calendars at the beginning of every year as a sign of good will. Many local administrative units in Huantai believe that this provides an extra source of income, and invest their own money in printing calendars. However, not everyone succeeds in making profit; many of these units, in fact, end up with substantial losses. In order to reduce the damage, TVEs are put under pressure to buy as many calendars as they can afford. And the burden can be quite heavy. Shi, for example, has spent 8,000 yuan overall for this purpose.[43]

Some of these extra extractions come with a more legitimate camouflage, under the name of administrative surcharges. For instance, one township government has imposed a "status transfer fee" on enterprises for every peasant worker they employ. The surcharge is 1,000 yuan per worker. The administration claims that it is necessary to compensate for the administrative expense involved in reclassifying the peasants as enterprise workers.[44] There are numerous examples of such ad hoc surcharges, including road maintenance fees, transport management fees, town construction fees, middle and primary school fees, to name a few. TVEs are, in short, targeted as a means of supporting the general welfare expenses of the community.

In a way, the local government is using the TVEs to relieve the financial burden of the local population. As contributions by enterprises now provide a significant portion of its total income, the local government can relax its levies on individual households. The taxes and tax-like surcharges collected from enterprise are redistributed among the local people in the form of public expenditures and improvements in local facilities. Some townships go a step further by simply transferring those levies, which used to be shouldered by peasants, to TVEs. For instance, TVEs in Tangshan and Qifeng townships have to pay the unified levy for their staff. Costing ninety yuan per worker, these levies used to be paid directly by the peasants. Thus, the residents of each township are relieved of a financial burden of about two million yuan a year.[45]

The township government, however, does show self-restraint in milking these enterprises. As mentioned above, the needs of the enterprises and personal incentives for managers are well taken into account. The township government is particularly eager to reduce the enterprises' burden when its own income will not be affected. Revenues that have to be shared with higher levels are particularly vulnerable, and flexibility in the enforcement of tax laws is a common phenomenon.[46] Given the sensitive nature of the issue, it is unsurprising that little local evidence of such practices has been found. However, several reports concerning tax collection may suggest a certain degree of leniency in law enforcement, or even collaboration by the township government in tax evasion in order to reduce the burden on enterprises.

Tax payments are, in principle, calculated by using a specific formula stipulated in the relevant tax regulation. However, implementation in the countryside is not always in accordance with the rules. Under certain circumstances, usually at the request of the enterprise concerned, a fixed-amount method will be employed in tax assessment.[47] Although the tax office is, according to the law, the only administrative unit responsible for the assessment, there is much room for negotiation over the final figure. One major factor affecting the process is pressure from the township government. A local tax official disclosed that tax officers are subject to constant pressure from the township government to lower the assessment whenever this method is applied in collective enterprises. Even when the normal procedure is applied, tax offices are under pressure from the township government to be lenient in taxing TVEs. The pressure is particularly intense when the quota imposed from the higher level has been satisfied. Although tax officers are appointed directly through the vertical line of command at the county level and, hence, are free from the direct influence of the township government, the views of the latter, or of the local Party secretary, still cannot be completely ignored. Many tax officials are willing to do the local bosses a favor by relaxing their squeeze on collective enterprises, especially when their basic assignments have been accomplished.[48]

Another case shows the flexibility of the township government in its enforcement of tax regulations. One township enterprise manager came up with an amazingly creative way to compensate the staff after his proposal for a substantial wage increase was rejected. Although there was no immediate shortage of cash or financial difficulty, the enterprise borrowed more than 1,000 yuan from each worker, at an interest rate twice as high as the current bank rate. The reason was that, as the increase in wages had been disapproved, the higher interest payment offered to the workers could provide them some form of financial compensation for them. The ETC was aware of the irregularity but decided to keep quiet. The tacit consent of the ETC was crucial, as such high-interest internal loans are forbidden by state tax regulations. In fact, the ETC even intervened to secure a lenient penalty on the enterprise when the local tax office discovered the irregularity later.[49]

All these stories seem to suggest that the township government is ready to maintain a balance between local needs and enterprises' interests, at the expense of revenue for the higher levels. The township government prefers to keep enterprise resources in the local community, either in the form of bonuses or wages, fixed investment, direct contributions to local finance, or social donations. By diverting enterprise resources from extraction by the higher levels of administration, the township government can reserve valuable resources for the enjoyment of the local community without increasing the burden on the enterprises.

Control of staffing decision

The importance of personnel control needs no explanation. As the appointment of managers has been examined previously, this section will concentrate on management of the general staff. More specifically, two major areas of

personnel management will be the focus: control over the size of the establishment, and the appointment and dismissal of staff. In general, although there is
a restriction on the size of the labor force, managers enjoy substantial freedom
in internal personnel matters.

The township government maintains tight control over the size of the labor
force employed by enterprises. An upper limit is imposed for each enterprise
and any increase has to be approved by the ETC in advance. In addition, the
mix of staff is under the control of the local administration. The creation of
new posts, especially those in the management category, has to be approved too.
The ETC is thus also involved in determining the organizational structure of
the company, as internal restructuring always implies the creation or removal
of posts. The rationale for tight control in this area is simple; it is a reflection
of the local government's primary concern of over enterprise resources. The
size of an enterprise's labor force is directly related to its expenditure on wages
and bonuses. Thus, a tight grip on the growth of an enterprise's labor force is
essential for maintaining control over enterprise finances.

Managers certainly have a role to play in determining the upper limit.
Their recommendations on the necessary increase in labor input are, in most
cases, respected. At the beginning of each financial year, managers have to
submit a labor plan for their enterprises, which contains an estimate of the
labor force needed and proposals for changes in the personnel management
structure. These proposals have to be submitted before economic targets for
their enterprises are finalized. Amendment afterwards is difficult, as it affects
the original distribution of resources. For this reason, changes in personnel
planning usually have to wait until the next financial year.

Managers' limitations in expanding staff size are well compensated by
their high level of discretion in the choice of specific staff. In the appointment
of both management and ordinary staff, managers played a dominant part.
Managers enjoy substantial freedom in choosing the core of the management
team. Local officials call the existing practice the "cabinet system" (*neiguozhi*)
– once the manager has been appointed, he or she is free to choose his or her
own management team. In principle, the appointment of major management
personnel, including deputies, departmental managers and chief accountants
is within the jurisdiction of the ETC. However, in practice, the manager's
choice is always respected, though the township ETC has to be informed of
any major change in personnel.

The township government has an even more relaxed attitude toward the
appointment of ordinary staff. Within the limits laid down by the ETC, the
manager basically has a free hand in deciding whom to employ. Workers can be
recruited through the county labor bureau, or via the market. As staff turnover
is relatively slow in rural enterprises, personal recommendation remains the
major recruitment channel. It is noteworthy, however, that recruits from the
local community constitute the overwhelming majority of the enterprises'
workforce. In all the township-level enterprises visited by this author, 80–90
percent of workers came from within the township boundaries, and the same

phenomenon can be found among village enterprises. Workers from other counties are rare because, as mentioned above, personal recommendation is the major recruitment channel and the spread of employment information is greatly hindered by the relatively narrow social connections of most workers. In addition, employment of outside workers is discouraged by the extra expenditure required in order to provide accommodations and other welfare benefits for these outsiders.

There is also a strong pressure to reserve employment opportunities for local people, and the local government's attitude is a constant reminder of this concern. Providing more jobs for the local population is, after all, one of the primary objectives of developing local industries. For the local government, this employment pattern also guarantees that the bulk of the wealth generated by these ventures is distributed within the community rather than leaking out to other areas. This is reflected in the official position of the county government. Administrative guidelines on local employment have been issued to all potential employers in the area, stressing that priority should be given to local residents when recruiting graduates of technical high schools and universities. It emphasizes that, only when local supply cannot satisfy the demand, should outside sources be tried. Even then higher educational requirements are stipulated for outsiders.[50]

The official position of priority for locals affects not only the pattern of employment, but also the managers' attitudes toward the enforcement of internal discipline. In theory, a manager has the power to dismiss anyone in the factory, and no prior approval from any administrative unit is needed. However, in reality, managers are still hesitant to dismiss their workers, especially when the trouble-makers are local residents. Potential social pressure from the community, which believes that the provision of employment is a duty of the collective enterprise, and knowledge of the local government's disapproval of such actions are strong enough to deter the managers. Thus, though it is the managers' right to dismiss anyone in the factory, they seem to approach this matter in a tactful and compromising fashion. In most cases, wage deductions and fines are imposed on workers and dismissal is rare.[51]

However, this does not mean that managers are completely helpless when it comes to readjusting the size and the mix of their work force. There have been cases of massive lay-offs of workers in Zibo. For instance, Huantai Food Processing Company recently sent home more than 80 percent of its workers because of its poor performance. A loss of more than a million yuan had accumulated over the past few years and a massive reduction in staff size was the best way to cut down the operational losses of the enterprise. The lay-off was regarded by the enterprise management as temporary, as these workers were still officially employed by the factory, though no benefits would be given during the lay-off period.[52] This is, in fact, a competitive advantage of TVEs over the state sector; they can make swift adjustments without major social consequences. The lack of benefits for TVE workers implies that, unlike their counterparts in state-owned enterprises, peasant-workers are not solely dependent on the workplace for subsistence. Access to shelter and food inherent in land entitlement makes dismissal a less painful and disturbing process in the countryside. Thus, as in the above case, temporary lay-offs are common, though the scale is usually quite small and they last only for a short period during the off-peak production season.

Local enterprises are, in fact, becoming more responsive to market needs in recent years, rendering the principle of priority for locals less imperative. The diverse origins of the senior technical staff of Dongyue Fluorine Chemical, one of the largest collective enterprises in the county, is revealing. All thirteen senior engineers were recruited from outside – from Jinan, Qingdao and Shanghai.[53] The enterprise's need for high caliber staff obviously could not be met locally.[54] These cases show that the local government's concern for the financial implications and developmental needs of an enterprise can prevail over the employment needs of the local population. The need to maintain a balance between conflicting claims requires flexibility from the township government and gives managers more room to maneuver.

However, the role of managers in staff appointments should not be measured solely by their power to appoint someone they like. The real test is, can they reject someone recommended by the local government? As shown by the analysis of the background of enterprise managers in Chapter 3, direct transfers from the administration into the enterprise management rank are rare, and managers coming through this route are a minority. The local government, in other words, remains restrained in this area. This probably reflects its respect for professional competence in the delegation of management power. However, there are several circumstances under which the local government may request that an enterprise accept certain personnel.

First, there is the state policy of sending cadres to the countryside. The Communist administration has a long tradition of transferring cadres to rural areas, dating back to Mao's years. During those radical years, this move was motivated by the urge to strike the right balance between "reds and experts"; in the reform period, the contribution of local experience to strengthening cadres' competence and exposure was equally highly valued. In addition, this policy was regarded by the central state as an indication of its support and concern for rural development.[55] Development of rural enterprises was targeted as one of the major areas deserving extra support. A similar practice was adopted by provincial as well as prefectural level governments across the country. In 1988, the Zibo Party Committee formally introduced the policy of sending down cadres to assist with the development of rural areas.[56] By 1993, 4,960 cadres from the prefecture and county levels had been appointed to township governments or below for a two-year period.[57] The paucity of educated and skilled personnel in local infant enterprises during the early period of rural industrialization explains the lack of complaints against these administrative transfers among managers. According to the third census in Zibo conducted in 1982, during these early post Mao-years, only 1.29 percent of those managers involved in non-agricultural activities in the countryside were university graduates, and those holding high school diplomas were confined to 17.5 percent. Relatively speaking, the local administration possessed better educated staff than its rural counterpart. Within the local public service, 4 percent were degree holders and 27.1 percent were high school graduates.[58] With the general reluctance to work at the rural grass roots level,[59] the administrative allocation of cadres appeared to be the most convenient option for improving the quality of the labor force in rural enterprises.

Ex-servicemen were another potential source of personnel bestowed on enterprises by the government. Pressure to accommodate these personnel was at its peak during the first half of the 1980s, when the central government was determined to cut the size of its military force by one million. Between 1986 and 1997, the Zibo government had accommodated at least 2,346 veterans into their establishment, and most of them were dispersed to the lower levels.[60] Like the cadres sent from the urban areas, these veterans are not necessarily unwelcome. Military service was one of the options that attracted most of the ambitious youth in the countryside in the pre-reform period, as it offered one of the few routes to glamorous city life. Military training also provided unique exposure to technical skills and literacy for rural recruits, and this knowledge turned out to be an important ingredient for producing good enterprise management personnel. In addition, the success stories of several ex-servicemen certainly affect the local perception. For instance, one of the local celebrities of our story, Zhang Jian – the young managing director of Dongyue Fluorine Chemical – was a veteran-turned-manager.

Most of these personnel were assigned to enterprise-related destinations. For the first batch of the 186 sent-down cadres from the prefecture government in 1986, 124 were assigned to economic commissions, bureaucratic units responsible for rural enterprise development. The subsequent batch of 1,025 cadres provided even more direct assistance to rural enterprises; most of them were assigned to 517 enterprises over ninety-six townships.[61] In addition to the fact that they were usually better educated and relatively competent, they also represented a contact with the higher level of bureaucracy that could be useful for business. Modest enterprises, especially private or village-level enterprises, responded quite favorably to the scheme. Zhenhua Factory, one of the most successful private ventures in Zibo, accepted a cadre three years ago and this turned out to be a blessing. The manager was keen to keep the cadre on a permanent basis, and offered him a deputy post with an attractive income package for his continued service.[62] Even if the quality of these cadres is less than might be desired, the harm they do is temporary at most. Usually their service lasts from six months to two years. In addition, enterprise managers can always negotiate the entry points for these personnel. All these arrangements imply that, if there is any potential damage, it can be kept within reasonable limits.

Summary

As seen from the previous discussion, it is evident that at least until the mid-1990s, the local government was still playing an active role in the operation of TVEs. For local officials, such a role was hardly conceived of as "intervention" or "intrusion"; it was simply a matter of responsibility. It was about delegating and sharing power with managers, while trying to accommodate conflicting claims on these collective properties. Local government was driven by its main aim of an uninterrupted supply of revenue, and anything that might have disturbed this justified close involvement. This was well reflected in its control over the wage bill and the size of staff establishment, investment in fixed assets and the setting of targets for financial obligations. The financial implication of these matters justified a hands-on approach.

The local government's preoccupation with revenue, however, also accounted for its tolerance and pragmatism. The trump card possessed by managers was their knowledge and skills – credentials highly respected by the local government and regarded as the key to prosperity. As long as its revenues were fully guaranteed, the local state appeared willing to go to great lengths to accommodate the managers' views. A universal rule, based on the nature of the ownership or other criteria, seemed inappropriate, as the extent of power-sharing depended on the specific details of the interaction – the financial contribution of the enterprise and the competence of the manager. In short, talented managers could earn their power over internal management through good performance. Managerial success, in other words, was not only the key to social privilege and political status; it was the determinant of the manager's power and discretion in internal management.

Although a secure supply of revenue and respect for managers' entrepreneurship set the limits for administrative involvement in enterprise management, the concern for equitable redistribution of resources and general development of the local community, and the obligations imposed by the higher level of administration both pushed it in opposite directions. The former necessitated more non profit-oriented measures, particularly in the area of employment and remuneration, to ensure "fairness" in distribution; whereas the latter demanded a greater degree of regularity in enterprise practice and greater consistency with national laws, and hence a more rigid approach to the regulation of local TVEs. Taken together, both factors limited the enterprise managers. The local administration tried to eradicate the tensions inherent in its conflicting tasks and to maintain the right balance by showing tactful flexibility over different areas of TVE management. With this carefully crafted balance, it hoped that the professional judgment of managers could be fully expressed amid the conflicting claims. This task was, however, not an easy one. It was further complicated by the continued growth of TVEs in the second half of the 1990s. Growth implied extra revenues and more economic opportunities for the local community, but it also entailed greater difficulty in maintaining the right balance between differing interests. Specifically, the rising importance of TVEs meant greater bargaining power for the managers, who, as seen in this chapter, were always prepared to exploit their favorable position in order to gain extra advantages. This dynamism of managers and their insatiable drive for rewards were the seeds of change in rural institutions. As will be seen in Chapters 6 and 7, the need to accommodate the rising demands of these managers was the driving force behind experimentation with the intensified shareholding reforms in rural China in the second half of the 1990s.

6 Evaluating enterprise reform

A local perspective

Our story so far reveals that the symbiotic relationship between local state and enterprise managers is the key to local economic development, and the functional indispensability of managers has earned them a strategic place in the local economic and political hierarchy. This chapter and the one that follows will continue to evaluate the increasingly important role of enterprise managers and the complexity inherent in the redefinition of the state's role in the market reform era. My contention is that the rise of managers does not stop with the improvement of their personal economic and political position; their ascent also increases pressure for institutional change in economic management.

The forthcoming discussion will focus on the shareholding enterprise reform experiment in Zibo prefecture, and will demonstrate how managers capitalized on their influence through the organizational restructuring of TVEs. This research suggests that shareholding reform in rural China was hijacked by local interests; local government and managers manipulated the reform momentum unleashed by the central government and moved it in the direction that best suited their own interests – accommodating the managers' demand for better rewards and protecting a steady supply of revenues, even at the expense of the original aim of the reforms. Whiting provides a compelling account of the development of shareholding cooperative reforms in rural Shanghai, Jiangsu, and Zhejiang. She argues that the trajectory of corporate restructuring of TVEs in these localities was predominantly a result of local government responses to the changes in the central extractive mechanism and desire of local governments to maintain control over the local economy. In spite of the persuasiveness of the account, it suffers the same statist parochialism criticized earlier in this discussion. Managers, who played a significant role in TVE development in the reform era, are irrelevant in Whiting's account.[1] This author argues that, although it is true that the process of TVE ownership reform was a deliberate attempt by local governments to defend their interests, it was also shaped by the rising role of managers. And this author would further argue that it is also in the interest of the local government to accommodate the managers' interest in the restructuring process. It was the managers' know-how that turned these assets into a steady stream of revenue and economic resources. The give-and-take reflected in the following analysis of reforms again confirms the symbolic nature of their exchanges and the prospect of mutual empowerment for both parties. Local governments in Zibo share much of Bates's observation on the political economy of development:

> [T]he political roots of development productively join with the economic when specialists in violence realize that they can best survive and prevail by promoting the prosperity of their economic base. Under such circumstances, owners of capital will believe their promises to refrain from predation. Knowing that predation would be politically unproductive, they will be willing to invest. In such circumstances, those with power will also be willing to delegate authority to those with resources and skills, enabling them to combine and to organize and, literally, to govern economic organizations. When their ability to survive, politically, depends upon the capacity of others to produce, economically, then specialists in violence will vest their power in those who will invest their capital.[2]

In the case of Zibo, managers may not be the owners of financial capital, but their invaluable stock of human capital – their managerial skills, know-how, and entrepreneurial instinct – is no less decisive for local economic well-being. As we will see, there is evidence of delegation of corporate control to managers via share distribution, but whether widespread privatization is emerging in rural China is debatable. Although it is certainly the case that share ownership by managers of rural businesses is increasing, local governments' presence in the local economy can still be felt. Barzel's distinction between economic property rights and legal property rights is pertinent to our understanding here. Though the economic right that people have over assets is the substantive ability to enjoy a piece of property, legal property rights are the rights recognized and enforced in part by the government. The legal rights are formal rules, which may enhance the economic rights, but the former is not sufficient for the latter. The economic property right is fundamentally dependent on the individual's own capability to protect his assets.[3] In the case of TVE managers, such protection is a function of their contribution to local prosperity and finance and their degree of self-sufficiency in operations. Formal share distribution alone may not provide a perfect depiction of control over TVEs; one needs to put this interaction into the context of rural China.

This chapter starts with an analysis of the rationale behind shareholding reform. This part of the discussion will concentrate on the theoretical promises of this idea; it aims to provide an account of the expectations of central government. A brief review of the progress of shareholding reform so far will follow. Central government's pragmatism and indecisiveness, features that have important implications for the implementation of shareholding reform at the grass-roots level, will be revealed. The discussion will then put reforms into the rural grass-roots context. It will examine how this specific reform proposal is evaluated by local interests – the local government and managers

– and reveal how the potential benefits of the reform initiative are offset by the functional necessity of maintaining the mutual dependence between the two parties. The inconsistency between the concerns of the reformers at the top and the local interests at the rural grass-roots level explains the lack of enthusiasm for this brand of shareholding reform, which theoretically represents an important step toward a greater degree of marketization of the Chinese economy. Instead, as will be discussed in Chapter 7, a unique version of shareholding reform, the shareholding cooperative system, has emerged. This is, however, an option mainly designed to serve the local interests and hardly meets most of the expectations of the central reformers in its potential impact on enterprise management.

A brief review of enterprise reforms in post-Mao China

Since 1978, China has experimented with a wide range of measures aimed at improving public enterprise efficiency. Industrial enterprises in Mao's China were not market oriented. The primary concern of enterprise managers in the pre-reform period was meeting the targets and orders imposed by administrative superiors, rather than achieving financial results and satisfying customer demand. Enterprises were regarded as subsidiaries of the administrative system and subjected to mandatory plans and direct governmental control.[4] This traditional socialist system exhibited several major defects: lack of autonomy and labor incentives, soft budget constraints,[5] and a lack of price signals and market mechanisms.[6] All these defects were identified as major reasons for the failure of the planned economy.

Following Mao's death, China started to experiment with various reforms intended to reverse the situation. The development of Chinese enterprise reform can be divided into three stages:

1   The initial stage (1979–83) was intended to give enterprises greater autonomy and to expand the role of financial incentives while maintaining the traditional planning system. Measures such as the profit retention scheme and performance-related bonuses for employees were introduced, and enterprises were also allowed to produce outside the mandatory plan.

2   The second stage (1984–6) shifted the focus to the increasing role of economic instruments and greater exposure of enterprises to market pressure. Major experiments included the introduction of the tax-for-profit scheme, the rationalization of indirect taxes, and the establishment of the dual-track system. It was at this stage that market transactions were formally introduced, alongside the traditional planning system, to influence enterprise output decisions.

3   During the third stage (1987 to the present), the issue of ownership system has dominated the reform agenda.[7] Experimentation with a contract responsibility system was among the earliest attempts to revitalize the

economy along this line. Its proponents argued that such a system could improve the economy by separating the use right of public property from the ownership right, i.e., although the enterprise remained a public asset, it could now be operated by a non-public agent, who is theoretically more vulnerable to market pressure and competition. Nonetheless, the limitations of this experiment soon emerged. Among these were the prevalence of "short-sighted behavior" (*duanqi xingwei*) by enterprise operators and the persistence of administrative intervention.[8] Its viability as a long-term strategy for enterprise reform was in doubt,[9] and a more audacious attempt has been gaining momentum.

Shareholding reform: a big step forward

Amid general dissatisfaction with the previous attempts at enterprise reform, the more daring option of shareholding reform quietly gathered a following. Unsystematic experiments were carried out in Beijing and Shanghai during the early 1980s and the idea managed to attract more serious consideration by the late 1980s.[10] The most important signal of recognition was the 1987 endorsement given by the former General Secretary of the Chinese Communist Party, Zhao Ziyang. In his report to the 13th National Congress of the Chinese Communist Party, Zhao said:

> Some of the things we have introduced in the process of reform, such as expanded markets for means of production, funds, technology and labor service and *the issuance of stocks and bonds* [author's italics], are phenomena which are not peculiar to capitalism but are bound to appear in the wake of large-scale, socialized production and the development of the commodity economy. Socialism can and should make use of them, trying at the same time to minimize their negative effects in practice.[11]

The legal status of shareholding enterprises was formally confirmed by the Enterprise Law (*Qiyefa*), passed in the 7th National People's Congress in 1988. The opening of the Shanghai Securities Exchange and the Shenzhen Stock Exchange in 1990 and 1991, respectively, marked a new stage in China's shareholding experiment. Several rules and regulations concerning the management of shareholding companies were promulgated, and a high-caliber Security Affairs Committee, consisting of top officials from seven relevant government departments, was also established directly under the State Council in 1992.[12] The Company Law (*Gongxifa*), passed in 1993, which imitates many key features of the organizational structure of a shareholding enterprise in a capitalist economy, clearly demonstrated the intention to develop this new enterprise system in China.[13] All these signified the central leadership's inclination to push forward with the shareholding reform experiment.[14]

Property theorists believe that the new arrangement can improve enterprise efficiency by minimizing the agency problem and clarifying property ownership.[15] According to Eggertson, "an agency relationship is established when a principal delegates some rights – for example, user rights over a resource – to an agent who is bound by a [formal or informal] contract to represent the principal's interests in return for payment of some kind."[16] Agency problems arise when the agent does not act in the best interest of the principal, or tries to pursue its own interests at the principal's expense. The relationship between enterprise managers and the owner of public enterprises, the state, is a good example. The agency problem can be improved by the shareholding system in two ways. First, it creates a greater incentive to monitor managerial performance. Shareholders, the ultimate risk-bearers of potential managerial failure, should have the incentive to supervise the performance of the enterprise management. In addition, as the returns on the investment made by each shareholder, in terms of dividends and interest earnings (whether an individual or public agency), are now determined by the general financial condition of the company, there should be a higher degree of financial transparency and accountability. Consequently, the management should be under greater internal pressure to perform.[17] Second, the reduced incentive for the managers to shirk responsibilities can also minimize the agency problem. The simplest way to achieve this is to make managers shareholders too. By doing so, the managers' incomes is correlated with the company's performance, which is, theoretically, dependent on the efficiency of the enterprises under their stewardship. This profit sharing gives managers some incentive to curtail voluntarily the degree of responsibility shirking.[18]

Property rights theorists also argue that a well-defined system of private property rights[19] is a precondition for improving enterprise efficiency and the proper functioning of a market economy. Property rights are clearly delineated if every property is assigned a well-defined owner or owners with usage, income, and transfer rights. According to property rights theorists, the absence of these rights is conducive to poor performance of the enterprise.[20]

These theoretical arguments are particularly appealing to the reform advocates, who are concerned with the efficiency of Chinese enterprises. One of the major indictments of the socialist economy is the inherent danger of public ownership; there are no clearly identified owners to pay for mistakes or bad luck. Someone else pays, and it is usually the state. The negative implications of the state bailing out inefficient enterprises are obvious. The resultant soft-budget constraint is, understandably, conducive to poor financial discipline and is a disincentive to improvements. State-owned enterprises are "owned by the people," yet it is obvious that this is too abstract and does not provide sufficient incentive for workers and managers to make the best use of resources. After all, they do not enjoy the income rights of the property (i.e. the enterprise), so why should they care? Or what will they lose if the enterprise performs badly? However, by converting these enterprises into shareholding enterprises, it becomes clear that shareholders are the clear residual claimants, as well as the ones who ultimately pay for managerial mistakes or failures. They have, in other words, all the incentive required to make sure that appropriate measures are taken to increase the profitability of the enterprise and to avoid inefficiency.

The potential contribution of the shareholding system in clarifying ownership rights also has unique appeal to the socialist enterprise in China, as it should minimize administrative intervention in enterprise management. Introduction of the shareholding system theoretically redefines the basis of participation in enterprise management. The right to involvement in the decision-making process of a shareholding enterprise should be determined by the holding of shares, rather than by the bureaucratic status of the individuals or organizations concerned, and each share should carry an equal privilege. These enterprises are no longer appendages of an administrative unit, but are financially independent economic entities accountable to their shareholders, who may or may not be administrative units. In the terminology used by Chinese economists, such an enterprise should become a so-called "enterprise without an administrative supervisor" (*wu zhuguan bumen qiye*), in contrast to the pre-reform arrangement, under which all public enterprises were under the direct supervision of a specific administrative unit.[21]

A general comparison of the principles of operating state-owned enterprises in Mao's period and shareholding enterprises in the reform period[22] may best summarize the theoretical promises of the new system and show how the reforms can revitalize Chinese enterprises. Notwithstanding the variations and complications in the actual operation of state-owned enterprises and shareholding enterprises, Table 6.1 provides a simplified comparison. A pattern of extensive administrative penetration in enterprise management is evident in state-owned enterprises. The administrative unit entrusted by the central government to supervise the enterprise is heavily involved in its management and operation. It acts as a bridge between the central planning mechanism and the enterprise via its administrative presence, and the quotas of production and financial extraction are transmitted from the former to the latter effectively. The fundamental role of the enterprise manager is to make sure that these quotas are dutifully fulfilled, and this is the major yardstick with which to evaluate a manager's performance. The owners, the people of China, are not involved, in any sense, in management and gain no direct benefits from the production of any specific enterprise. In short, the state-owned enterprises are simply rendered administrative appendages, serving mainly as a means of fulfilling the state plan. Those who "own" the enterprises are not involved in their management, and those with control and who make decisions are not held responsible for the enterprises' profits and losses, because financial balance is not the primary burden on their shoulders. In the worst case, a contingent financial subsidy is always available.

The description of the shareholding enterprise in Table 6.1 reveals a contrasting image. The administrative unit has no formal role in internal management. In addition, there is a clear link between the different ownership rights in the enterprise. The owners, i.e. the shareholders, can participate in the decision-making process through various means and define the general

Table 6.1 Comparison of the operation and management structure of state-owned enterprises and shareholding enterprises in Mao's China

	State-owned enterprise	*Shareholding enterprise*
Owner	All people of China	Shareholders
Executive control	Under the supervision of specific administrative unit; manager with limited autonomy in operation	Shareholders' assembly, supervisory committee[a] and board of directors are the bodies which make major decisions; manager is held accountable to these internal institutions
Residual claimant	The supervising adminstrative unit; enterprise retains a small share	Shareholders
Production orientation	Fulfillment of the quotas of production imposed by the state plan	Profit-making; market signals as the major reference for production
Ultimate financial responsibility	Possibility of bailing out by the state treasury, and budgetary constraint is elastic	Hard budgetary constraint, and bankruptcy as the final resort in financial difficulties

Note

a The Supervisory Committee (*Jianshihui*) is a unique innovation in the Chinese shareholding system. According to the Company Law, all shareholding enterprises have to establish this institution, which is composed of representatives of shareholders and workers of the company. Workers' representatives have to be elected democratically by workers. This institution enjoys many important powers including access to the financial records of the company, the right to request answers from the directors and manager, and the right to call for an emergency shareholders' assembly.

policy of the company. They are also directly responsible for profits and losses, as the company is financially independent. Thus, in order to survive, they have to make sure that the one they entrust with steering the company on the path toward prosperity – the manager – is doing the right thing and reacts rationally to any market signals.

Though it is debatable whether these potential benefits of the shareholding system are ever fully realized in any of the capitalist economies,[23] expectations of this new idea remain high in China. This optimism may best be summarized by Dong Fureng, a senior economic adviser to the Chinese government. According to Dong:

> This [shareholding reform] releases the enterprise from appendage status and enables it to be self-managing. Their asset relations are unambiguous, and ultimately every shareholder is responsible for profit and loss. Budget constraints are hard or nearly as hard as in privately owned enterprises.

Consequently, these enterprises can become subject to market forces and the market system can expand. This is a hopeful experiment.[24]

Another major attraction of the shareholding system is its potential contribution, as a financial lever, in converting idle capital for productive purposes. One of the most spectacular developments of the Chinese economy since the commencement of the reform program is the tremendous increase in savings by individuals and enterprises. Savings deposits of urban and rural individuals increased from twenty-one billion yuan in 1978 to 1,476 billion yuan in 1993,[25] and enterprise deposits increased from 207 billion yuan to 1,147 billion between 1985 and 1994.[26] The accumulation of such a huge amount of capital necessitated the development of a system to recycle this money for more productive purposes. The shareholding system can provide a financial tool to channel this capital into the development of Chinese enterprises.

In addition, the declining financial capacity of the Chinese government also made the search for an effective capital mobilization tool a more urgent task. The sustainable and steady growth of Chinese enterprises has to depend on the availability of new sources of financing, as they can no longer rely on the state to provide sufficient funding. The proportion of government finances in GNP has decreased sharply during the reform period,[27] and hence it is simply unrealistic to expect the state to continue its policy of heavy subsidies for enterprises as in the pre-reform era. In fact, the Chinese government has introduced numerous financial instruments in order to reduce financial pressure. The extensive use of treasury bonds is a good illustration. By 1990, a total of 2,573 billion yuan in bonds was issued, of which more than half had been issued by administrative units.[28] These figures show the Chinese state's eagerness to find an alternative source of funding to support the bureaucracy and to promote economic development. Put in this perspective, the function of the shareholding system in channeling capital for enterprise development is important.

Indecisiveness of the central government

Despite these high expectations, the approach of the Chinese leadership remained indecisive toward the full development of the shareholding system during the early years of reform. Although the establishment of several stock exchange centers has attracted worldwide attention, along with speculation about the irresistible advance of capitalism in China, progress during the first half of the 1990s was moderate. By 1993, only 4,580 state-owned and collectively owned enterprises at the county level or above had converted to the shareholding system, constituting only 4.5 percent of the total number of enterprises in this category.[29] In addition, for most of these enterprises, shares can be sold only to employees or related companies. Only a very small number of these enterprises (124) are listed on the two stock exchanges in Shanghai and Shenzhen.[30] In other words, an effective secondary market for company shares has yet to be established, and the absence of this development has limited the potential contributions. More important, it reflects the Chinese government's hesitation and indecisiveness, for which there are several explanations.

Decades of central planning have nourished a false sense of economic certainty and stability among economic bureaucrats in China. The resultant anxiety over financial stability and the apparent lack of experience in dealing with the inherent volatility and unpredictability of financial markets may account for the bureaucrats' concerns about and cautiousness toward the newly developed stock market. Their paranoia is likely to be reinforced by memories of the several recent confrontations with the people, such as the political turbulence during the summer of 1989, which was to a large extent ignited by growing economic frustration, particularly over inflation. Anxiety is evident even among top leaders. For instance, Premier Zhu Rongji, who has been generally regarded by the world media as one of the more reform-minded leaders, and who has been nicknamed the "Gorbachev of China," has shown reservations about the rapid development of shareholding reform and has warned against the danger of "stock fever."[31] Overcautiousness is, however, part of a vicious cycle. The reluctance to expand the size of the stock market has unintentionally sown seeds of instability in the market. The simple fact is that there is simply too much money chasing too few shares in the Chinese stock market. The huge discrepancy between supply and demand and the administrative interference blocking market adjustment have led to the anticipation of great returns from these shares. The following observation by a Chinese stock watcher is revealing:

> As soon as new stocks have been put on sale, residents have rushed to buy but have seldom sold them, feeling free from any worry or risk or crisis . . . . Many people do not understand what stock is all about. One Shanghai resident who bought some stocks said, "The price of stocks is rising every day. Buying stocks can make money, I don't care how things will stand in the future. I'll just wait and see."[32]

This ignorance and the chronic imbalance between supply and demand can sometimes lead to explosive situations. The "8/10 riot" in Shenzhen, in August 1992, is an example of such a situation. More than one million Chinese stood for days in the summer heat to buy shares of newly listed companies. As it became apparent that supply could satisfy only a small fraction of these potential buyers, frustration in the street mounted. Thus, when rumors spread about officials withholding application forms for buying shares for themselves, riots broke out.[33]

Ideologically, it is also noteworthy that China, unlike its counterparts in Central Europe, has never fully admitted officially that privatization is the ultimate goal of economic reforms. The private sector is booming, yet it is still premature to say that the irreversible trend toward full-fledged privatization seen in other post-communist states is evident in China; at least officially, the issue remains unsettled.[34] The Party is still struggling to hammer out a powerful and persuasive argument on the ideological compatibility of implementing economic reforms with strong capitalist features under the official advocacy of the superiority of socialism. The Party has, however, made various attempts. In the 13th National Congress of the Chinese Communist Party (CCP) in 1987, Zhao Ziyang, one of the most enthusiastic of Chinese premiers toward market reform, put forward his theory of a "primary stage of socialism" as the ideological justification for economic reforms. In the 14th National Congress in 1992, Jiang Zemin tabled his vision of a "socialist market economy."[35] Cynics may say that these arguments are simply toying with terms and lack real substance, but the legacy of socialist principles remains a significant factor in the development of China's reform program. Insistence on public ownership may sound rhetorical, but reform is proceeding in a historical context of continuity and discontinuity. The progress of market reforms and the exposure to new ideas and concepts may keep pulling the country in a new direction, but the persistence of the CCP leadership is the most powerful guarantee of continuity with the "socialist past." These different attempts at ideological justifications by Party leaders hint that there still exists a powerful audience among the ruling elites who care about this ideological discourse. In other words, ideology is still a variable to be reckoned with in the process of economic reform.

Consequently, on the issue of ownership reform and the shareholding experiment, the central government is pragmatic in two senses. On the one hand, dogmatic adherence to the traditional planned economy has been discarded; on the other, there is no unreserved faith in full-scale privatization. The famous dictum of the "chief architect of reform," Deng Xiaoping, is still a useful indicator of the pragmatism of the present leadership. Deng said, "the color of a cat doesn't really matter; if it can catch mice, it's a good cat." With the improvement of economic performance being the Party leadership's fundamental concern, pragmatism still exerts its influence among Chinese statesmen. As long as dynamic economic growth is maintained, local variations in the implementation of shareholding reforms are likely to be tolerated. This mentality has provided an opening for local interests in rural China to maneuver and a chance for them to exert their influence on the shape of enterprise reform. The impact of this factor will be more vividly illustrated in the next chapter.

Relevance for the rural economy

Although the state sector in urban areas is the primary target of enterprise reforms, this does not mean that the reforms are irrelevant in the rural context. The promise of revitalizing enterprise efficiency and the capital mobilization function of shareholding reform is equally appealing to the rural sector. A similar, yet even more spectacular, rise in rural savings has been observed in the countryside. There has been phenomenal growth in rural savings in the post-Mao years – a sixty-four-fold increase between 1978 and 1993 alone.

The total amount of rural savings increased from less than six billion yuan to 358 billion yuan during this period.[36] The demise of People's Communes and their fundamental mechanism of distribution (the work-point system), the introduction of the household responsibility system, and purchase price increases for agricultural products have all contributed to this growth. The rural population's relative ignorance about and lack of access to different financial instruments makes the search for a means to tap into this capital for productive use an urgent task. The introduction of the shareholding system has provided a possible means through which to channel this capital into rural enterprise development. The capital would otherwise be used for less productive purposes, such as the purchase of imported items, extravagant furnishings for houses, elaborate banquets or other luxury items, or it would simply be left idle.

The need to improve the efficiency of TVEs is also high on the agenda of local administrators in rural China. It is important to note that TVEs differ from their state-owned counterparts in urban areas in one important respect: they developed outside the state plan. In other words, they are less affected by the defects of conventional socialist enterprise management, such as a huge burden of welfare responsibility and tight control over production. However, the fact that TVEs are publicly owned means that they face some problems similar to those faced by their urban counterparts in the state sector. Among these are the issues of possible administrative intervention, disincentive among staff, and ambiguous property rights. It is for this reason that the idea of shareholding reform is also relevant for the development of TVEs in the countryside.

The track record shows that the local government in rural China shares the central government's concern for enterprise efficiency. As argued previously, the financial contribution of local industry has been an indispensable component of local revenues and thus the local state has every reason to improve the performance of these enterprises. The relatively weaker financial status of the rural administrations also makes them less capable of bailing out inefficient enterprises than their counterparts in the higher administrative levels. TVEs have to go bankrupt if they fail to survive in the face of tense market competition. For the rural administrations this is the last resort to cut losses, yet the financial damage is significant.

The local administrators have been adventurous in their pursuit of property rights reform since the early years of economic reform. If the issue is not simply to identify who the owners are, but also how the bundle of property rights is being disintegrated and recombined,[37] then progress in rural China has been substantial. There has been significant downward reassignment of the usage rights of collective enterprises, from the local state to non-state operators. The wide variety of contractual arrangements providing the *de facto* owner, i.e. the local government, with a specific compensatory payment, in return for its consent to the leaseholders or contractors managing its assets with a considerable degree of autonomy, have in effect removed part of the usage rights from the local government. The practice of a contractually specified payment to the owner also implies a parallel downward reassignment of the income rights. In many cases, the contracting agents agree to pay a fixed quota of income to the owner, and accept in advance a formula for sharing any returns above the quota.[38]

A double-edged sword

Local government's eagerness to improve the enterprise management system has to be balanced with its concern for maintaining control over local enterprises. For this reason, progress in reassigning transfer rights has been limited. Various experiments, such as leasing out enterprises and the contract responsibility system, are common in collective enterprise management, but privatization of collective enterprises is the exception rather than the rule. The latter represents an irrevocable move that could terminate the local government's control over the assets, and it is apparent that the local government is not ready to go that far. Several reasons may account for its reluctance to give up its control over TVEs.

In addition to concerns with maintaining a steady supply of TVE revenues, the ideological factor also plays a major role in local government's reluctance to relinquish its control over and ownership of TVEs. "If absolute property means exemption from social control it has never existed," argues Elizondo.[39] According to this argument, all property has a social aspect and limitations on private property do exist, especially when the notion of public interest is involved. As Furubotn and Pejovich insightfully point out, "ownership is not, and can hardly be expected to be, an unrestricted right. The right of ownership is an exclusive right in the sense that it is limited only by those restrictions that are explicitly stated in the law as it is interpreted from time to time."[40] In other words, the perception of public interest plays a key role in defining the relationship between the state and enterprise. Put like this, it is easy to understand the active state intervention in TVE operation under socialism, given the paternalism inherent in the vanguard nature of the Party-state.

In rural China, the concept of public interest is significantly affected by the socialist legacy of Mao's era. Maoist radicalism has been diluted significantly by the advent of market reform, but some ideological traits are arguably still detectable in rural society. Most notable is the principle of egalitarianism. This was revealed in the pattern of local government's involvement in enterprise management evaluated in Chapter 5. Residents of the local community feel entitled to employment and income opportunities in local TVEs. Under socialist principles, they are right to think so, as collective ownership implies that they are the owners of these TVEs. This enduring impact of the socialist ideology in the reform era provides an extra impetus for local government to maintain its presence in TVE operation. The presence of local government is an indispensable part of the local economy; it is crucial for upholding the distributive fairness of the socialist economy, and is thus necessary and legitimate. As argued by North, informal elements may have "tenacious survival ability" and, despite radical change in formal rules, they somehow persist.[41] In the case of rural China, the Maoist legacy retains a place in defining the grammar of local governance. Such a perspective has proven to be an important factor affecting the evaluation of the proposed shareholding reforms.

A comparison of the role of the local government in enterprise management under two different organizational structures may help to explain further the local reservations about shareholding reforms. The pattern of local government involvement in TVE management, revealed in Chapter 5, will be contrasted with shareholding enterprises, as stipulated in the Company Law.[42] As summarized in Table 6.2, four areas of control are of particular concern for local government: managerial appointments, profit distribution, fiscal extraction, and operational management.

In non-shareholding TVEs, the power of appointing a manager is enjoyed solely by the township ETC. Its consent is an indispensable part of the appointment process. However, under the new system, the ETC has less say in this matter because its share of the company is reduced. The power of appointment belongs either to the shareholders' assembly or to the board of directors. In both cases, the dominant role of local government is not guaranteed, given its minority share.

Local government's bargaining position with respect to profit distribution appears to be much stronger in the TVE management system than under the shareholding mechanism. Under the new system, what the local government can get from a enterprise is determined by its share ownership. The barriers are more rigid and impersonal. There is also a new complexity in the process of dividing the "cake," as the interests of the numerous shareholders must now be taken into account. With the new requirements of greater financial transparency and discipline, and with the shareholders' incentive to protect their own financial interests, local officials are likely to have less room for maneuver.

Given the same tax rate for enterprises under the different ownership systems, the financial impact of the new system on the local government should be minimal. However, one significant aspect – the collection of a management fee (*guanlifei*) – may be affected. Calculated on the basis of a fixed percentage of the enterprise's turnover, the fee is collected by different administrative units according to the ownership system. The township ETC is entitled only to those fees paid by collective enterprises, whereas private-sector fees go to the township Industry and Commerce Administration (ICA) (*Gongshang Guanliju*), which is under the vertical command of the central ministry. Local government is aware that there remains a big question mark over the nature of the ownership of the newly formed shareholding enterprises – are they private or collective? This controversy, and its possible financial implications, has reinforced local government's reservations about shareholding reform.[43]

In terms of operational management, as with the distribution of profits, local government is in a more comfortable position in the pre-shareholding

Table 6.2 Comparison of the role of the local government in enterprise management in different forms of enterprise

	TVE	*Shareholding*
Appointment of manager	Approved by the ETC	Approved by the board of directors
Distribution of profits	Stipulated in the contract or agreement determined and approved by the ETC	Determined by the board on the basis of distribution of shares
Fiscal extraction	The ETC is entitled to a share of collected management fees	The issue of fee collection remains unsettled
Operational management	The scope of autonomy enjoyed by the manager is largely deter mined by the ETC	The board of directors determines the scope of freedom of the operators

scenario, even if it is constrained by bargaining with enterprise staff. As a shareholder, the local government can be sure that its involvement in and control over major decisions concerning the development of the enterprise are guaranteed. The problem is that it is no longer the only owner – a more dispersed ownership arises with the introduction of shareholding reform – and, worse still, it may become a minority owner. These factors are likely to contain the influence of the local government.

In short, local government's incentive to introduce shareholding reform is very much offset by its fear of losing control over local industry. Local government's reservations about shareholding reforms are understandable, as the reforms are basically aimed at tying the hands of local government in the management of collective enterprises. Unlike previous reform measures, the new idea challenges local government's exclusive role in the reassignment of property rights. Once an enterprise is transformed into a shareholding company, there is a possibility that the local government will lose control of more shares and it will eventually be condemned to a minority position. A lukewarm response, if not total rejection of the idea as an option for collective enterprise reform, should not be too surprising to neutral observers.

Calculations of the enterprise managers

Although local government may have reasons to resist shareholding reform, it still has to seek an improved organizational structure to enhance the efficiency of enterprises. On the one hand, the agency and incentive problems concerning enterprise managers are genuine issues that need to be tackled. On the other hand, a proper balance between control and managerial autonomy has to be maintained if the dynamism and entrepreneurial talents of managers are to be freely expressed. In this respect, the attitude of enterprise managers toward the new reform is crucial. Theoretically, shareholding promises a rose garden for managers, and there seems to be little reason for their objection to the adoption of the shareholding scheme. The proposed system of shareholding can improve the position of enterprise managers by elevating their social status and providing them with better financial prospects and greater managerial autonomy.

The new mechanism provides TVE managers a chance to become co-owners of the enterprise through buying shares. It can transform managers from subordinate appointees of the local government into equals on the board of directors. Rather than being a *dagongzi*, a slang term imported from southern China that refers to an employee, they can now become a genuine *laoban*, an expression of recognition and respect, which the locals use to refer to the owner-boss. The social value and psychological satisfaction attached to such a status can be enormous. The new system may also increase the personal income of managers in several ways. First, the chance to buy shares in the company provides managers with an extra source of income other than wages and bonuses. For companies in good financial condition, such income can be substantial. Second, as the "take" of the local government becomes more predictable and more proportional to its shareholding, a closer linkage between a manager's efforts and his income is to be expected. Lastly, the new system also promises greater managerial autonomy. The conventional system of collective enterprise management is characterized by relative intimacy between the local government and the manager, even at the operational level. As seen in Chapters 4 and 5, the local government's presence may not always be resented and, on some occasions, its involvement is welcomed. However, the problem of when and how such involvement is conducted is not totally regulated by enterprise managers; the cost of securing the local administration's blessing is accepting the unpredictability and arbitrariness of its involvement. This is, unsurprisingly, a source of tension between the two parties and an irritation for managers, particularly for those managers who are running leading profit-making enterprises. It may be seen as a lack of trust in the manager's ability or as a disruption to his well-thought-out plans. The shareholding system, which aims to reduce administrative interference in enterprise management, appeals to managers for this reason. The local government is only one of the many shareholders on the board of directors, and the presence of other shareholders should provide a buffer against its arbitrary interventions.

However tempting the shareholding system may appear, the implications of its introduction for managers can be comprehended only when the rural context is considered. In short, the interdependence between the local government and enterprise managers, as revealed in the previous discussion, leads to a different interpretation of the meaning of the prospective organizational change for local interests. This interdependence contributes to a mutual sanctioning mechanism by which each party is bound to act with restraint when making claims against the other. Managers can make their discontent felt by working less, shirking responsibilities, and being indecisive. Between the limits of passive satisfaction of the basic output targets imposed by the local government and a passionate performance as a motor of local economic development, enterprise managers enjoy substantial room in defining their own role. The revenue implications of an enterprise's performance are an effective form of pressure on the local government. Nevertheless, a concern for personal financial status and career prospects obliges managers to be sensitive to officials' feelings. Withdrawal of official blessing can certainly have a negative impact on business. The local government can, of course, make life even more difficult for managers by administrative means such as wage freezes, or even dismissal as a last resort.

Managers are likely to agree that arbitrary intervention by local government is annoying, yet the proposal to separate the enterprise from politics, through the adoption of formal rules on property relations, seems to miss a crucial point in the definition of the proper boundary between enterprise and local government. The latter's involvement in the operation of an enterprise is mainly confined to its ability to replace the existing management, rather than being determined by a legally defined framework. Local governments avoid being "back-seat drivers" and monopolizing the economic rewards mainly because they does not feel they can do so without damaging the local economy. Thus, administrative intervention is maintained at an acceptable level as long as the economic role of managers remains indispensable and the fundamental feature of local finance (i.e. the financial contribution of TVEs constitutes an indispensable proportion of the total revenues generated locally) remains intact. With these conditions for interdependence remaining constant, managers can be confident that local government will be aware of the limits of its involvement in the local economy.

However, managers also have a part to play in ensuring that the local government acts with restraint. They must let the local government know that they too will exercise self-restraint. In other words, both parties must know that reciprocity will be observed. Each side can then be sure what to expect and can act strategically. Thus, the opportunity offered by the proposed shareholding scheme has to be handled with great caution. A basic strategy that managers must follow is to avoid setting out to take maximum advantage of this opportunity. If the local government feels that reasonable limits have been breached – i.e. if managers are enthusiastic about the idea of buying majority shares in companies – the delicate balance will be destroyed. Seen from this perspective, unless managers are completely confident that they can live without the support of local government, it is dangerous for them to embrace shareholding reform too enthusiastically and to attempt to reap the full benefits.

The reservations of enterprise managers about the new scheme are also affected by the security of the proposed property relations. The major contribution of a clearly defined property rights relationship is that it "makes possible legal expectations with respect to things."[44] However, if such expectations are to be met, the right to property has to be secured. This is related to another issue that is critical for the success of property rights reform: enforcement.

Two alternative forms of enforcement, internal and external, are possible. "Enforcement poses no problem when it is in the interests of the other party to live up to agreements," argues North.[45] The consent of the local government is crucial for implementation of the reform. However, whether such consent is given on a voluntary basis is a different matter. The local government may, as a result of immense pressure from above or for other reasons, make reluctant concessions. Even if the endorsement is given voluntarily in the first place, it does not mean that continued commitment can be taken for granted. As discussed above, there are many reasons why the local government may find the new arrangement to be working against its interests. The dilution of its control and influence over enterprise operations, the growing danger of becoming a minority shareholder, or the frustration resulting from the new organizational barrier against its involvement, for example, may all incite the local government to try to bypass the new system.

If internal enforcement is not reliable, external enforcement is needed. Here the issue of the policing agent matters. Who will act as the third party to arbitrate in a dispute between shareholders, particularly when the local government is the culprit? The Chinese court is obviously a legitimate candidate. The critical question is "Will other shareholders, such as the managers, initiate legal proceedings when a dispute arises?" It would be surprising if many managers were to go to court for arbitration under such circumstances. In the case of enterprise managers who rely on local government assistance, the cost of upholding their shareholder rights may be too high.

Seen from this perspective, the potential benefits of the new system are greatly devalued. Put simply, the fatal flaw of shareholding reform is the attempt to "tie the king's hands" without an effective enforcement mechanism. One has to depend on the good faith and, most importantly, the self-restraint of local government in committing itself to the new arrangement. "Policy proposals that neglect the problem of enforcement are, therefore, incomplete,"[46] and for enterprise managers the debate over productive potential of shareholding reform remains abstract and academic. The informal mechanism of property relations mentioned above might sound inferior and insecure for those property theorists who believe that a clearly defined and legally protected division of rights is the only basis for stable expectations or market transactions. However, in reality, the choice is always constrained by the limited options available.

The unique context in rural China has produced a distinct property rights arrangement for TVEs. The delineation of rights pertaining to collective enterprises is determined not by impersonal and universal rules enforced by legal means, but by continuous bargaining between local state and enterprise managers. The interdependence of the two parties in the development of TVEs is the basis of this interaction. The need to unleash the synergy from this *entente cordiale* accounts for the readiness to compromise and cooperation on the part of both parties. The mutual benefits and possibility of mutual sanctions define the appropriate balance between local government's interventionist tendency and managers' search for autonomy. Although managers are not the sole proprietors, their income rights and control rights are guaranteed as long as they can deliver profits. The close financial linkage between performance and income explains how the incentive problem can be tackled without a fundamental change in TVE property rights arrangements. In addition, the structure of TVEs also allows a unique punishment mechanism, despite their collective nature. The community nature of TVEs, as elaborated upon in previous chapters, gives rise to a unique opportunity structure for managers. That is, failure to perform will greatly jeopardize a manager's career in business as well as in administration. The limited number of TVEs in the local community makes a second chance in another enterprise unlikely, and the parochialism of TVE development means that a new beginning in another enterprise outside the community is almost an impossibility. In short, the appeal of the shareholding system seems to be diffused by the effectiveness of this unconventional arrangement.

Summary

The foregoing analysis points to an important aspect of the politics of market transformation in post-Mao China. It reflects fundamentally the existence of different concerns and priorities between the central and local governments, and also between different actors at the local level, i.e. managers and the local bureaucracy. These elements constitute the basic ingredients of the dynamics of the politics of socialist transformation. The discussion exposes the danger of overemphasizing the authoritarian character of the Chinese state, which tends to overlook the potential difference between state agencies and the role played by subordinate local administrations. In a similar vein, the discussion also draws attention to the role played by social interests during the reform era. Politically speaking, local government still maintains its general control over the local polity, and society shows little sign of or interest in confronting the local government and posing a direct challenge to its authority. Economically, social interests are exerting their influence by making themselves functionally indispensable, as are TVE managers. This constitutes a basic framework for understanding the prospects for market reform in rural China.

The discussion also puts the evaluation of attitudes toward market reform among the parties concerned back into the unique context of rural China, which, this study argues, is an important analytical perspective. It provides an important frame of reference for understanding local concerns and the cost–benefit calculations of specific economic changes. More importantly, this perspective uncovers the interactive relationship between state and society at the rural grass-roots level. That is, on the issue of shareholding reform, neither the local government nor enterprise managers assess the situation in isolation; instead, as affected by the condition of interdependence, each party takes the concerns of the other seriously in evaluating the cost and benefits of the proposed changes. Neither side is trying to maximize benefit in this interaction. Shareholding reform elevates managers to a higher social status and better financial position, but their newly granted formal status is not going to be their only frame of reference for interacting with local officials, and they are not planning to fully utilize these formal rights to contain government involvement in enterprise affairs. The perimeter of exchanges is still defined by state–enterprise interdependence and the options, resources, and opportunities available to the players. Nevertheless, for local government, corporate restructuring is not all negative, and shareholding reform should not be viewed simply as a triumphant pomp of manager empowerment. It is, in fact, a mutual empowerment process in which the local government's position is also strengthened by a corps of more contented and capable managerial experts. The state and society are, in other words, engaging each other and mutually constituting. Thus, as argued in Chapter 1, the state-in-society approach is crucial for understanding the dynamics of market transformation.

The next chapter will uncover how the different priorities at the rural grassroots level, and the momentum unleashed from above, combined to produce a unique variant of the shareholding enterprise, the shareholding cooperative system, which, this study argues, mainly serves the local interests and moves along a direction less than desirable to the central reformers.

7 Managers cashing in

Shareholding reform in rural China

This chapter continues to explore the dynamics of enterprise reform in rural China. It will focus on how the different agendas and priorities of the local actors discussed in Chapter 6 are expressed in concrete action, in shaping the development of shareholding reform in the countryside. This chapter argues that the reform initiative has been exploited by local interests – local government and TVE managers – for their own purposes. Development of rural enterprises since the mid-1990s has further reinforced the bargaining position of managers vis-à-vis the local administration, and hence the old balance between them has to be reformulated. These local calculations have determined the shape of the outcome of reforms. Rather than restructuring the enterprise organization along the lines of the shareholding enterprises in the urban sector, a variant known as the shareholding cooperative system (*gufenhezuozhi*) has been adopted. *The reform has, in fact, been hijacked by local forces*; the ultimate outcome serves the local interests rather than the central reformers' intentions. The central government's indecisiveness and pragmatism provides the room for these local maneuvers. The collaboration of these two parties has significantly diffused the impact of the shareholding reform, and the local government maintains its grip over TVE income rights, while enterprise managers have turned out to be the major winners. Nevertheless, the process, as discussed in Chapter 6, is a story of mutual empowerment. Managers' positions have been strengthened by the corporate restructuring, whereas the financial compromise with the local government also guarantees the latter resources for effective governance. It is far from conclusive to argue that a sweeping privatization is emerging, in spite of the gradual disappearance of the local government's "formal" control over TVEs.

The forthcoming discussion will also reveal the impact of the historical legacy; the inheritance of the socialist experience has affected the interaction patterns of enterprise reform. The habitual paternalism and the options available for the local government, the concept of distributive fairness in the local community, the indecisiveness of the central government toward full-blown marketization, and the managers' perceptions of the fairness of their financial claims are all, to a certain extent, conditioned by socialist ideology. As pointed out in Chapter 1, history matters. And in this chapter it proves to be the key to understanding the reform process.

The discussion will start with an account of what has really been happening in enterprise reform in rural China. The historical review shows that shareholding reform has never taken root in the countryside. Instead, a special brand of reform has emerged: the shareholding cooperative system. Two explanations have been offered to account for the emergence of this rural variant: the capital requirement argument and the control argument. However, neither of these arguments succeeds in providing a satisfactory account of the direction and final outcome of the developments at the rural grass-roots level. An alternative argument, concerning managers' power, offers the key to a better understanding. This discussion will proceed with an account of the enterprise managers' mounting dissatisfaction with their individual financial status, and will argue that this frustration and the managers' growing importance to the local economy exert pressure on local government. The subsequent analysis of the options available to and constraints on the local government in accommodating managers' demands will explain why the local variant – the shareholding cooperative system – is preferable. How the new enterprise system is restructured to satisfy the local state's concern with balancing conflicting claims will be fully elaborated in the last part of the discussion.

The shareholding cooperative system: background and development

Instead of the shareholding system advocated by the central reformers, who believed that this innovation could move the Chinese economy a step closer to a market economy, the development of enterprise reform in rural China moved in a different direction. Zibo is a good illustration of this. By 1995, out of a total of 1,402 TVEs in prefecture's industrial and commercial sectors, 651, or 45 percent, had already been reorganized along the lines of the shareholding system. Yet a sober analysis reveals that little genuine progress had been made along the path expected by the central reformers. Officials in charge of enterprise reform in Zibo concede that most of the shareholding changes introduced in these "reformed" enterprises were not very "standardized" (*guifan*), meaning that these "shareholding" enterprises do not fully comply with the legal requirements stipulated in the Company Law – an official blueprint for enterprise reform that emulates most of the key features of the corporate structure of enterprises in a capitalist economy. Only one-sixth of these reformed enterprises were reorganized along the lines of genuine shareholding reform. The rest are shareholding cooperative enterprises (*gufenhezuozhi qiye*).[1]

What, then, is the shareholding cooperative system? The shareholding cooperative system is a mixture. It incorporates certain features of the corporate structure of a shareholding enterprise in a market economy, but the design of its organizational structure is deeply embedded in the rural context. Its distinctively collective characteristics are clearly demonstrated by the contrast with shareholding enterprises, as summarized in Table 7.1.

Table 7.1   Contrast between a shareholding enterprise and a shareholding cooperative enterprise

	Shareholding enterprise	Shareholding cooperative enterprise
Shareholders	Anybody	Mainly restricted to enterprise staff and local government
Shares	Mainly capital	Capital and other resources, particularly labor
Relationship between shareholders and staff	No preferred pattern	Deliberate overlapping
Risk for shareholders	Loss of capital	Loss of capital, other investment, and employment
Circulation of shares	Internal or external	Restricted to staff
Return	Dividends and interest	Dividends, interest ,and employment
Social function	Profit-making	Community responsibility as statutory requirement
Corporate governance	Shareholders' assembly, board of directors	Shareholders' assembly, board of directors, and supervisory committee

Again, this is a very simplified picture, and a wide range of variations exist in practice. In addition, as we are mainly concerned with state–society relations in the collective sector, the subsequent comparison is also restricted to collective-oriented enterprises, in which the shareholding cooperative enterprise is a company converted from collective ownership.

As seen in Table 7.1, the shareholding cooperative system assembles several important features of the shareholding system. First, it provides leverage for gaining resources for the enterprises; selling shares provides a convenient means by which new investment can be brought in. Second, it contributes to the clarification of property rights of the enterprise concerned. Shareholders are the owners of the enterprise and their ownership rights are closely linked to the firm's financial status. They are liable for financial loss in bad years and will be rewarded in good years. The shareholders' status also provides those who hold the shares in these two types of enterprises with certain participation rights.

However, the shareholding cooperative system is distinguished from the shareholding system by one defining characteristic – the preservation of a strong flavor of the collective economy. It is important to note that the rationale behind the application of the shareholding principle in rural enterprises was to convert collective ownership into a more efficient form of organization. The collective origin leaves obvious marks on the outlook of the reform process. According to the orthodox socialist view, labor creates wealth; thus, if shareholding is to be introduced, workers in the enterprise should be given shares, as they are the ones who create the wealth in the first place. In addition, the role of local government, which is the guardian of the collective interest and is also heavily involved in operations, should also be recognized. These concerns are, in fact, well endorsed in the reformed enterprises' share composition, in Zibo as well as in other areas practicing this system. There are two major categories of shares in most cases: collective shares (*jitigu*) and employee shares (*zhigonggu*). The collective will be assigned a certain number of shares in the newly transformed enterprise. This is justified on the grounds that the shareholding experiment is not meant to involve the dispersal of public resources into private hands, but only a redelineation of property rights. Thus, the collective, being the original owner, should not be deprived of its original stake in the process. These shares will naturally go to the local government, the guardian of the collective interest of the community. Another portion of company shares will go to the company's staff. This is another reflection of the impact of the socialist ethos on the reform process. The principle of "to each according to his work" still matters here, and due respect is given to the workers' contribution to the accumulation of the enterprise's assets. Thus, each worker is entitled to a share.

Consequently, unlike in a shareholding enterprise, a shareholding cooperative enterprise evolves around a closed system. Its shareholders are mostly confined to the staff of the enterprise, and the circulation of shares is highly restricted. Resale is, in many cases, permissible only among workers in the same company, and anyone who leaves the company has to sell the shares back. The unique feature of the overlapping of staff and shareholders reinforces the welfare function of the enterprise, despite the introduction of the shareholding principle into the organizational structure.

The central government's endorsement contributes to the development of this hybrid form of shareholding. The idea first officially appeared in the *No. 1 Document of the Central Committee of the CCP* in 1985, which recognized it as a legitimate form of enterprise organization in the countryside after the innovation had become popular in some areas of rural China, particularly in the localities where private enterprises were well developed.[2] The continued expansion of its application led to the setting up of a test point in Zhoucun district, Zibo, in 1987, which aimed at experimenting with TVE ownership reform.[3] In 1990, the Ministry of Agriculture issued a tentative regulation that provided the first clear guidelines on rural shareholding cooperatives.[4] This official recognition provided powerful reinforcement for the development of the shareholding cooperative system in the countryside.

Two features of central government involvement are noteworthy. First, its intervention was mainly reactive in nature. That is, the innovation was mainly a local initiative by which rural enterprises, privately or collectively owned, tried to increase their competitiveness and chances of survival. It was not the result of any grand design from above; rather, it emerged before any official policy on this issue existed. Second, the indecisiveness of the central government is obvious. The aforementioned *Document No. 1* was a measure to contain the development of private enterprise, though, ironically, official permission for its development had just been granted. In a similar vein, the regulation that was passed in 1990 tried to incorporate some features of the corporate structure of a shareholding enterprise, while preserving a strong flavor of the collective economy. The central government, in short, was torn between marketization and the preservation of a collective economy. Although realizing the problems inherent in public ownership, the Party still could not commit itself to curtailing the collective sector in rural China. This indecisiveness provided scope for the emergence of the hybrid form of shareholding depicted above.

Explaining the sluggish development

An important question is why the trend was not reversed when the central government geared up its efforts at shareholding reform. As seen in Chapter 6, a more adventurous approach to experimentation with the new idea was evident in the early 1990s. Stock exchanges were set up and more regulations and laws were put in place to provide a legal framework for shareholding development. Given the rising importance of rural enterprise in the national economy, enterprise reform in this direction was certainly on the agenda of the central reformers. This is, in fact, reflected in the regulations for shareholding cooperatives mentioned above, in which elements of the corporate structure of a shareholding company in a capitalist economy are present. However, as pointed out previously, the shareholding cooperative system remains dominant in rural areas. Why? There are two possible explanations: the capital requirement argument and the control argument.

A straightforward explanation for the general failure to meet the statutory requirements of a standard shareholding enterprise is the restriction of the legal minimum capital requirement stipulated in the Company Law of the People's Republic of China. The minimum capital requirement of ten million yuan simply deprives many interested enterprises of the chance to restructure and register as a shareholding company.[5] A non-standard arrangement is the second best option.

This is surely a valid argument for the situation before the mid-1990s, as most TVEs in China during this period were generally small in scale and operated with few resources; few had resource totals over the ten million yuan mark. It is certainly true in the Zibo case that the degree of standardization among shareholding enterprises remains low. For instance, even in Zhoucun, one of the prefecture's most advanced areas in terms of enterprise reform, local officials disclosed that, although shareholding reform was introduced in sixty-four industrial TVEs, only 25 percent met all the statutory requirements. Most of them failed in terms of either developing an appropriate organizational structure or complying with standard accounting requirements or other financial regularities. Nevertheless, for these enterprises, the financial requirement argument is hardly persuasive because their official registration in this category implies that they are financially eligible, at least on paper. It is even more puzzling to see the lack of improvement in terms of standardization among these enterprises, despite the incentives provided by the Zibo government. Anxious to gather substantial momentum for the new drive toward enterprise reform, there was growing pressure from higher authorities to improve the standardization rate of shareholding reform.[6] In response to the central directive, Zibo issued several local regulations and documents in order to encourage a greater degree of consistency within standardized shareholding enterprises. Inducements for greater standardization, such as priority in loan allocation and in the supply of energy and raw materials, were proposed, but with little success.[7] There were, in other words, some other considerations for the local actors in sticking to the shareholding cooperative option instead.

The control argument centers on the township government's concern with its control over the reform process, and Figure 7.1 clearly illustrates the crux

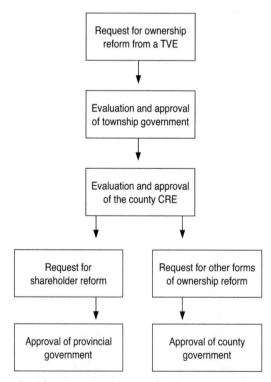

Figure 7.1 Administrative procedure of TVE ownership reform.

of this argument. It shows that conversion into a standardized shareholding reform entails approval from above the county administration, whereas endorsement of the establishment of a shareholding cooperative enterprise falls within the jurisdiction of county authorities. Thus, although control over the ownership reform process is beyond the township administration's jurisdiction, the involvement of the provincial authority in genuine shareholding reform erects an extra barrier to the township administration's influence. Put simply, the provincial authority, which is three levels higher, is too remote for the township administration, which lies at the bottom layer of the state machinery. The county-level administration, its immediate superior in the hierarchy, is, however, more susceptible to its influence. At an individual level, officials are likely to be in frequent contact with each other. The possibility of working in the same office in the future, and the probable personal friendship between officials, can provide scope for lobbying from the lower level. Institutionally speaking, the immediate financial and administrative connection between the two levels also gives the township administration more to bargain with. All these favorable factors are absent from the province–township relationship.

The concern for managers' grievances

However persuasive these explanations may be, their fundamental limitation is their failure to account for the specific pattern of development. That is, though these two arguments may be able to explain the underdevelopment of shareholding reform in rural China, they do not offer any hint as to why shareholding cooperatives should be the alternative. Even more important is that they fail to account for the detailed arrangements of this local variant. As will be seen in the case of Zibo, the shareholding system has evolved in such a way that the balance of interests between the local government and enterprise managers can be skillfully maintained. In other words, the deviation from the standard type of shareholding enterprise cannot be fully explained only in terms of the interests and choices of the enterprise, or those of the local government; it is, rather, a result of the collaboration between enterprise managers and the local government. And, more importantly, the collaboration goes beyond the formal arrangements of the shareholding cooperative. Tacit agreement between the two further diffuses the impact of this hybrid form of enterprise development, and eventually the limited effect of the innovation in terms of changing state–enterprise relations is largely subdued.

This chapter contends that the enterprise managers' concern for their individual financial interest is the most important driving force behind local support for the shareholding cooperative reform in Zibo. A striking finding of the interviews is the general frustration among enterprise managers about their financial status. All managers interviewed considered themselves to be underpaid. Although, as seen in the previous discussion, there exists a huge income gap between enterprise managers and workers, a feeling of being unfairly remunerated prevails among managers, who believe that they are underpaid for their important contribution to the enterprises and for bearing the immense pressure inherent in management. It is interesting to see that the better an enterprise's financial conditions, i.e. the higher the income likely to be enjoyed by the manager concerned, the greater the grievance.

This finding reflects managers' rising expectations, and such a sentiment, this study would argue, is very much fueled by the rise of the private sector. The emergence of the private sector has had two effects on managers' evaluation of their own financial situation. First, the financial status of their counterparts in the private sector always serves as a frame of reference for defining a fair income. The living standards and lifestyles of local private entrepreneurs are frequently quoted as examples of what constitutes a decent and comfortable life. More importantly, the existence of an alternative arena for business skills also affects these managers' evaluation of the opportunity cost of staying in their present jobs. There appears to be a general perception that a lucrative alternative is always there for anyone who bothers to make a move. Such optimism is best reflected by a manager interviewed of one of the county's most lucrative firms:

> I don't think the company could have developed into its present level without my contribution. It's me, not the township government, who steers the company into the right track. It's me, not the township mayor or Party secretary, who finds the buyers and makes money. But I don't think I have been fairly treated. I believe I can easily earn a million a year if I quit my job and start my own company.[8]

The more competent people are, understandably, more confident about their prospects in the private sector. This may explain the paradox in which frustration is even greater among the better-off managers.

The private alternative can be more than a reference point. The requirement for a substantial amount of initial capital, and the possible loss of official blessing and of other related operational advantages, may deter many discontented managers from making the move to the private sector, but it is not impossible. Such a possibility adds greater credibility to their threat of resignation at the bargaining table. Local officials are well aware of the sentiment, and worry about the danger of brain drain the private sector. A local official in Wangcunzhen township admitted:

> [T]he danger of enterprise managers starting their own businesses is imminent. "Setting up their own turf and building a new stove" (*zilashantou lingqiluzao*) is a common dream shared by managers. The stabilization of the management team (*wenzhu guanli duiwu*) has occupied a dominant place in our agenda.

Shareholding cooperative system as a way out

Given all the reasons for the local government to stand against shareholding reform, isn't it easier to dismiss these "troublemakers" instead of launching the reform? The simple truth is that it is too costly to do so. As pointed out in Chapter 3, the shortage of managerial talent in the rural community is the fundamental basis of this constraint. The hands of the local government are further tied by the phenomenon of information asymmetry in enterprise management and the high cost involved in finding a replacement. Worse still, the normative constraint on distribution limits the option of a substantial salary increase for managers. Shareholding is a way out of this predicament.

Information asymmetry between the asset owner and the agent who is entrusted to manage the asset is a constant source of tension between the two parties. In an enterprise context, the manager, who is on the front-line of daily operations and the center of transactions, can gather much useful information concerning the company's strengths and weaknesses, information that is unknown to the company owner. Collective enterprises in rural China operate in much the same manner. Chapters 3, 4, and 5 have shown that TVE managers enjoy a substantial degree of autonomy, and hence the problem of information asymmetry is expected. What may further distinguish rural enterprise in China from other contexts is the local government's tolerance of certain financial irregularities. For instance, as pointed out in Chapter 5, the local government acquiesces in cases of underreported enterprise profits for tax purposes, in order to enable enterprises to reduce their tax burdens. However, by doing so, the local government is also contributing to a greater degree of information asymmetry. It is likely that the enterprise manager will be the only person who has accurate information about the firm's financial conditions.

Enterprise managers, in other words, develop a significant amount of specific knowledge of the firms under their stewardship. Although the specificity of this knowledge may increase the cost of resignation, as this workplace-specific information will lose much of its value when the manager moves to another enterprise, it also implies that, if the manager is to be dismissed, certain crucial knowledge about the operation of the enterprise is likely to be lost too. It may require a substantial effort to recover the consequent loss. Information asymmetry should move further in the direction of favoring managers if the scale of enterprise production increases.

Finding a replacement for manager is another difficult task. First, not only is the mobility of managerial talent restricted by the administrative barriers to the free movement of human resources (the *hukou* system), but the sense of inferiority and underdevelopment attached to the countryside may also diminish the attractiveness of career opportunities offered in this sector.[9] The trend may be changing, but any rural enterprise still has to make an extra effort to lure managerial talent from the city. Second, the exchange of market information concerning the availability of managerial personnel across communities is far from satisfactory. This is partly a result of the underdevelopment of market mechanisms in rural China, but is to a larger extent attributable to the general reluctance to employ non-natives in these top managerial posts. It seems difficult for the local government to entrust responsibility for the management of such an important local asset to outsiders. Occupation of these posts implies not only influence over crucial resources, but access to a unique bargaining position vis-à-vis the local authority as well, as suggested by the interdependence thesis. This is consistent with the previous discussion on the managers' origins. As pointed out in Chapter 3, all TVE managers are natives of their local communities. Thus, there is little incentive to supply or demand information about managerial vacancies or the availability of personnel across the region. Consequently, the pool of potential recruits is restricted and an extensive searching process is likely.

A direct increase in managers' salaries or bonuses is a convenient alternative to replacement. Yet, as argued in Chapter 5, the redistributive norm of egalitarianism in the countryside has affected enterprise decisions. Local cadres involved in industrial management repeatedly emphasized the importance of public opinion and agreed that a certain degree of balance between managers and popular sentiment has to be maintained. Cadres do not want to be accused of favoritism.[10] The principle of "letting some people get rich first" (*rang yibufenren xianfuqilai*), a catchphrase summarizing the gist of the liberal policies toward all kinds of entrepreneurial energies unleashed in the countryside by reforms, may still prevail, but rising income inequality in the local community and its political repercussions still trouble local officials, for whom socialism is still the official ideology.

This normative constraint is felt not only by the local administrators, but also by managers. A good illustration is the self-imposed redistributive measure introduced by one of the top managers in Zibo. It is a Chinese tradition for a superior to give subordinates a red packet during the Chinese New Year, as a token of good fortune. What is distinctive about this case is the huge amount of money involved. Instead of the average amount of less than 100 yuan, this manager gave 10,000 yuan to each to each of his five deputies. What is even more striking is that he gave the money out of his own pocket. He explained that this was necessary, as he did not want to be accused by the others of "earning too much."[11] Though details of the potential social pressure on managers with "unfair" incomes are not available, the above story hints that some "everyday forms of resistance"[12] from local peasants are likely, and that the pressure to conform is substantial.

Thus, local government is caught between mounting pressure from aggrieved managers and the limited options available. Action must be taken lest enterprise performance is affected. Seen from this perspective, the shareholding cooperative system has a unique appeal. Shares are conceived of as a new instrument with which to improve the financial status of enterprise managers in a socially acceptable way. A manager is entitled to buy company shares when the enterprise is reorganized according to the shareholding principle, and then gains the dividends from the shares that they hold. There may be jealousy or even resentment toward high wages, but the attitude toward higher income generated from shares is different. Many rural workers still fail to recognize the specific rights or privileges with respect to the company inherent in these financial documents, particularly during the early stage of implementation; instead, company shares are simply regarded as a form of high-interest loans to the company or some kind of compulsory company bond that they have little incentive to buy.[13] Their ignorance of the new financial concept, their relative inferiority in terms of what they can afford, and, most important of all, the limited transferability of these shares make the workers, in general, uninterested in buying these shares.[14] In addition, some also regard investment in these shares as considerably risky. These company shares usually bring a return higher than other forms of investment, such as a savings deposit in the bank, but this is not guaranteed. Thus, a higher return for those who have invested more in shares is justified because the more shares one has, the greater risk one has to bear.[15] This perception has great significance for aggrieved managers and presents a means for the local government to escape from its predicament. Not only can this instrument strengthen the linkage between a manager's income and the enterprise's performance, an incentive for more efficient service that discourages managers from shirking responsibility, but it also provides the local government a means by which to accommodate the managers' financial demands without much community discontent.

In other words, for local governments, the reform process is not particularly guided by an image of a perfect corporate form, which is what economists may imagine. Instead, the trajectory of enterprise restructuring is very much dictated by concerns with accommodating the diverse claims of managers, the local government, and the local community; this is the yardstick for measuring options for change. Put into this perspective, one may understand why another possible form of corporate restructuring, limited liability, has also been discarded. At a glance, limited liability companies provide an ideal vehicle for reforming TVEs. Limited liability requires little capital and provides leverage for raising capital, clarification of ownership, promises of greater transparency and accountability, and, most important of all, the prospect of enhancing a manager's position. However, TVE reforms did not start from scratch, but grew out of decades of collective ownership. This implies entrenchment of local government's interest and, for local government, the ownership reform process entails a search for the best option for balancing its claims with other interests. Here, the Company Law, the national law regulating the operation of limited company liability, imposes a number of handicaps on local governments. Several clauses of the Law are particularly noteworthy. Article 58 of the Company Law stipulates, "government functionaries may not concurrently serve as directors, supervisors or managers of companies." Article 61 also specifies, "directors and managers shall not engage personally in or operate for others the same category of business as the company they are serving."[16] It is obvious that these two restrictions will severely limit local government flexibility if TVEs become limited liability companies. Although, as argued earlier, cadre-turned-managers are rare in Zibo, a formal barrier to local government's freedom to replace rebellious managers with more trusted officials in one or several enterprises is hardly an appealing option. In a similar vein, the right to appoint officials to boards of directors of newly reformed enterprises is certainly a more preferable arrangement.

The limited liability option also implies less freedom in internal financial arrangements for the restructured company. The Company Law also stipulates a stringent procedure for mergers and divisions. The provision of a detailed balance sheet and an inventory of assets is compulsory, as are a public announcement of restructuring and a notice to creditors within a specific time limit, and there is also a long list of mandatory financial propriety and legal requirements. And, as will be seen in the forthcoming discussion, mergers have, in fact, become a development strategy for TVEs since the late 1990s. It is debatable how many mergers of rural enterprises in Zibo can live up to these legal requirements, given that rural enterprises are not particularly known for their accounting accuracy and financial regularity, and considering the general laxity of the asset validation process in China. Other financial leverages, such as the issuing of company bonds, face no less regulation.

Thus, compared with the local innovation of the shareholding cooperative, limited liability companies imply a more regimented and formal option, heavily regulated by national authorities. The inherent loss of room for maneuver, and the consequent invitation to scrutiny and regulation from higher authorities, will definitely make the delicate act of balancing conflicting claims over TVEs an even more difficult task, accounting for the less than enthusiastic response from local governments toward this option. For managers, although the more regulated format may imply a more refined boundary, barricading them from administrative interference, it will be argued in the forthcoming discussion that it is doubtful, given the endurance of the stage of interdependence between even local state and enterprise, whether this more "advanced" form of corporate restructuring can attract managers.

Dividing the cake: a balancing act

As argued earlier, the essence of local governance in rural China is maintenance of the ideal balance between conflicting claims. Managers' discontent was the catalyst for the introduction of the specific variant of reform, yet it is hardly the only concern; local government is understandably anxious to protect its own interests. In addition, the expectations of the local population must be, in one way or another, taken into consideration if popular discontent is to be avoided. These considerations again require a skillful balancing act by the local government. It is these conflicting concerns determining the ultimate shape of the local variant that, in turn, offset most of the impact that shareholding reform is expected to have on the state–enterprise relationship. As we will see shortly, the balance is maintained, in part, by a formal guarantee of fundamental improvements in the managers' financial position. It is also reinforced by an informal arrangement between managers and local government, which ensures that the former will continue to take up their community obligations in spite of the change in ownership structure. This logic remains in place even with the intensification of ownership reforms in the late 1990s.

Managers as the major winners

As seen in the experience in Zibo, enterprise managers are, unsurprisingly, the major winners in the shareholding cooperative reform process. Several features concerning the exact arrangement of shareholding reforms confirm this argument. First, there is an inherent bias favoring the enterprise managers in employee share distribution. As observed in Zibo, there are two subcategories of employee shares. Basic shares (*jibengu*) are distributed to the employees freely as a gratuity for their previous efforts. An individual's entitlement is calculated on the basis of length of service, seniority of position, and salary.[17] However, this offer is not unconditional. In order to enjoy this right, the individual concerned is required to buy a certain number of shares proportional to his or her basic share entitlement. In most cases, the former is one to two times the value of the latter. The second type of shares is generally known as the risk share (*fengxiangu*); the worker is asked to share a certain degree of risk under the new system. If the enterprise performs badly, the worker risks losing some of the money invested in these shares, as returns in the form of dividends and bonuses are unlikely under such circumstances. Under this arrangement, managers are likely to be the largest individual shareholders in the company for various reasons. First, managers hold the most senior company staff positions and usually have the longest service record. The requirement of an extra share purchase also enables managers to use their entitlements fully. They are also more likely to be able to afford the purchase. In addition, managers' specific knowledge of their enterprises' potential gives them greater awareness of their company's prospects, further reinforcing their willingness to invest. In some cases, special shares are allocated to managers as an extra remuneration package. Pengyang township, for example, has introduced special allotments of efficiency shares (*xiaoyigu*) and value-added shares (*zengzhigu*) for managers. The former refers to extra shares awarded to managers when above-quota production is achieved, while the latter are granted when a substantial increase in the fixed assets of the enterprise is achieved.[18] As a result, a substantial number of these newly issued shares in Zibo's reformed enterprises are concentrated in the hands of the manager, making him the individual who holds the largest number of shares in the reformed company.[19]

Affordability is another crucial factor affecting the number of shares held by managers. That is, if the value of the net assets of the company is astronomical, it simply cannot be swallowed by managers, no matter how eager they are to buy shares. The asset valuation process is flawed in many respects. The underdevelopment of the accounting profession is partly responsible for this problem. More importantly, the absence of a fully developed stock market in the area deprives accountants of an important reference point.[20] However, as seen in Zibo, the local government may deliberately choose to maintain the asset value at a low level. Its intervention or the toleration of an improper valuation process justifies this suspicion. Legally speaking, the valuation process should be handled by a professional auditing agency. It is supposed to be an impartial process. The enterprise management will be consulted, but the actual valuation work should be conducted independently by professional auditors who have no direct interest in the enterprise.[21] Yet there are many complaints about managers' intervention in the process.[22] Officials of Zibo CRE (*tigaiwei*) revealed that refusal to provide financial details or clarification of accounting irregularities, attempted bribery, unsolicited luxurious hospitality for assessors, or even threats by enterprise management were not unheard of.[23] Worse still, local government is frequently quite prepared to scrap the independent auditing process altogether, and to transfer the responsibility to the management personnel of the enterprise concerned. For instance, the Zhoucun district government admits that non-listed shareholding enterprises, i.e. those companies that do not circulate their shares on the stock exchange, can be exempted from external auditing for asset valuation. Instead, an assessment team consisting mainly of internal staff will be set up for this task. However, this is not only a violation of the relevant national regulation, but is also inconsistent with local regulations.[24] The local government, in short, simply opens the door for the management personnel, who have so much interest in keeping the value of the enterprise down, to influence the valuation process.

Lastly, the better transparency promised by shareholding reform has never been fulfilled. Workplace democracy is an honored principle in the socialist regime, and the designers of shareholding reform are keen to preserve such an element. In addition to the institutions of a board of directors and a shareholders' assembly, a new mechanism, the supervisory committee (*jianshihui*), has been introduced.[25] However, in Zibo, most of these participatory institutions seldom function effectively. In many cases, the shareholders' assembly and the supervisory committee have never convened a meeting. Even the "functioning" institutions do not perform the watchdog role properly. In most cases, the financial condition of the enterprise remains a secret confined to a few top management personnel, and no further details are disclosed at the annual shareholders' meeting either.[26] Managers retain their unchallenged position in the operation of the enterprise, and the decision-making process remains a black box for the numerous ordinary shareholders. This is, in fact, consistent with the national picture. A national survey shows that shareholders' assemblies are established in less than two-thirds of the reformed enterprises, and only about half have set up a board of directors. Unsurprisingly, only 41 percent of these enterprises disclose their financial figures annually.[27]

Protecting the interests of the local government

The remaining problem is how to protect the township government's interests. In short, there exist formal and informal arrangements between the local government and enterprise managers that largely diffuse the negative impact of shareholding reform on the local government's role in local economic management.

The most direct and effective way for the local government to preserve its influence in enterprise management is by holding majority shares in the reformed enterprises. This is exactly the case in Zibo. Like other areas experimenting with the shareholding reform, Zibo showed a high ratio of collective shares, i.e. shares owned by the local government, during the early 1990s.[28] In general, the rate is more than 70 percent in most reformed enterprises. According to a survey of 496 shareholding cooperative TVEs in one district administration in Zibo, collective shares constitute about 77 percent of the total shares of these companies.[29] During the early 1990s, the central government decided to gear up its shareholding reform efforts and demanded the lowering of the collective share ratio.[30] However, the central request appears to have fallen on deaf ears. Local documents and directives have been issued by these local administrations calling for a reduction in the ratio of collective shares,[31] but the efforts are evidently half-hearted. Huantai county, for instance, claims to have achieved remarkable progress in this direction, and officially 49.2 percent of its reformed township enterprises have zero collective shares.[32] Though this evidence may appear to illustrate the local government's determination to intensify reform, closer scrutiny shows that many of the enterprises concerned make an insignificant financial contribution or are on the brink of bankruptcy. Zibo Dongfang Enterprise is a case the Huantai county government is fond of using as proof of its sincere desire to reform. Founded in 1954, this collective enterprise was converted into a shareholding enterprise with zero collective shares in 1993. However, it is noteworthy that the financial condition of the enterprise was very poor before the conversion. In the first five months of 1993, it sustained total losses of more than five million yuan. In fact, the assessed asset value of the enterprise was negative.[33] For most important enterprises, in contrast, the local government still maintains a dominant shareholding position, with more than 51 percent of reformed enterprises' shares in its pocket.[34]

The status of a shareholding cooperative enterprise also fails to exempt the reformed companies in these areas from their duty to meet the local government's various demands for community welfare. As pointed out in Chapter 5, collective enterprises are seen as a convenient source of resources for solving pressing community problems. Unemployment and a shortage of funds for necessary public works are high on the list, and it is almost obligatory for collective enterprises to make contributions toward these needs. Zibo's experience shows that enterprise reform does not bring about a fundamental change in this respect. Regulations concerning the management of shareholding cooperative enterprises have laid down specific instructions regarding the use of profits, including restrictions on the division of profits and an allotment for enterprise development.[35] Again, this shows the government's indecision between the preservation of the collective economy and privatization. However, the Zibo case shows that the local government sometimes goes further than this. For example, shareholding enterprises are obliged to employ retired veterans and their relatives,[36] and 10 percent of gross profits must be used for "voluntary" social donations.[37] In short, the local government has made sure that enterprise reform will not deprive it of access to enterprise resources for community welfare development.

Share distribution provides little information for measuring an enterprise's financial obligations to local government. Ideally, the local government's direct financial extraction from a shareholding enterprise should be determined by the number of shares it holds. The pre-reform practice of a profit remittance quota – an annual amount of money an enterprise was theoretically obliged to submit to the local government, irrespective of its financial condition at the end of the fiscal year – was to have been abandoned. However, the Zibo case shows that this practice is still in place in many reformed enterprises, though the amount owed is somewhat lower than the pre-reform level.[38] In other words, on top of the dividend to which the local government is entitled by virtue of its shareholder status, another lump sum is guaranteed. By this arrangement, the potentially negative impact of shareholding reform on its flow of income is very much diluted. This preserves a safety net, and at the same time it introduces a new lever enabling the local government to grasp a greater slice of local prosperity during good years.

Reform intensification since the mid-1990s

The above discussion shows how a compromise enhancing managers' income rights without fundamentally upsetting the pre-reform balance of enterprise usage rights was reached during the early 1990s. However, further changes at macro and micro levels since the mid-1990s have worked in favor of the enterprise managers and hence necessitated a balance readjustment. The reform momentum unleashed by the new initiative from the very top of the Party leadership, together with the growing concentration of enterprise development, required further organizational restructuring of enterprises to accommodate the rise of managers. This round of reform was characterized by the further dilution of local government's shares in enterprises and the consolidation of managers' dominance. However, some forms of give and take between managers and local government remain evident, thus demonstrating that interdependence might still be a valid depiction of the relationship.

Jiang Zemin's endorsement of the shareholding system at the CCP's 15th National Congress in 1997 provided impetus for further reform in this direction. His report stated:

The shareholding system is a form of capital organization of modern enterprises, which is favorable to separating ownership from management and raising the efficiency of the operation of enterprise and capital. It can be used both under capitalism and under socialism.[39]

Jiang went on to comment on the diverse forms of shareholding cooperative enterprises in urban and rural areas. Jiang regarded them as a new reforming phenomenon and felt that their progress should be encouraged, guided, and promoted.[40] In other words, ownership reform was reconfirmed as being necessary for developing the economy, and, more importantly, the shareholding cooperative system was now considered as a possible and legitimate option.

There has also been, in recent years, a growing consensus among Chinese researchers and practitioners in rural economic management advocating a greater concentration of shares in the hands of managers. The rationale is that, although shareholding cooperative reform did achieve a relatively clearer delineation of ownership, share distribution, particularly with local government retaining most of the shares, failed to achieve the expected motivational effect on management. Operator holding majority share (*Jingyingzhe zhan dagu*) was recommended as the guiding principle for prospective reform. With this arrangement, it was argued, a greater incentive effect and a strong chain of financial accountability could be achieved.[41]

However, two inter-related developments have made the allocation of more shares to enterprise operators urgent: the declining rate of profit and the expansion of the production scale. Competition among rural enterprise has become more intense since the mid-1990s. The profit rate for rural enterprises, defined as profit per unit output, has been declining since the mid-1990s.[42] Given the significant contribution of rural enterprise to national economic growth, this is alarming for the CCP. The intensity of competition is also reflected in the decrease in the number of enterprises. The total number of collective enterprises dropped between 1995 and 1997, from 1.62 million to 1.29 million. Put in this context, any proposals that may help to revitalize their efficiency will be received positively.

This national picture is consistent with the local scenario in Zibo, where the deceleration of growth and a decrease in the number of enterprises is evident. Industrial output growth of township enterprises in Huantai, for instance, decreased by one-third between 1994 and 1998. The situation in Zhoucun, another leading industrialized district in Zibo, is no better; growth has stagnated since 1995.[43] Local officials expressed anxiety about these trends and identified two possible remedies: enterprise mergers and greater incentives for enterprise managers.

The growing concentration of enterprises is visible in Zibo. The total asset value of rural enterprises in the prefecture increased by 18 percent between 1994 and 1997, whereas the average asset value per enterprise jumped by 60 percent during the same period. In addition to the pressure of competition, the policy of encouraging formation of enterprise groups (*qiye jituan*) also contributes to this trend.[44] Local officials assert that this is necessary to maintain steady economic growth. One official explained:

> [I]n the past, we emphasized the flexibility of having enterprises of medium and small size. It is just like travelling in a small boat; it is easy to turn around twists and corners (*chuanxiao hao diaotou*) and is, hence, more adaptable to market fluctuation. But now, we need a bigger boat to withstand storms of fierce market competition (*chuanda kang fenglang*) and so we need large enterprises. That's crucial for survival and growth.[45]

By 1997, there were sixty-two enterprise groups in Zibo.[46] These business groups were composed of enterprises with asset values ranging from 78 to over 200 million yuan, with an average workforce of about 1,000.[47] They became the engines of local economic growth. For instance, ten enterprise groups provided about a quarter of the total tax and profits generated in Zhoucun district.[48] The formation of enterprise groups is usually started with the absorption of several small enterprises by one large one. First, asset valuation of the smaller enterprises is conducted, and then shares are issued. Then follows the transfer of the controlling shares of these enterprises to a big enterprise, which forms the core of the group. In most cases, two or three enterprise groups are formed in a township. Local officials state that, by doing so, they hope that the competitiveness of the local enterprises can be strengthened by the better management of the core enterprise and the increase in the enterprise group's collective resources.

The local government's strategy of the further utilization of local managerial talent has to be accompanied by the granting of greater financial rewards, so more dilution of collective shares seems inevitable. For those managers who are now in charge of the local business conglomerates, greater responsibilities must come with more rights. The fact that local governments are now more reliant on fewer enterprises does put managers running these key firms in a much improved bargaining position. And this is clearly reflected in the new round of ownership reform in Zibo initiated in 1998. Two major goals are particularly noteworthy: the further dilution of collective shares and the larger portion of shares assigned to managers. These objectives are clearly reflected in the policies introduced by the Huantai government. A zero percent collective shares policy in reformed enterprises was stipulated as the guiding principle for shareholding restructuring, and the end of the year 1998 was targeted as the deadline for its implementation.[49] In addition, the principle of operator holding majority share (*Jingyingzhe zhan dagu*) was enshrined in the county government's reform strategies. In Huantai, 30 percent of total shares for managers was the benchmark for a reasonable proportion of distribution.[50] By mid-1999, most of the shareholding cooperative enterprises had been restructured along these lines.

Collective shares also disappear in more reformed enterprises. Managers, consequently, are made the largest single shareholders of their enterprises in most cases. By early 1999, shareholding reorganization was completed in more than 60 percent of Zibo as a whole.[51] The case of Yingwei Textiles is a good example. The enterprise is managed by Zhang Ying and her husband. Zhang is a legendary figure in the area, not only because she is one of the few women managers, but also because she is also running one of the largest enterprises in Zibo; the company is ranked among the fifty largest tax-paying enterprises in Zibo. But Zhang's recognition comes mostly from her success in transforming the company from a factory with a two million yuan debt into a local giant with 100 million yuan in assets. In 1992, when share-holding reform was introduced into this company, she and her husband were given less than 20 percent of the shares. Between 1992 and 1998, the amount of tax and profits submitted by this company increased from one million to eleven million yuan. The township mayor admitted that the Zhang family's complaints about their unfair financial rewards increased with the growth of the company. In 1998, Zhang and her husband were given 51 percent of the shares; the township simply sold all its shares to the enterprise management and staff.

The insistence of higher authorities provides the major drive for this transformation. A senior official at county level admitted that they have a strong faith in the ability of managers of the leading enterprises, and believe that they can help to revitalize the local economy if proper incentives are given to them. This explains the urgency and the anxiety for reform. As one township mayor recalled:

> [T]he county authority was really serious in this reform. In early 1998, we were summoned to a meeting chaired by the county secretary and were told that the intensification of shareholding reform must be accomplished by the end of that year. The secretary stressed that this was a matter of life and death for township enterprises. It was followed by a study class on the necessity and principles of the reform. The message was very clear: change your enterprise or we should be fired![52]

However, the managers' tacit financial concessions accounted for the smooth transition. In essence, managers "voluntarily" agreed to honor certain new financial obligations, which in turn minimized the township government's losses in the new round of ownership reform. Again, compromises between local government and managers, whose positions had been reinforced by the latest round of enterprise reform, were struck in order to accommodate the demands from both parties. Two approaches have commonly been adopted. First, enterprises might agree to contribute regularly to community welfare. Such donations can be enormous. In one case, the amount was more than one million yuan a year.[53] Second, managers might also agree to pay new charges. One particularly common area is the charge for land use. As mentioned earlier, though most reformed enterprises enjoyed favorable rates or even free land use when local government was still the major shareholder, during the last round of shareholding reform substantial charges were imposed on most enterprises. The situation of Gouli township is illustrative. The total expenditure of the township administration in 1998 was 5.6 million yuan. Unfortunately, its budgetary income could only provide 3.4 million yuan. In the past, the government would maintain its balance by imposing a surcharge for rural households (*tiliu*) and extracting profits from its enterprises. From 1998 onward, the government signed new land leases of forty years with local enterprises, which guaranteed a steady income of one million yuan a year.[54] Again, arrangements between managers and local government are in place to compensate the latter for their loss of formal rights over enterprises as a result of enterprise reform.

Summary

The case of enterprise reform in Zibo shows how the central initiative of marketization can be diffused by local maneuvering. The pragmatism of the central government allowed local interests to develop a unique brand of shareholding system that best suited their own agendas. Local interests, the local government and managers, who are mutually dependent, have different agendas and concerns in mind in tailoring the organizational structure of local enterprises. For them, the relevance of the theoretical promise of the corporate structure of the shareholding system is limited. Instead, the innovation and initiative imposed from above provided them with a chance to pursue their own interests. Consequently, the end product defies most of the central reformers' expectations.

The rise of managers with proven success, and the fact that they are the major winners in the shareholding reform process, are the most important messages of the story. The change in the asymmetry of power was the fundamental catalyst for institutional change, and the party that holds more strategic resources can always shape the outcome in its favor. The case of Zibo demonstrates how the organizational structure of rural collective enterprises has been transformed along lines advantageous to managers, whose valuable enterprise management expertise is the key to local economic prosperity. Although the interdependence between managers and local government contributed to half-hearted reform during the first half of the 1990s, further enterprise growth and the consequent sophistication of operation in the late 1990s consolidated the managers' dominant role.

Managers have gained substantially from the conversion into the new enterprise structure; they are, however, always aware of the limits. In return for the generosity of the local government, they are restrained in asserting their rights as shareholders and remain pragmatic in handling their relationship with local authorities. They tolerate the continued presence of the township government, which theoretically can be excluded under this new enterprise structure. Managers adjust their position vis-à-vis local government not according to their shares position, but according to their functional indispensability to the local economy. It is the degree of interdependence of the local government and the managers that determines the right balance of autonomy and intervention, not the formal change in enterprise structure. Managers' concessions to side payments, such as generous donations to local welfare, are, in effect, sharing the *de facto* income rights over enterprise with local government. It is still too costly to insist on their full legal entitlement over their enterprises, as they still need local government support in one way or another. Managers are definitely on the rise, but their concessions imply that the outcome of tug-of-war with local government remains indeterminate. The trend of diluting collective shares certainly fuels the argument that sweeping privatization in rural China is evident, but it is doubtful that we are witnessing the intended effect of demarcation between the state and business. This resonates with Rawski's insight into the problem of preoccupation with formal institutional change. He warns against the confident determinism of the "Nirvana approach" posited by Demsetz, who has strong faith in the superiority of privatization. Rawski argues that the expected impact of privatization may not be achieved simply by the formal delineation of property rights.[55] Similarly, as implied in this case study, rights over TVEs are more a result of a bargaining process between government, managers, and the local community. The intricacies of the process requires one to go beyond the simple analysis of a formal property rights regime and focus on the larger context of the local political economy.

The collaboration between local government and managers is revealing. It defies the expectations of the civil society argument that empowered social interests will seek to expand their autonomy, even in confrontational ways. Managers in Zibo fail to meet these expectations. Instead, they collaborate with the local government in advancing their interests and the endurance of interdependence renders autonomy less attractive than it would be otherwise. This also rekindles the debate over the market transition argument raised in Chapter 1. The Zibo case shows clearly that economic rationality or macro benefits alone cannot account for the progress of market reform. All these exchanges and interactions are conducted within a larger institutional and historical framework. It also shows that analysis of the implications of distributional benefits and how concerned parties mobilized their resources to bargain and negotiate the shape of the final outcome of interaction is crucial for this understanding. The case of enterprise reform shows that the historical legacy of socialism and interdependence are crucial contextual variables that significantly determine the direction of development. This is a powerful warning against the danger of the institutional determinism raised at the very beginning of this discussion.

8   Prospects of the local
state–manager alliance

This study is an exploration of the enduring puzzle of connections between economic transformation and political change. It aims to enhance understanding of this matter by focusing on the case of rural China in the reform period, a desirable subject for observation given the tremendous changes in the economic realm during the two decades since Mao Zedong's death in 1976. In order to explore these important theoretical issues, the research concentrates on one aspect of rural transformation – the pattern of interaction between enterprise managers and the local state in rural China and the consequent redefinition of the role of the socialist state in the era of market reform. The lessons drawn from the Zibo case study must, of course, be treated with caution. The nature of the qualitative approach, based on a small sample, and the regional variation across the vast territory of China, raise the possibility of overgeneralization. Nonetheless, the focus on a locality with a dominant collective sector retreating from the local state's strong presence during the reform era – a pattern common to most rural communities in China – implies that the findings should contain a certain degree of generality and, thus, are useful for the understanding of the politics of a reforming socialist state. This original, focused study can serve as the starting point for further research on this subject.

This chapter will evaluate the major lessons learned from the analysis presented so far. In brief, a new pattern of state–society interaction has emerged in China. Social interests, enterprise managers in this case, have been empowered by the changes taking place in the market reform era. Their rise has necessitated a redefinition of the role of the state in the local context, from a pattern of domination and control to one of collaboration and cooperation. The findings, however, also provoke deeper theoretical reflections on the issues of socialist transformation and institutional change. They challenge the prevailing teleological views concerning the reform process in China. In the economic realm, the evidence does not fit well with the "market transition" argument, which assumes that full marketization is inevitable. There are many diversions and sidetracks along the market reform path, and the emergence and persistence of many unorthodox economic mechanisms raises doubts about the economic argument. In the political realm, the findings also defy the expectations of advocates for a civil society; social actors do gain greater autonomy, yet they also exhibit an equal interest in maintaining harmonious relations with the state. Both perspectives fail to capture the complexity and dynamics of the reform process and the multidimensional connection between economic and political changes. Instead, a delicate process of mutual empowerment of state and social actors is evident. This study argues that a historical institutional approach, which emphasizes the impact of historical legacies, the constraints and incentives imposed by the institutional setting, and the choices of actors concerned, can provide a more powerful framework.

The second part of this conclusion will evaluate the prospect of the local alliance between state and managers. This author believes that into the 1990s, with the advent of intensified market reforms and further integration of rural enterprises into the national economy, the local strategy of co-optation was hardly sustainable. The political implications of manager empowerment had to be accommodated at levels beyond local administration.

History matters

The implications of the simple fact that economic reform in China is growing out of the experience of a planned economy are far greater than its rhetorical value for propaganda purposes. It may be premature to jump to the conclusion that the findings confirm the argument of path dependence in institutional development,[1] but history definitely matters in this case and helps in understanding the course of development. History, or more specifically in this case socialist legacy, matters not as a fatalistic or deterministic constraint on the course of events, but because it affects the availability of options, the costs and benefits of choices, and the framework within which calculations are made. A substantial degree of openness or indeterminacy exists for the actors concerned, and, ultimately, it is the actor who decides what to do.

Socialist legacy affects the interaction between managers and the local state in at least three ways. First, the ideological legacy inherited from the pre-reform period continues to haunt the Party leadership, and the resultant ambiguity and indecisiveness contained in the reform program have had the unintended effect of impeding its progress. Out of either genuine faith in the socialist ideal, prudence in the unprecedented task, or even intellectual inertia, the Chinese leadership, unlike the post-socialist regimes in Poland, the Czech Republic, or Russia, has continued to honor the ideological superiority of socialism and has yet to endorse full-scale privatization as the ultimate reform goal.[2] Unlike many of its formerly socialist counterparts, the Chinese Communist Party is still (at the time of writing) guiding reforms, and the sainthood of the first generation of revolutionary cult figures, such as Mao Zedong, remains officially untouched. The Russian lesson, which demonstrated the risks of the total collapse of the socialist regime, has only reinforced the Chinese Communist Party's faith in the strategy of avoiding a dramatic departure from socialist legacy. Right or wrong, the Party is not yet prepared to launch a comprehensive denial of its past. A disjointed incrementalism in the reform program, which is characterized by pragmatism and a toleration of unauthorized initiatives, is the logical alternative. On the positive side, this can provide an opening for greater spontaneity from below.[3] However, as seen in the implementation of the shareholding reform, it can also be exploited to block progress toward further marketization. For the local interests, which have different agendas and concerns, such an accommodating stance at the higher level provides more room to maneuver.

Second, in more concrete terms, the economic framework designed according to the Maoist ideal of a planned economy has also deprived the reform regime of a desirable infrastructure on which to build an effective market mechanism, and has therefore increased the cost of economic transformation. A poorly developed transportation and communication network, underinvestment in commercial facilities across the country, and other problems inherited from Mao's economy are hardly compatible with the standard requirements of an effective market mechanism. The industrial foundation inherited from the collective era also exhibits a strong parochial orientation, with businesses confined in reach by their intimate relationship with local state.

In cognitive terms, the general experience of the planned economy has generated further difficulties for the reform process. Anti-market traits of the pre-reform economy limited the exposure to market operations for most economic actors and, thus, deprived them of the chance to acquire the necessary cognitive skills and experience. In addition, the enduring values inherited from the Mao era have also diverted the course of reform by affecting the valuation of costs and benefits and limiting available options. The persistence of the normative pressure to maintain a certain degree of egalitarianism in the rural community is a good example. It affects the local state's evaluation of the feasibility of various options in satisfying discontented managers as well as the managers' perceptions of a legitimate claim on enterprise profits and the enterprise's obligations to the local community. It is debatable whether it is a pretext for extortion or an issue of genuine concern. However, it is definitely relevant in the local discourse regarding a fair share of the fruits of rural industrialization.

The combined effect of partial market reforms and the historical legacy has produced a unique setting, containing both continuities and discontinuities, for the interaction between state and society. The resulting relationship is more complicated than the scenario envisioned by the notion of civil society, which assumes an inevitable battle for a clear demarcation of the boundary between the two. Nor can one be absolutely confident that an inevitable trend toward full-scale marketization is emerging, as assumed by the market transition theorists. The intermingling of the old and the new economic orders gives rise to fluidity, indeterminacy, and ambiguity in development, which may or may not be in line with the neat and tidy theoretical constructs assumed to be relevant for understanding the phenomenon. By giving full respect to details and specificity, this analysis has hopefully enhanced understanding of the subject matter.

Toward a synergetic perspective

The rise of managers epitomizes the challenges that the new economic order poses for the local state. It reflects the emergence of a new incentive structure and new opportunities, as well as new pressures created by changes in the post-Mao institutional setting. A retuning of governing style is necessary, as the local state has to act with greater restraint and delegate more political and economic power to managers. Such concessions reveal the local state's perplexity in comprehending the new logic of economic management – market competitiveness, profitability, innovation, unemployment and labor redundancy, etc. – and its inadequacy in governing without the assistance of new social actors endowed with the right attributes.

Dali Yang, in his summary of the major studies on rural governance, insightfully points out that the role of the state is very much affected by contextual factors, primarily the financial importance of rural enterprise and the level of economic development of the local community.[4] However, Yang's assumption that the local state decides the governance style of local economic management is debatable. A similar statist bias can be detected in Jean Oi's notion of local state corporatism, in which the role of managers is very much limited or is indistinguishable from the state. The Zibo case, however, points in a different direction; the local state's level of involvement in enterprise management is contingent upon the balance between conflicting claims, and concern for the fullest utilization of the managers' entrepreneurial drive is of great importance. In other words, social actors, the managers in this case, play an important role in defining and regulating the extent of the local state's presence in the local economy. Enterprise managers, for example, now have certain leverage (management skills and knowledge) with which they can regulate their relationship with the state. Instead of being a passive recipient, or a client under the patronage of individual officials,[5] they have been provided with a more solid foundation on which they can pursue their own interests. Their contribution to economic development has earned them command over important local resources, a more equal footing in relation to the local state, and even access to the formal decision-making process at the local level. What has really happened is that, with the advent of economic reform, particularly toward the end of the twentieth century, the cost to the state of neglecting or suppressing the role played by these social actors has become much higher than in the pre-reform era. In some cases, as with the managers in the development of rural enterprises, it has reached such a high level that the state simply cannot afford to alienate this potential ally. Through action (the threat of resignation by managers) or inaction (lowered work effort), social actors can now bargain for a more comfortable distance between the state and themselves. This analysis, therefore, highlights the importance of the development stage argument in understanding state–business relationships. The statist explanation for TVE growth provides a persuasive account for the early stage of reform, but overlooks the potential transformation of business actors. As seen in the case of Zibo, the dynamics of the state–manager relationship are closely related to growth in the size of enterprise operations, the degree of integration between local enterprises and the national economy, and the degree of marketization. The inter-related development of enterprise growth and independence fosters a new bargaining position vis-à-vis state actors. Shafer's research on the role of *chaebol,* or conglomerates, in Korea is revealing. He argues that it is undeniable that these *chaebol* owe much of their rapid rise to the Korean government's ambitious Heavy and Chemical Industrial Development Plan; the official blessings of cheap loans, export subsidies, preferential tax treatment, monopoly markets, and protection were key to their success. However, once these *chaebol* had established their precarious financial positions and importance, state leverage against them was constrained. The state has been forced into the role of "lender of the last resort" because the bankruptcy of a *chaebol* would threaten the financial and economic stability of the country. Furthermore, these *chaebol* have also shown strong interest in the policy process, as they see politics as a way to protect their interests.[6]

The relationship between managers and the local state is, of course, far from friction-less. However, as shown in this analysis, the former seldom pursue their interests through direct confrontation with the latter. Instead, the managers' approach involves greater subtlety and goes beyond the prescribed mode of interaction depicted by the dichotomous view of the state–society relationship. The indispensability of their managerial skills to the progress of the local economy provides managers with unique leverage for making their views known: the withdrawal of professional service or cooperation. Managers are the key to transforming idle and underutilized industrial capacity into a steady stream of income and revenue, and they possess the means to convert the meaningless ownership rights of the publicly owned resources into concrete and tangible benefits for members of the local community. Although actual resignations are few and far between, the availability of alternative careers in the private sector adds much credibility to such a threat. The fact that their contribution is highly valued is well reflected in their gradual ascendancy up the local political hierarchy, their increasing discretion in internal management, and the significant impact they make on the outcome of reform, as shown in the study of the implementation of the shareholding cooperative system. With a panoply of options ranging from "setting up a new stove" (i.e. starting a personal business) to lowered performance or indifference, managers are making their opinions known and asserting themselves silently. Unspectacular though these options may be, they are definitely no less effective in achieving the intended goal of pressuring the local state.

Manager advancement is, certainly, not without constraints. With so much personal interest at stake in the performance of the enterprises under their management, the managers' strategy limitations are obvious. More fundamentally, the success of their strategies hinges upon the self-restraint of the local state. Managership *per se* does not guarantee access to influence and status; discretionary power in management, political titles, and various forms of recognition are awarded selectively, on the basis of managers' performance. Individual managers' ability to deliver desirable performances determines their position in the local community, sets the tolerance threshold of the local officials, and hence defines their particularistic relationship with the local state. In other words, they have to earn the self-restraint of the local state through diligence and sound managerial judgments.

The relationship involves two-way traffic, and enterprise managers have their part to play too. As financial and economic concerns are the basic foundation upon which the prevailing relationship with the managers is built, the local state's acquiescence and tolerance can also be revoked if these primary goals are not fulfilled owing to the managers' excessive demands. The relationship between the two parties is not necessarily zero-sum by nature, but the allocation of enterprise resources can be. When the fruit of economic success appears to be mostly consumed by greedy managers, it makes little sense for the local state to remain forgiving. Managers, in other words, have to be aware of the local state's bottom line when pursuing their interests, and to act with self-restraint. As reflected in the case of shareholding reforms, this seems to be common knowledge and has been well respected. The shareholding reform initiative seems to offer a rose garden for managers. However, as reflected in our analysis, managers have reacted with great restraint. They have made use of the chance to improve their position, taken significant shares of the newly converted companies, and acquired a new legitimate basis for earning higher income. However, they seldom fully exploit the potential institutional effect of the new system in minimizing the continued presence of the local state in enterprise operation. With managers' cooperation, the local state's financial stake has been well protected, despite the change in the organizational outlook of these newly converted shareholding enterprises. Both parties, are, in short, optimizing rather than maximizing the potential benefits offered by the opportunity.

This self-restraint is not simply a result of fearing local state retaliation – the local state can be useful for business operation too. The relationship between the two parties is best summarized as one of mutual dependence reinforced by mutual sanctions. It is a delicate balance that both parties have to work hard to maintain. And within this general framework, neither party can afford to antagonize the other. In fact, it is interesting to see that the Zibo case has much in common with the "duality of leadership" of businessmen and officials under capitalism, as described by Charles Lindblom:

> Because public functions in the market system rest in the hands of businessmen, it follows that jobs, prices, production, growth, the standard of living, and the economic security of everyone all rest in their hands. Consequently, government officials cannot be indifferent to how well business performs its functions ... In the eyes of government officials, therefore, businessmen do not appear simply as the representatives of a

special interest, as representatives of interest groups do. They appear as functionaries performing functions that government officials regard as indispensable . . . Collaboration and deference between the two are at the heart of politics in such systems. Businessmen cannot be left knocking at the doors of the political system; they must be invited.[7]

However, the underdeveloped market system and the shortage of managerial talent in rural China produces an even more intimate relationship between business and politics than is suggested by Lindblom's description. In a way, they are inherent parts of each other. In this distinct pattern of interaction, a simple dichotomous view of state–society confrontation can hardly capture the complexity of the overall picture.

The corollary of this reflection is the evaluation of the importance of political capital in the reform era. Whereas Victor Nee has suggested that the value of political capital has been declining with the advent of market reform, the majority of commentators concur with Jean Oi's contrasting view of the persistence of bureaucratic influence. As reflected in this study, this may be an important question, but an understanding of the issue may be undermined by these polarized views. The Zibo case shows that local development is influenced more by the synergy unleashed by the transforming political and economic order than by political or social capital alone. Put simply, a skillful combination of these assets can produce the best possible result at the current stage of economic reform. This is reflected at both the individual and institutional level, as demonstrated in this analysis. At the individual level, both ex-cadre experience and apprenticeship in commune-brigade enterprises during the pre-reform period are among the major credentials of key management personnel. At the institutional level, though managers appear to be the dominant source of entrepreneurial drive in the booming business sector, the official blessing of the local state continues to function as a useful supplement in reducing transaction costs and securing greater economic predictability. This new strategy of "walking on two legs" enables both parties to fully exploit the opportunity offered by economic transformation, and explains why the new social actors, as mentioned above, show little enthusiasm for distancing themselves from the local state, as well as explaining why the local state is willing to adopt a more restrained stance. In short, one needs to go beyond the state to comprehend the dynamic of rural governance in reform China.

The story also demonstrates the Chinese Communist Party's adaptability. Decollectivization and marketization do restrain the leverage available for local state actors, but the state actors in Zibo show immense vitality in adjusting to new challenges, and remarkable flexibility in accommodating the rise of managers. The willingness to twist reform initiative unleashed by the higher authorities, and the co-optation strategy of admitting managers' into the local policy process, has enabled the local state to maintain its governance with a more steady supply of revenues, resources, and legitimacy. Nevertheless, if one puts this into a larger context, it is hardly a local phenomenon. The Zibo story also highlights the central Party leadership's audacity in opening its door to private entrepreneurs in the new millennium. The implication of the ideological offensive of the "three representation" theory launched by Jiang Zemin goes beyond the personal satisfaction of the Party Secretary; it also reflects the sensitivity of the Party to the changing political reality and its pragmatic view of the reforms.[8] This provokes a reflection on the possibility of the changing nature of the state and, as revealed by the Zibo story, the possible impact of socioeconomic changes on the formation of the Chinese Party-state and the consequent adaptation of the local officials.

Vulnerability of local collaboration

Looking to the future, the fundamental question concerns the sustainability of this local collaboration. This author's predicts that if the state–manager cordiality is a function of the degree of mutual dependence of the two parties, given the prospect of further reform and integration with the national economy, the future of this local collaboration is bleak and managerial empowerment will be an issue of political significance beyond the local level.

Mobilization of peasant-workers

The endurance of the entente cordiale between the local state and managers depends fundamentally on three conditions: the capacity of local business to deliver economic goods, the ability of the local state to maintain a balance between conflicting claims, and the passivity of peasant-workers. Although these variables are independently determined by different contingent factors, the likelihood that these conditions can be sustained is affected by general economic conditions. Economic downturn or the further concentration of rural business will heighten the tension between the parties, and a resultant change in the relationship requiring a more autonomous local state to retain the balance is possible.

The peasant-workers in Zibo appear to have a high tolerance threshold, as is evident in most developing countries. They are willing to work under unpleasant workplace conditions, characterized by poor ventilation facilities, substandard safety measures, and minimum protection against industrial hazards.[9] They accept long working hours and minimal welfare provisions,[10] and occasionally female workers are even asked to take up the undignified responsibility of accompanying potential investors or officials from higher levels to a karaoke or dance hall.[11] Chinese peasants, however, have demonstrated their ability to make their grievances known if necessary. There have been growing instances of rural unrest in the countryside in recent years; frustrated peasants are capable and willing to take justice into their own hands, even through direct and violent confrontations with local cadres,[12] which are obviously beyond the array of "everyday forms of resistance."[13] It is premature to conclude that there is an emerging crisis in rural China, but this vividly shows that the passivity of peasants simply cannot be taken for granted. There are, in fact, several developments that may breed potential activism among peasant-workers in rural China. First, the growing exposure to the urban situation of the rural population will certainly affect peasant-workers' assessment of their own position in the rural workplace. Increased contact with urban counterparts may provoke a sense of deprivation among rural workers; the knowledge of the discrepancy in welfare entitlement and the relative comfort in the urban workplace may sow the seeds of frustration and activism among peasant-workers. With the slowing down of TVE development in recent years and the growing linkages between urban and rural sectors, the outflow of rural workers, which is estimated to be 80–100 million per year, is likely to increase in coming years. Second, the growing importance of non-agricultural employment for rural households may also decrease rural workers' tolerance of any unfair distribution in the rural enterprise. The financial importance of factory employment's income contribution needs no repetition here, but there are other developments that may simply reinforce the peasants' participation rate in rural enterprises. Among these is the growing freedom of the rural population from agricultural production. Decollectivization renews incentives for Chinese farmers, but also deprives China of the benefit of production economies of scale and sustained enthusiasm for investment. There have been numerous experiments to address the problem, with the intention of concentrating more land in the hands of the more motivated farmers and at the same time relieving the farming duties of those who find their energy to be better rewarded elsewhere.[14] Consequently, a greater participation rate in rural enterprises is expected.

However, the foregoing analysis does not suggest that peasant-workers' activism is simply inevitable. These sentiments or anxieties are, after all, motivated by economic concerns and should ease off if economic benefits can be maintained at an acceptable level. The distribution of shares reflected in the implementation of shareholding reform in Zibo is a good example. By giving generous share offers and high dividends to workers, managers in Zibo's reformed enterprises demonstrated how a free hand in operations could be *bought*. However, the fact that low production costs are a major reason for the sector's success in outcompeting the state-owned sector has imposed a great constraint on the enterprises' ability to pacify aggrieved workers. Low wages, minimal welfare, and the evasion of expenses incurred in complying with national regulations on industrial safety or environmental control, all of which are crucial elements for keeping down costs, are in direct conflict with workers' interests. This may apply to any profit-oriented entity, but for rural enterprises, which are competing mainly on cost, this factor is of paramount importance.[15]

Tension may reach a breaking point when the business conditions of these enterprises deteriorate. Needless to say, it is more difficult to satisfy workers' growing expectations as the pie gets smaller. Worse still, there are several distinct features of rural enterprises that may make them particularly vulnerable to economic downturns. First, as most rural enterprises are, in general, still involved in production with primitive technology and are small in size, entry into business is relative easy. In other words, the profitability of the industry can quickly be diluted by a sudden increase in the number of competitors.[16] This is motivation for improving efficiency, but it also means that the buffer against the potential reversal of business is, in general, small. Second, local protectionism has contributed to a high degree of duplication in the mix of local industry across the country.[17] The spontaneous and uncoordinated development of rural industries supported by parochial local governments has defied the economic rule of comparative advantage and has obstructed the emergence of a more healthy industrial structure. Such unnatural concentration exerts a similar pressure by enhancing competition and decreasing the profitability of specific industries. Lastly, unlike their capitalist counterparts, peasant-workers in China regard their employment in collective enterprises as a right – an entitlement derived from collective ownership. Thus, any reduction in benefits which may be necessitated by poor market conditions is likely to be met with great resentment in the rural context. Unfortunately, the trend of slowed TVE growth since the mid-1990s, described earlier in this discussion, heralds little comfort for local governments in China. The intensifying competition between enterprises, as reflected in Table 2.1, makes it even less assuring for those who are concerned with peasant-workers' sentiments.

Worse still, the danger that workplace tensions will intensify exists even during good years. The fundamental root of this tension is the instinct to minimize costs, inherent in profit-oriented enterprise. The local state, as seen throughout this discussion, has tried to maintain the right balance between economic growth and workers' interests. This task, however, will become more delicate if there is a fundamental change in terms of the bargaining power for local enterprises. The question is, if enterprise managers, who have already established their influence in the local political and economic order, are becoming even more powerful, does the local state still have the will and ability to contain any unjust exploitation of workers? It has yet to be confirmed whether or not the exploitation of workers is increasing, but TVE managers are undoubtedly gaining strength. Most notably is the trend toward the formation of enterprise groups (*qiye jituan*) among TVEs in rural China, as described earlier. As seen in Zibo's case, political power comes with economic strength, so this development implies a rise in managerial bargaining power.

In short, peasant-worker activism, whether triggered by deteriorating economic conditions, growing awareness of their deprivation, or the growing aggression of the enterprises, will compound the position of the local state as the mediator between conflicting claims. There is, on the one hand, a need to support managers in maintaining the competitiveness of their enterprises. On the other hand, the local state is not immune to popular pressure. The task faced by the local state is unprecedented: it has to maintain the momentum of local industrial development, which rests heavily on state tolerance of the evils evident in the early experience of capitalist development for a polity with a socialist legacy. Growing labor restlessness increases the burden on its shoulders and may necessitate a re-examination of its relationship with the business sector in order to get the balance right. Particularly worrying for the local state is the potential eruption of tension in the workplace and the consequent disorder in the countryside. With the central government's growing concern over rural political stability in recent years, potential intervention from a higher level renders indifference to popular sentiment impossible.[18] Even for individual cadres, who have great personal interest in the business sector through moonlighting or various forms of kickbacks, it is in their interest to see the "necessary capitalist evils" contained within reasonable limits. Their business connection probably makes them easy targets for any rectification effort in the aftermath of a workplace-related confrontation. As their access to these business opportunities rests on their possession of public authority, dismissal from their official capacity would mean the end of their administrative as well as their business careers.

Consequently, one plausible scenario is a distancing between business and politics. The new variable of activated peasant-workers would require the local state to act with a greater degree of autonomy in regulating the operation of local enterprises or with a greater readiness to suppress any ruthless exploitative measures adopted by local enterprises. More specifically, the local state may have to play a more intervening role, especially in matters concerning conflict resolution in the workplace or other areas of potential tension; managers' freedom in certain aspects of enterprise management are, consequently, likely to be restricted. Certainly, the fundamental symbiotic relationship between the local state and local business should not be discarded, as the basis of mutual dependence remains intact in the present stage of marketization. However, the requirement of a more autonomous role in the face of peasant-worker activism may offset some of the momentum toward a greater consolidation of the local alliance.

Extending the reach of the central state

As the local alliance between business and politics is contingent upon the limited availability of alternatives and the substantial cost attached to them, gearing up marketization efforts is likely to make enterprise managers less inclined to adhere to the existing relationship with the local state. A greater degree of marketization can provide more alternatives and a free flow of resources, and this can in turn weaken the degree of mutual dependence between the local state and managers, decreasing the attraction of the status quo. Greater liberalization of foreign investment, a more comprehensive price reform package, a higher degree of commercialization of the credit supply, and the abolition of various administrative barriers to the flow of resources, can all bring fundamental changes to the economic basis of the entente cordiale between the local interests. The pace of marketization is also likely to be accelerated by China's admission into the World Trade Organization in 2001.

All these measures will depoliticize the mobility of resources and minimize the role of the local state in different aspects of enterprise operation. With less to be gained from their collaboration with the local state, enterprise managers will certainly readjust their position accordingly. A freer flow of resources and minimized administrative interference lower the hurdle for entering into a wider business context, and the managers' quest for greater profits makes an increase in cross-community transactions inevitable. However, an expanded market requires constant interaction with unfamiliar counterparts. As a reasonable degree of certainty and predictability in economic life are crucial for entrepreneurial activities, managers are eager to find alternative mechanisms with which to build their businesses. This may in turn provide a new constituency for the appeal of the new economic system, which is based on impersonal, universal, and formal rules – the basic ingredients of an effective market economy.

The proliferation of universal rules and standards was evident in the 1990s. Table 8.1 provides a summary of a survey on the rules and directives concerning the regulation of rural enterprise development issued by commissions or ministries at central level between 1977 and 1998. Into the 1990s, rural enterprises transformed from backyard workshops supplementing agricultural incomes into a key component of the national economy. The economic contribution of rural enterprises is now indispensable for national growth. For instance, in 1998, the total export value of rural enterprises reached 680 billion yuan, constituting a third of China's total exports.[19] Rural markets are no longer sufficient for this booming sector. Rural consumption can only absorb about one-third of the total rural industrial output.[20] Consequently, the central government has become more actively involved in regulating their development. These developments mean that interaction between local enterprises and higher levels of government is more likely and, in some cases, inevitable. This also implies that, more and more, administrative matters can no longer be handled by local officials alone. New obligations, standards, and requirements defined by the central bureaucracy have restricted local officials' room to maneuver.

Further integration with larger political and economic orders also coincided with the changing concerns of enterprise managers. Another study by this author has revealed that enterprise managers have now become more preoccupied with issues requiring policy or institutional changes, instead of the parochial matters of the past.[21] Excessive extraction and administrative interference were managers' main concerns in the 1980s, and they asked for a favorable administrative framework to promote market development in the 1990s. The latter requires policy changes and institutional reform, which can only be sanctioned and endorsed by higher levels. In other words, though interaction with the state remains crucial, the target for lobbying or pressure has changed. Cordiality with the local bureaucracy may still make life easier, but managers are also aware that local administration alone cannot solve all their problems.

Table 8.1 Central rules and directives on TVE development, 1977–98

Policy area	Number of rules and directives issued	
	1977–89	*1990–8*
Property rights reform	3	17
Ownership change	3	10
Asset valuation	0	6
Enterprise group formation	0	1
Internal enterprise management	14	52
Financial management	1	7
Product quality control	3	8
Technology upgrading	1	8
Industrial safety	4	6
Environment/hygiene	2	6
Staff training	0	2
Staff welfare	0	2
Political education	0	1
Others	3	12
Macro-development	2	19
Overall development	1	10
Sectoral priority	1	1
Inter-regional collaboration	0	8
Administrative regulation	1	7
Foreign trade	2	2
Credit supply	4	3
Taxation	10	1
Land	1	0
Enterprise/entrepreneur honors	0	6
Total	37	107

Source: Ray Yep, "Towards a Symbiotic State–Enterprise Relationship in Rural China: Changes and Prospect," *Hong Kong Journal of Social Sciences* (Autumn/2000), No. 17, p. 9.

The growing demands for the introduction of Rural Enterprise Law is illustrative. One could hear scattered calls for greater protection of enterprise interests during the late 1980s,[22] and the sentiments have intensified since. The unabated administrative extortion and the growing amount of wealth accumulated by rural businesses have certainly exacerbated the conflict between enterprise and bureaucracy. Managers, who feel they have more and more at stake in protecting enterprise resources, have also become more vocal on this matter. Although there was already a national regulation in place stating the importance of separating politics from enterprise and of respecting the independent legal personal status of enterprises by 1990,[23] managers never stopped asking for a more secure legal protection – a national law on rural enterprise. The issue became, more or less, a regular proposal made by managers in local or national people's congress in the 1990s.[24] Whether the Rural Enterprise Law passed in the National People's Congress in 1997 can meet all the managers' expectations certainly requires a separate discussion, but managers' enthusiasm for this piece of legislation is evident.

Enterprise development in the 1990s also denoted a different expectation on behalf of administrative departments. Whereas defense against excessive extraction and arbitrary intervention were the themes of the 1980s, the expectations of rural business administration became more positive and forward-looking in the 1990s. In short, rural enterprises desired a better coordination between administrative departments. For them, the fact that numerous departments enjoyed overlapping jurisdiction over rural enterprises, and the long list of bureaucratic units that could obstruct their business in one way or another were hardly desirable, for this not only implied huge transaction costs in getting through all the hurdles, but also meant an impediment to efficient administrative services.[25] In the 1980s, when most business activities were confined to local or nearby areas, the issue of bureaucratic communication and coordination may not have caused so much concern. At that time, enterprises surely had to go through webs of bureaucratic actors, but local government support may have been enough to enlist cooperation. Involvement of units at the county or municipal levels may have been needed occasionally, but they were still within the reach of the township administration. Personal friendship, kinship ties, past experience, or the possibility of working in the same office all provided access for lobbying from the grass-roots level. However, with the exposure of rural enterprises to national or even international markets, the problem has become acute. Local administration, at the township level or below, with its limited jurisdiction and low status in bureaucratic hierarchy, can do little to provide the support necessary for these expanding enterprises. For instance, there exists a common concern for a better flow of information on nationwide market demand and material supply.[26] One concrete proposal suggests the formation of an administrative unit responsible for equipment swapping among enterprises. In other words, the new service must ensure communication and coordination between offices across the countryside, instead of local or nearby bureaucratic units.

The demands for policy and institutional changes in the 1990s entailed a different mode of action. Collective action became a more appropriate strategy for expressing common concerns. The Zibo case shows that, far from being a homogenous group, managers differ in terms of their path of ascendancy, their endowment with managerial skills, and their prior affiliation with the bureaucracy. Their heterogeneity is further exacerbated by the fact that economic, social, and political power are distributed according to an individual's success in enterprise management. A hierarchy of status among managers is evident. The relationship between the manager and the local state remains particularistic in nature. For ambitious managers concerned with local issues and guaranteed direct access to local officials, collective action is hardly necessary. However, with the changing concerns of policy and institutional changes, some form of collective voice among managers may be to their advantage. The very first instance of these initiatives can be traced back to an open letter signed by twenty-six outstanding managers in 1987. While attending a forum organized by the Ministry of Agriculture, Forestry and Fishery, these managers took the opportunity to issue a letter reiterating their faith in socialism and the new wave of economic reform introduced by the Party.[27] Subsequent joint efforts touched upon issues of wider concern, including industrial safety,[28] problems of unclear ownership,[29] ideological legitimacy,[30] legal reform,[31] and product quality,[32] and the number of managers involved also increased – in one case, 1,000 managers were involved.[33] In other words, managers now regarded collective action as one of the possible options for pursuing interests, particularly for those matters of wider policy concern.

Thus, the inevitable trend of further integration of TVEs into national or even international economic order will certainly lead to a different habitat for state–manager exchange. A possible effect of the central state's enthusiasm in imposing universal standards and practices, inherent in the marketization process, entails devaluation of the local state's official blessing. With more transactions regulated and facilitated by higher authorities, and the enterprises' growing business contact with the outside world, the balance of interdependence between managers and local state may move further in the favor of the former. Nevertheless, the outcome is not preordained. The innovativeness and adaptability exhibited by the local state in Zibo is proof that one should not underestimate the local state's offensive ability in the face of challenges. This definitely warrants more research in future.

Concluding remarks

Our story began with concerns about the political implications of managerial empowerment at the rural grass-roots level and ended with the recognition of its significance for the national political economy. The predictions made in the last part of this discussion foresee the further rise of enterprise managers and envision a changing pattern of articulation and accommodation of the interests of these managerial elites. The "final" outcome of the unfolding of Chinese capitalism remains to be determined. This author believes that the analysis of the case of Zibo should help to enhance one's understanding of the intricacies of the connection between economic change and political development in reform China. But the major lesson of this story is that it is ultimately the choice of actors that determines the outcome of reform. Economic changes do affect the setting of interaction, incentives, and calculations, but their impact is neither mechanical nor deterministic. Market transition entails a paradigmatic shift for all economic and political actors concerned, but teleological arguments which assume that certain economic trends and political changes are inevitable on the basis of economic rationality and objective needs are hardly consistent with the analysis presented here. The Zibo experience shows that *demand* for marketization can be perceived differently by, on the one hand, market reformers at the central level, or property rights theorists who believe a clearer property relation is the prerequisite for growth, and, on the other hand, the local actors – enterprise managers and the local state – who find the problem less urgent. The Zibo case also demonstrates the importance of evaluating the *supply* side of economic reform. With different agendas and interests in mind, those at the grass-roots level have not necessarily embraced the reform momentum unleashed from above. Its implementation may be deliberately delayed, twisted, or even hijacked as a result. Paradoxically, the basic questions of who gets what and when provide us with an illuminating framework for analyzing one of the most sophisticated issues for political scientists of our time: the political economy of market transformation.

Notes

1 Understanding rural transformation

1 "Rural Entrepreneurs Write Letter to Deng," Foreign Broadcasting and Information Services (*FBIS*) (China), Vol. 92, No. 194, 10/6/1992, p. 41.
2 Ibid., p. 42.
3 For examples on the economic and social consequences of rural industrialization, see W. Byrd and Lin Qinsong (eds), *China's Rural Industry: Structure, Development, and Reform*, New York: Oxford University Press, 1990; S. Ho, *Rural China in Transition: Non-Agricultural Development in Rural Jiangsu, 1978–1990*, Oxford: Clarendon Press, 1994; Ma Rong, Wang Hanshang, and Liu Shiding (eds), *Jiushi Niandai Zhongguo Xiangzhen Qiye Tiaocha (Survey of China's Rural Enterprise in the Nineties)*, Hong Kong: Oxford University Press, 1994; Zhou Yimiao and Zhang Yulin (eds), *Zhongguo Chengxiang Xietiao Fazhan Yanjiu (Research on the Rural–Urban Coordinated Development in China)*, Hong Kong: Oxford University Press, 1994; G. Guldin (ed.), *Farewell to China's Peasantry: Rural, Urban and Social Change in the Late Twentieth Century*, Armonk, NJ: M. E. Sharpe, 1997.
4 O. Odgaard, "Entrepreneurs and Elite Formation in Rural China," *Australian Journal of Chinese Affairs*, No. 28, July 1992, pp. 89–108; O. Brunn, *Business and Bureaucracy in a Chinese City: an Ethnography of Private Business Households in Contemporary China*, Berkeley, CA: Institute of East Asian Studies, 1993; S. Young, *Private Business and Economic Reform in China*, Armonk, NJ: M. E. Sharpe, 1995; and M. Pearson, *China's New Business Elites: The Political Consequences of Economic Reform*, Berkeley, CA: University of California Press, 1997.
5 D. North, *Institutions, Institutional Change and Economic Performance*, New York: Cambridge University Press, 1990, pp. 73–82.
6 B. Moore, *Social Origins of Dictatorship and Democracy*, Boston: Beacon Press, 1966; K. Polanyi, *The Great Transformation: the Political and Economic Origins of Our Time*, Boston: Beacon Press, 1957; S. Lipset, *Political Man* (expanded edition), Baltimore: Johns Hopkins University Press, 1981; and C. Lindblom, *Politics and Markets*, New York: Basic Books, 1977.
7 G. O'Donnell, P. Schmitter and L. Whitehead (eds), *Transition from Authoritarian Rule: Comparative Perspectives*, Baltimore: Johns Hopkins University Press, 1986; and G. O'Donnell and P. Schmitter (eds), *Transition from Authoritarian Rule: Tentative Conclusions about Uncertain Democracies*, Baltimore: Johns Hopkins University Press, 1986.
8 F. Fukuyama, *The End of History and the Last Man*, London: Penguin Books, 1992.
9 A. Smith, *The Wealth of Nations*, London: Penguin Books, 1986, p. 380. The classic work on the linkage between property rights and economic growth is, of course, by Douglass North: D. North and R. Thomas, *The Rise of the Western World: A New Economic History*, New York: Cambridge University Press, 1973.

10　Here Barzel distinguishes between economic property rights and legal property rights. An economic right refers to an individual's ability to enjoy the property – to consume the asset directly or indirectly through exchange. This is the essential right over a property. A legal right is what the state assigns to a person. The former is the end whereas the latter is the means, but, as pointed out in the quotation, not the only means. Y. Barzel, *Economic Analysis of Property Rights*, New York: Cambridge University Press, 1997, p. 2.

11　M. Olson, *The Logic of Collective Action*, Cambridge, MA: Harvard University Press, 1965.

12　J. Knight, *Institutions and Social Conflict*, New York: Cambridge University Press, 1992.

13　B. Naughton, "Chinese Institutional Innovation and Privatization From Below," *American Economic Review, Papers and Perspectives*, Vol. 84, No. 2, 1994, p. 267.

14　Susan Whiting has emphasized the importance of state support for the development of rural enterprises in Mao's era. Still, it is justified to argue that rural enterprises, in general, do not enjoy the security of material supply and product outlet to which their counterparts in the state sector are entitled. S. Whiting, *Power and Wealth in Rural China*, New York: Cambridge University Press, 2001.

15　A. Walder, "Local Government as Industrial Firms: an Organizational Analysis of China's Transitional Economy," *American Journal of Sociology*, Vol. 101, No. 2, September 1995, pp. 263–301.

16　K. Lieberthal and M. Oksenberg, *Policy Making in China: Leaders, Structures and Processes*, Princeton, NJ: Princeton University Press, 1988, Chapters 1 and 2.

17　For the critique of the "old" statist view, see H. Eckstein, "On the Science of the State," *Daedalus*, Vol. 108, No. 4, 1979, pp. 1–20; D. Easton, "The Political System Besieged by the State," *Political Theory*, Vol. 9, No. 3981, pp. 305–25; and G. Almond, "The Return to the State," *American Political Science Review*, Vol. 82, No. 3, 1988, pp. 853–73.

18　Although it is admitted that society does have its impact on the process of state formation, the neo-statists stress that, once institutionalized, the state tends to be relatively permanent through time and can no longer be seen simply as the reflection of societal demands. Instead, incongruence between the needs and the expressed demands of the state and various societal groups becomes the norm, not the exception. S. Krasner, "Approaches to the State: Alternative Conceptions and Historical Dynamics," *Comparative Politics*, Vol. 16, No. 2, 1984, pp. 223–46.

19　J. March and J. Olsen, "The New Institutionalism: Organizational Factors in Political Life," *American Political Science Review*, Vol. 78, No. 3, 1984, pp. 737–49.

20　For a vivid description of such dependence, see J. Oi, *State and Peasant in Contemporary China*, Berkeley, CA: University of California Press, 1989, p. 42; and K. Xiao Zhou, *How the Farmers Changed China: Power of the People*, Boulder, CO: Westview Press, 1996, Chapter 2.

21　C. K. Yang estimated that in the 1950s there were twelve million members of the CCP and twenty-three million members of the (Communist) Youth League, which adds up to a total of thirty-five million. This is 5.83 percent of China's total population of 600 million, the figure produced by the Communist Party in 1957, compared with 2.14 percent of the population constituted by the gentry in the last century. In addition, the 1.5 million communist officials represent an immeasurably larger bureaucracy than the 40,000 official positions in nineteenth-century China. C. K. Yang, *A Chinese Village in the Early Communist Transition*, Cambridge, MA: Technology Press, 1959, pp. 255–6.

22　C. K. Yang, *The Chinese Family in the Communist Revolution*, MIT, Cambridge, MA: Technology Press, 1959, pp. 137–82.

23　During the early years of rural collectivization, the Party deliberately made use of existing ties of friendship and family to reinforce trust in the new arrangement and the commitment of its participants. See E. Friedman, P. Pickowicz, and M. Selden, *Chinese Village, Socialist State*, New Haven, CT: Yale University Press, 1991, pp. 54–8; V. Shue, *Peasant China in Transition*, Berkeley, CA: University of California Press, 1980, pp. 144–91; and S. Heins Potter and J. Potter, *China's Peasants: The Anthropology of a Revolution*, New York: Cambridge University Press, 1990, pp. 131–2.

24   For an account of the intermediation role of local gentry in imperial China, see P. Duara, *Culture, Power and the State: Rural North China, 1900–1942*, Stanford, CA: Stanford University Press, 1988; S. Naguin and E. Rawski, *Chinese Society in the Eighteenth Century*, New Haven, CT: Yale University Press, 1987; J. Esherick and M. Backus Rankin (eds), *Chinese Local Elites and Pattern of Dominance*, Berkeley, CA: University of California Press, 1990; and M. Park Redfield (ed.), *China's Gentry: Essays in Rural Urban Relations by Fei Xiaotong*, Chicago, IL: University of Chicago Press, 1953.

25   V. Shue, *The Reach of the State: Sketches of the Chinese Body Politic*, Stanford, CA: Stanford University Press, 1988, pp. 130–1.

26   For other accounts of this phenomenon, see J. Burns, *Political Participation in Rural China*, Berkeley, CA: University of California Press, 1988; A. Chan, R. Madsen, and J. Unger, *Chen Village: The Recent History of a Peasant Community in Mao's China*, Berkeley, CA: University of California Press, 1984.

27   J. Migdal, "The State in Society: an Approach to Struggle in Domination," in J. Migdal *et al.* (eds), *State Power and Social Forces: Domination and Transformation in the Third World*, Cambridge: Cambridge University Press, 1994, p. 10.

28   P. Schmitter, "Still the Century of Corporatism?," in F. Pike and T. Stritch (eds), *The New Corporatism: Social-Political Structures in the Iberian World*, Notre Dame, IN: University of Notre Dame Press, 1974, pp. 93–4.

29   M. Pearson, "The Janus Face of Business Associations in China: Socialist Corporatism in Foreign Enterprises," *Australian Journal of Chinese Affairs*, No. 31, January 1994, pp. 25–46; and J. Unger and A. Chan, "China, Corporatism, and the East Asian Model," *Australian Journal of Chinese Affairs*, No. 33, January 1995, pp. 29–53. Lowell Dittmer also uses the term loosely when he argues that the united front policy adopted by the Party is "neocorporatist." L. Dittmer, "Public and Private Interests and the Participatory Ethic in China," in V. Falkenheim (ed.), *Citizens and Groups in Contemporary China*, Ann Arbor, MI: Center for Chinese Studies, University of Michigan, 1987, p. 20.

30   For instance, J. Unger and A. Chan ("China, Corporation and the East Asian Model," *The Australian Journal of Chinese Affairs*, No. 33, 1995, p. 52) argue that "at least some of the old 'mass organizations' and new associations are gradually coming under the influence of, and beginning to speak on behalf of, their designated constituencies. Some of them are, in short, shifting gradually but perceptibly in a 'societal corporatist' direction."

31   For examples, see K. Lieberthal and M. Oksenberg, *Policy Making in China*, in K. Lieberthal and D. Lampton (eds), *Bureaucracy, Politics, and Decision Making in Post-Mao China*, Berkeley, CA: University of California Press, 1992; and D. Goodman and G. Segal (eds), *China Deconstructs: Politics, Trade and Regionalism*, London: Routledge, 1994.

32   G. White, J. Howell, and Shang Xiaoyuan, *In Search of Civil Society: Market Reform and Social Change in Contemporary China*, Oxford: Clarendon Press, 1996, pp. 211–15.

33   A. Cawson, *Corporatism and Political Theory*, Oxford: Basil Blackwell, 1988, p. 19.

34   C. Johnson, *MITI and the Japanese Miracle: The Growth of Industrial Policy 1925–1975*, Stanford, CA: Stanford University Press, 1982; A. Amsden, *Asia's Next Giant: South Korea and Late Industrialization*, Oxford: Oxford University Press, 1989; and

R. Wade, *Governing the Market: Economic Theory and the Role of Government in East Asian Industrialization*, Princeton, NJ: Princeton University Press, 1990.

35 S. Maxfield and B. Ross Schneider (eds), *Business and the State in Developing Countries*, Ithaca, NY: Cornell University Press, 1997.

36 M. Blecher and V. Shue, *Tethered Deer: Government and Economy in a Chinese County*, Stanford, CA: Stanford University Press, 1996.

37 M. Blecher, "Developmental State, Entrepreneurial State: The Political Economy of Socialist Reform in Xinju Municipality and Guanghan County," in G. White (ed.), *The Chinese State in the Era of Economic Reform: The Road to Crisis*, London: Macmillan, 1991, pp. 265–91.

38 J. Duckett, *The Entrepreneurial State in China: Real Estate and Commerce Departments in Reform Era Tianjin*, London: Routledge, 1998.

39 J. Howell, *China Opens its Doors: The Politics of Economic Transition*, Boulder, CO: Lynne Rienner, 1993.

40 Ma Shu-yun, "The State, Foreign Capital and Privatization in China," *The Journal of Communist Studies and Transition Politics*, 15 (3), pp. 54–79.

41 D. Wank, *Commodifying Communism: Business, Trust, and Politics in a Chinese City*, New York: Cambridge University Press, 1999.

42 M. Pearson, *China's New Business Elite: The Political Consequences of Economic Reform*, Berkeley, CA: University of California Press, 1997.

43 W. Niskanen, *Bureaucracy: Servant or Master*, London: Institute of Economic Affairs, 1973.

44 M. Woo-Cummings, "Introduction: Chalmers Johnson and the Politics of Nationalism and Development," in M. Woo-Cummings (ed.), *The Developmental State*, Ithaca, NY: Cornell University Press, 1999, pp. 1–31.

45 Maxfield and Schneider, *Business and the State in Developing Countries*, op. cit.

46 This ideal type refers to a system of intermediary organizations that are relatively independent of the state, firms, and families, which are capable of collective action in promoting their own interests, which do not seek to replace the state (so political parties are excluded), and which act in a civil fashion. P. Schmitter, "Ten Propositions Concerning Civil Society and the Consolidation of Democracy," unpublished paper, Stanford University, 1996.

47 J. Hall, "In Search of Civil Society," in J. Hall (ed.), *Civil Society: Theory, History and Comparison*, Cambridge: Polity Press, 1995, pp. 1–31; J. Keane, *Democracy and Civil Society*, London: Verso, 1988; C. Hann, "Introduction: Political Society and Civil Anthropology," in C. Hann and E. Dunn (eds), *Civil Society: Challenging Western Models*, London: Routledge, 1996, pp. 1–26; A. Arato and J. Cohen, *Civil Society and Political Theory*, Cambridge, MA: MIT Press, 1992; and A. Seligman, *The Idea of Civil Society: Resolving the Battle of Private Interests and the Common Good*, New York: Free Press, 1992.

48 J. Keane (ed.), *Civil Society and the State: New European Perspectives*, London: Verso, 1988; R. Miller (ed.), *The Development of Civil Society in Communist Systems*, St Leonards, NSW: Allen and Unwin, 1992; and Z. Rau (ed.), *The Re-emergence of Civil Society in Eastern Europe and the Soviet Union*, Boulder, CO: Westview Press, 1991.

49 T. Gold, "The Resurgence of Civil Society in China," *Journal of Democracy*, Vol. 1, No. 1, 1990, pp. 18–31; D. Solinger, *China's Transients and the State: a Form of Civil Society?* Hong Kong: Institute of Asian-Pacific Studies, Chinese University of Hong Kong, 1991; M. Bonnin and Y. Chevrier, "The Intellectual and the State: Social Dynamics of Intellectual Autonomy during the Post-Mao Era," *China Quarterly* No. 127, 1991, pp. 569–93; and G. White, "Prospects for Civil Society in China: A Case Study of Xiaoshan City," *The Australian Journal of Chinese Affairs*, No. 29, 1993, pp. 63–87.

50 G. White, "Prospects for Civil Society in China," op. cit.

51   There are, of course, other studies that interpret the concept of civil society with a greater emphasis on its integrative dimension. For instance, see "Symposium on 'Public Sphere/Civil Society' in China?," *Modern China,* Vol. 19, No. 2, April 1993. However, most of these works focus on historical episodes during the late Qing or Republican period. In most of the studies of the contemporary period, the issue of societal autonomy seems to be the major concern.

52   Walder's study of the workers' protest in Beijing during the summer of 1989 is illustrative. He demonstrates that the unprecedented autonomous workers' movement was very much a result of the cautious non-committal attitudes of the factory cadres, who were uncertain of the outcome of the power struggle at the top at that moment. As soon as martial law was imposed, these organized processions were immediately suppressed. A. Walder, "Urban Industrial Workers: Some Observations on the 1980s," in A. Rosenbaum (ed.), *State and Society in China: The Consequences of Reform,* Boulder, CO: Westview Press, 1992, pp. 103–20.

53   Whitehead argues that the entitlement to political rights without the corresponding constraint of the norms of civil society is likely to produce multiple variants of incivility which paradoxically endanger the development of civil society. L. Whitehead, "Bowling in the Bronx: The Uncivil Interstices between Civil and Political Society," in R. Fine and Shirin Rai (eds), *Civil Society: Democratic Perspectives,* London: Frank Cass, 1997, pp. 94–114.

54   D. Solinger, "Urban Entrepreneurs and the State: the Merger of State and Society," in A. Rosenbaum (ed.), *State and Society in China: The Consequences of Reform,* op. cit., pp. 121–41.

55   The debate on the "second economy" approach as a viable strategy of democratization in Hungary is relevant here. The idea of "bourgeois first, citizen second" was advocated by scholars such as Ivan Szelenyi, who believe that the second economy could breed autonomy in the political sphere too. But this idea of "autonomy breeds autonomy" is under attack from others who recognize the entrenched connection of interests between the state and the second economy. I. Szelenyi, *Socialist Entrepreneurs: Embourgeoisement in Rural Hungary,* Madison, WI: University of Wisconsin Press, 1988; C. Hann, "Second Economy and Civil Society," and N. Swain, "Small Cooperatives and Economic Work Partnership in the Computing Industries: Exception that Proves the Rule," *Journal of Communist Studies,* Vol. 6, No. 2, 1990, pp. 21–44 and 85–109, respectively.

56   V. Nee, "A Theory of Market Transition: From Redistributive to Markets in State Socialism," *American Sociological Review,* Vol. 54, October 1989, p. 663.

57   Ibid., p. 668.

58   V. Nee, "Social Inequalities in Reforming State Socialism: Between Redistribution and Markets in China," *American Sociological Review,* Vol. 56, June 1991, pp. 267–82.

59   A common non-economic activity of TVEs is keeping redundant labor. This is requested by local government, which always has the policy objective of providing full employment in the community. V. Nee and Su Sijin, "Institutional Change and Economic Growth in China: The View from the Villages," *Journal of Asian Studies,* Vol. 49, No. 1, February 1990, pp. 3–25. See also Qian Ying, "Defang Zhengfu Jingji Xingwei Guifanhua Wenti Yanjiu" (Research on the Problem of Routinization of the Economic Behavior of Local Government), *Nongcun Jingji Shehui (Rural Economy and Society),* No. 4, 1989, pp. 28–31.

60   V. Nee, "Organizational Dynamics of Market Transition: Hybrid Forms, Property Rights, and Mixed Economy in China," *Administrative Science Quarterly,* No. 37, 1992, p. 23. The idea is further elaborated in V. Nee and Sijin Su, "Institutions, Social Ties, and Commitment in China's Corporatist Transformation," Russell Sage Foundation and Cornell University, Working Paper No. 64, 1994.

61   V. Nee, "Organizational Dynamics of Market Transition," op. cit., p. 24.

62 I. Szelenyi and E. Kostello, "The Market Transition Debate: Toward a Synthesis?," *American Journal of Sociology*, Vol. 101, No. 4, January 1996, p. 1086.

63 Nan Lin, "Local Market Socialism: Local Corporatism in Action in Rural China," *Theory and Society*, No. 24, 1995, p. 305.

64 D. Stark, "Recombinant Property in East European Capitalism," *American Journal of Sociology*, Vol. 101, No. 4, January 1996, pp. 993–1027; A. Walder, "Local Governments as Industrial Firms: An Organizational Analysis of China's Transitional Economy," *American Journal of Sociology*, Vol. 101, No. 2, September 1995, pp. 263–301; M. Boisot and J. Child, "The Iron Law of Fiefs: Bureaucratic Failure and the Problem of Governance in the Chinese Economic Reforms," *Administrative Science Quarterly*, No. 33, 1988, pp. 507–27; and M. Boisot and J. Child, "From Fiefs to Clans and Network Capitalism: Explaining China's Emerging Economic Order," *Administrative Science Quarterly*, No. 41, 1996, pp. 600–28.

65 D. Stark, "Recombinant Property in East European Capitalism," op. cit., and N. Fligstein, "The Economic Sociology of the Transitions from Socialism," *American Journal of Sociology*, Vol. 101, No. 4, January 1996, pp. 1074–81.

66 W. Parish and E. Michelson, "Politics and Markets: Dual Transformations," and A. Walder, "Markets and Inequality in Transitional Economics: Toward Testable Theories," *American Journal of Sociology*, Vol. 101, No. 4, January 1996, pp. 1042–59 and 1060–73 respectively.

67 J. Oi, *Rural China Takes Off*, Berkeley, CA: University of California Press, 1999.

68 J. Oi, "Fiscal Reform and the Economic Foundations of Local State Corporatism in China," *World Politics*, No. 45, October 1992, pp. 100–1.

69 Ibid.

70 K. Xiao Zhou, *How the Farmers Changed China*, op. cit.

71 J. Oi, "The Role of the Local State in China's Transitional Economy," *China Quarterly*, No. 144, December 1995, p. 1145.

72 Ibid., p. 1136.

73 M. Blecher, "Developmental State, Entrepreneurial State: The Political Economy of Socialist Reform in Xinju Municipality and Guanghan County," in G. White (ed.), *The Chinese State in the Era of Economic Reform: The Road to Crisis*, London: Macmillan, 1991, pp. 265–91.

74 For instance, S. Young, *Private Business and Economic Reform in China*, op. cit.: M. E. Sharpe, an East Gate Book, 1995; O. Odgaard, "Entrepreneurs and Elite Formation in Rural China," *Australian Journal of Chinese Affairs*, No. 28, July 1992, pp. 89–108; O. Brunn, *Business and Bureaucracy in a Chinese City: an Ethnography of Private Business Households in Contemporary China*, Berkeley, CA: Institute of East Asian Studies, University of California, 1993; Zhongguo Qiyejia Tiaocha Xitong (Chinese Entrepreneurs Research Group), "Zhongguo Qiyejia Xianzhuang Fenxi ji Qiyejia tui Qiye Jingying Huanjing di Pingjia" (Analysis of the Present Conditions of Chinese Entrepreneurs and Their Assessment of the Business Environment), *Guanli Shejie* (*Management World*), No. 6, December 1993, pp. 128–9; Zhongguo Jingji Tizhi Gaige Yanjiuzuo Shehui Yanjiuzhi Shehui Yulun Tiaochazhi (Social Research Division and Social Opinion Research Division of China's Economic Reform Research Institute), *Gaige de Shehui Xinli Bianqian yu Xuanze* (*The Social Psychology of Reform: Change and Choice*), Chengdu: Sichuan Renmin Chubanshe, 1988, pp. 138–76; M. Pearson, *China's New Business Elite*, op. cit. For managers in the rural collective sector, a few exploratory works have been carried out. For example, D. Goodman, "New Economic Elites," in R. Benewick and P. Wingrove (eds), *China in the 1990*, London: Macmillan, 1995, pp. 132–44; and Zhang Gang, "Government Intervention vs. Marketization in China's Rural Industries: The Role of Local Governments," *China Information*, Vol. VIII, No. 1/2, 1993, pp. 45–73.

75 J. Burnham, *The Managerial Revolution*, Westport, CT: Greenwood Press, 1941, p. 82.

76 Ibid., pp. 102–3.

77 P. Sorokin, "What is a Social Class?" in R. Bendix and S. Lipset (eds), *Class, Status and Power*, Glencoe, IL: Free Press, 1953.

78 T. Parsons and N. Smesler, *Economy and Society*, London: Routledge & Kegan Paul, 1947.

79 For a challenge to this argument, see M. Zeitin, "Corporate Ownership and Control: The Large Corporation and the Capitalist Class," *American Journal of Sociology*, Vol. 79, No. 5, 1974, pp. 1073–119.

80 J. Scott, *Seeing Like a State: How Certain Schemes to Improve the Human Condition Have Failed*, New Haven, CT: Yale University Press, 1998, p. 49.

81 R. Bates, *Beyond the Miracle of the Market: The Political Economy of Agrarian Development in Kenya*, Cambridge: Cambridge University Press, 1989.

82 P. Evans, *Embedded Autonomy: States and Industrial Transformation*, Princeton, NJ: Princeton University Press, 1995.

83 J. Migdal, "The State in Society," op. cit.

84 J. Migdal, *State in Society: Studying how States and Societies Transform and Constitute One Another*, New York: Cambridge University Press, 2001, p. 57.

85 The unevenness of state strength among different policy areas is evident. For example, the implementation of population policy in China. Birth control measures in urban China have been implemented with reasonable success, whereas the situation in the countryside is far from satisfactory.

86 J. Migdal, "The State in Society," op. cit.

87 See W. Powell and P. Dimaggio (eds), *The New Institutionalism in Organizational Analysis*, Chicago: Chicago University Press, 1991; and L. Zucker (ed.), *Institutional Patterns and Organizations: Culture and Environment*, Cambridge, MA: Ballinger, 1988.

88 K. Thelen and S. Steinmo, "Historical Institutionalism in Comparative Politics," in S. Steinmo, K. Thelen, and F. Longstreth (eds), *Structuring Politics: Historical Institutionalism in Comparative Analysis*, Cambridge: Cambridge University Press, 1994, pp. 1–32.

89 For instance, a parliamentary system can produce completely different patterns of executive-legislature relations in different contexts. The difference between the Italian and the British system is an illustration.

90 For a discussion of the contrast between this version of institutionalism and other versions, see P. Hall and R. Taylor, "Political Science and the Three New Institutionalisms," *Political Studies*, XLIV, 1996, pp. 936–57.

91 R. Yin, *Case Study Research: Design and Methods*, Beverly Hills, CA: Sage Publications, 1984, p. 23.

92 H. Eckstein, "Case Study and Theory in Political Science," in F. Greenstein and N. Polsby (eds), *Handbook of Political Science*, Vol. 7: *Strategies of Inquiry*, Reading, MA: Addison-Wesley, 1975, pp. 79–137; and C. Ragin and H. Becker (eds), *What is a Case? Exploring the Foundations of Social Inquiry*, New York: Cambridge University Press, 1992.

93 There are at least three major patterns of TVE development in rural China. They can be loosely termed the Zhujiang model, the Sunan model, and the Wenzhou model. The first is characterized by the dominant role of foreign investment and is mostly found in the Pearl River delta in southern China, Fujian province and other coastal areas. The Sunan model depicts a different pattern in which the collective sector remains the backbone of the local economy and the local state plays a dominant role in its nurturing and development. In a nutshell, the process is very much community oriented. The concept was originally generalized from the experience of the southern part of the Jiangsu province. Lastly, the

Wenzhou model represents a pattern characterized by the dominance of private initiatives. Private ownership is the key foundation of the rural economy of the south-eastern part of Zhejiang province and a more mature market mechanism is in place there. For a review of these different patterns of rural development, see Zhou Yimiao and Zhang Yulin (eds), *Zhongguo Chengxiang Xietiao Fazhan Yanjiu* (Research on the Rural–Urban Coordinated Development in China), Hong Kong: Oxford University Press, 1994.

94 Calculated from data available in *Zhongguo Xiangzhen Qiye Nianjian* (*ZXQN*) (*China's Rural Enterprise Yearbook*), 1992: p. 136, 1993: p. 144, 1994: pp. 182–3 and 1995: p. 94.

95 *Xiangzhen Qiye* (*Rural Enterprise*) (Zibo), No. 1, June 1995, pp. 43–4.

96 Statistically, it is shown that the collective sector is in most cases still the dominant component of the local economy. The 1992 national figures show that more than two-thirds of total rural output value and about one-half of non-farm employment in rural China are contributed by the collective sector – TVEs, which are administered by local bureaucracy. The regional breakdowns also show a similar pattern. In terms of employment contribution, in only thirteen out of the total of thirty provinces does the private sector account for a dominant share of the employment, and, in terms of total output value, the number of provinces in which the contribution of the private sector is dominant is only five. *ZXQN* 1992, pp. 133 and 140–4.

2 Transformation in a historical perspective

1 D. Yang, *Calamity and Reform in China: State, Rural Society, and Institutional Change since the Great Leap Famine*, Stanford, CA: Stanford University Press, 1996, pp. 21–67.

2 C. Riskin, *China's Political Economy: The Quest for Development Since 1949*, Oxford: Oxford University Press, 1988, pp. 123–4.

3 S. Aziz, *Rural Development: Learning From China*, London: Macmillan, 1978, pp. 46–61.

4 R. Ash, "The Evolution of Agricultural Policy," *China Quarterly: Special Issue on Food and Agriculture in China During the Post-Mao Era*, No. 116, December 1988, pp. 529–55.

5 *Zhongguo Nongye Nianjian* (*China's Agricultural Yearbook*), 1989, Beijing: Zhongguo Nongye Chubanshe, p. 121.

6 K. Zhou, *How the Farmers Changed China: Power of the People*, Boulder, CO: Westview Press, 1996, p. 57. Daniel Kelliher shares a similar view on the spontaneity of Chinese peasants on this issue. D. Kelliher, *Peasant Power in China*, New Haven, CT: Yale University Press, 1992.

7 Y. Y. Kueh, "China's Second Land Reform," *China Quarterly*, No. 101, March 1985, p. 125.

8 "Zhonggong Zhongyang Guanyu Yijiubasinian Nongcun Gongzuo de Tongzhi" (Notice of the Central Committee Concerning Rural Work in 1984), in Guojia Gongshang Xingzheng Guanliju Xinxi Zhongxin (Information Center of the Bureau of Industry and Commerce) (ed.), *Geti Laodongzhe Shouce* (*Individual Laborers' Handbook*), Beijing: Beijing Ribao Chubanshe and Gongshang Chubanshe, 1984, pp. 188–201.

9 A. R. Khan, "The Responsibility System and Institutional Change," in K. Griffin (ed.), *Institutional Reform and Economic Development in the Chinese Countryside*, London: Macmillan, 1984, p. 86.

10 Du Haiyan, "Causes of Rapid Rural Industrial Development," in Byrd and Lin, *China's Rural Industry*, op. cit., pp. 47–62.

11 *Zhongguo Tongji Nianjian*, 1995, p. 224.

12 K. Walker, "Trends in Crop Production, 1978–86," *China Quarterly*, No. 116, December 1988, pp. 592–3.

13 G. White, *Riding the Tiger: The Politics of Economic Reform in Post-Mao China*, London: Macmillan, 1993, p. 97.

14 S. Ho, *Rural China in Transition: Non-agricultural Development in Rural Jiangsu, 1978–1990*, Oxford: Clarendon Press, 1994, p. 210.

15 Song Lina and Du He, "The Role of Township Governments in Rural Industrialization," in Byrd and Lin, *China's Rural Industry*, op. cit., pp. 339–57).

16 M. Blecher and V. Shue, *Tethered Deer: Government and Economy in a Chinese County*, Stanford, CA: Stanford University Press, 1996, pp. 71–2.

17 A. R. Khan, "The Responsibility System and Institutional Change," op. cit., p. 77.

18 Calculated from the data in *Zhongguo Tongji Zhaiyao (ZTZ) (China's Statistical Digest)*, 1993, p. 53.

19 Ibid., p. 55.

20 Ibid., p. 54.

21 M. Blecher and V. Shue, *Tethered Deer*, op. cit., p. 205.

22 R. Kojima, "Agricultural Organization: New Forms, New Contradictions," *China Quarterly*, No. 116, December 1988, p. 720.

23 See Qin Guangwu, "Ganqun Quanxi Beiwanlu"(Memorandum of the Relationship Between Cadres and the Masses) *Nongcun Gongzuo Tongxun (Rural Work Newsletter)*, No. 11, 1988, pp. 30–1. See also, Fan Fang, "Xin di Siluan Xianxiang Renxin Sizou Zhaungkuang" (*Phenomenon of Four New Sources of Chaos and Situation of Desertion*) *Nongcun Gongzuo Tongxun* (Rural Work Newsletter), No. 5, May 1993, pp. 38–9; and Yang Zhongyi, "Qianxi Cunganbu di Bazhong Xintai" (Analysis of Eight Kinds of Mentality of Village Cadres) *Xiangzhen Luntan* (Township Forum), No. 8, August 1991, p. 33.

24 A. Park, S. Rozelle, C. Wong and Changqing Ren, "Distributional Consequences of Reforming Local Public Finance in China," *China Quarterly*, No. 147, September 1996, pp. 751–78.

25 L. West, "Provision of Public Services in Rural China," in C. Wong (ed.), *Financing Local Government in the People's Republic of China*, Oxford: Oxford University Press, 1997, pp. 213–82.

26 Lianjiang Li and K. O'Brien, "Villagers and Popular Resistance in Contemporary China," *Modern China*, Vol. 22, No. 1, January 1996, pp. 28–61; Chen Baisong and Zhang Bun, "Nongmin Fudan Xianzhuang, Chengyin and Duice" (The Development, Causes and Remedies for the Problem of Peasants' Burden) *Nongye Jingji Wenti* (*Problems of Agricultural Economy*), No. 3, March 1993, pp. 37–41; and Li Qin, "Dui Woguo Nongmin Fudan Xianzhuang di Fenxi" (The Analysis of the Peasants' Burden in China), *Zhongguo Nongcun Jingji* (*Chinese Rural Economy*), No. 8, August 1992, pp. 47–51.

27 *ZTZ*, 1993, p. 50. Figures are in current price.

28 *ZTZ*, 1994, p. 50.

29 *ZGTN*, 1995, p. 575.

30 One *mu* is equivalent to one-sixteenth of a hectare.

31 Du Haiyan, "Causes of Rapid Rural Industrial Development," in Byrd and Lin (1990: 53).

32 Song Lina and Du He, "The Role of Township Governments in Rural Industrialization," in Byrd and Lin (1990: 339–57); and Wang Zhonghui, "Township Public Finance and its Impact on the Financial Burden of Rural Enterprises and Peasants in Mainland China," *Issues & Studies*, No. 31, August 1995, pp. 103–21.

33 *ZGTN*, 1993, p. 54.

34 *ZXQN*, 1992, Beijing: Nongye Chubanshe, p. 133.

35 *ZGTN*, 1995, pp. 329 and 364.
36 Dou Xianjun, "Guanyu Nongcun Shengyu Laodongli Zhuanyi Wenti di Yanjiu," (Study on the Issue of Transferring Surplus Rural Labor) *Nongye Jingji Wenti (Problems of Agricultural Economy)*, No. 172, April 1994, pp. 10–14; and "Jiuxiniandai Nongcun Gaige di Zhuti: Fang Nongyebu Nongcun Jingji Yanjiu Zhongxin Fuzhuren Du Ying,"(Theme of the Rural Reform in the 1990s: Interview with Du Ying, Deputy Director of the Rural Economy Research Center of the Ministry of Agriculture) *Zhongguo Nongcun Jingji* (Chinese Rural Economy), No. 109, January 1994, pp. 3–8. On the phenomenon of rural–urban migration in present-day China, see D. Solinger, *China's Transients and the State: A Form of Civil Society*, Hong Kong: Hong Kong Institute of Asia-Pacific Studies, Chinese University of Hong Kong, 1991.
37 C. Wong, C. Heady and Wing T. Woo, *Fiscal Management and Economic Reform in the People's Republic of China*, Hong Kong: Oxford University Press, 1995, p. 108.
38 Ibid., pp. 59 and 200–1.
39 S. Ho, *The Asian Experience in Rural Non-Agricultural Development and Its Relevance for China*, World Bank Staff Working Papers, No. 75, Washington, DC: The International Bank for Reconstruction and Development/The World Bank, 1986, pp. 42–3.
40 W. Byrd and Lin Qingsong, "China's Rural Industry: an Introduction," in Byrd and Lin, *China's Rural Industry*, op. cit., p. 9.
41 C. Riskin, "Political Conflict and Rural Industrialization in China," *World Development*, Vol. 6, No. 5, 1978, pp. 681–92.
42 In this way, scarce resources could be preserved for the development of heavy industries – the top priority at that time. S. Ho, *Rural China in Transition*, op. cit., pp. 14–15.
43 According to Griffin and Griffin, wastage and inefficiency were evident among these industries. K. Griffin and K. Griffin, "Commune- and Brigade Run Enterprises in Rural China," in K. Griffin (ed.), *Institutional Reform and Economic Development in the Chinese Countryside*, London: Macmillan, 1984.
44 C. Wong, "Rural Industrialization in the People's Republic of China: Lessons from the Cultural Revolution Decade" in Joint Committee, *China Under the Four Modernization*, cited in S. Ho, *The Asian Experience in Rural Non-Agricultural Development and Its Relevance for China*, op. cit., p. 42.
45 K. Griffin and K. Griffin, "Commune- and Brigade Run Enterprises in Rural China: An Overview," op. cit., pp. 210–11.
46 W. Skinner, "Marketing and Social Structure in Rural China," *Journal of Asian Studies*, Vol. 24, No. 1, 1964, pp. 3–24; Vol. 24, No. 2, 1964, pp. 195–228; and Vol. 24, No. 3, 1965, pp. 363–99.
47 A. Donnithorne, "China's Cellular Economy: Some Economic Trends Since the Cultural Revolution," *China Quarterly* No. 52, October/December 1972, p. 612.
48 Ibid., pp. 618–19.
49 Ibid., p. 274.
50 *ZGTN*, 1995, p. 145.
51 E. Tsang, "The Changing Role of Supply and Marketing Co-operatives in China," *Small Enterprise Development*, Vol. 5, No. 3, September 1994, pp. 35–42.
52 According to Kornai, shortage is an inherent feature of the socialist economy as growth is pursued at a forced rate, i.e. each industrial firm is instructed by its superior that it must grow. As a result of this expansive drive and hunger for investment, scarcity is inevitable. J. Kornai, *The Economics of Shortage*, Amsterdam: North Holland Publishing Company, 1980, two volumes.
53 Ibid., pp. 37 and 39.
54 *ZGTN*, 1995, p. 497.

55   D. Solinger, *Chinese Business Under Socialism: The Politics of Domestic Commerce, 1949–1980*, Berkeley, CA: University of California Press, 1984, Chapters 1 and 2.

56   Ibid., pp. 16–31.

57   *ZGTN*, 1995, p. 257.

58   D. Kelliher, "Chinese Communist Political Theory and the Rediscovery of the Peasantry," *Modern China*, Vol. 20, No. 4, December 1994, pp. 387–415.

59   For a discussion of the contrast between state cadres and local cadres, see D. Barnett, *Cadres, Bureaucracy, and Political Power in Communist China*, New York: Columbia University Press, 1967, pp. 38–41; and S. H. Potter and J. Porter, *China's Peasants: The Anthropology of a Revolution*, New York: Cambridge University Press, 1990, Chapter 13.

60   An excellent account of how such moral embeddedness can be an important ingredient for the effective exercise of political authority is, of course, R. Madsen, *Morality and Power in a Chinese Village*, Berkeley, CA: University of California Press, 1984. Huang Shu-min's anthropological work also provides an interesting account of how the respect for local morality is related to communist rule in the countryside. Huang Shu-min, *The Spiral Road: Change in a Chinese Village Through the Eyes of a Communist Party Leader*, Boulder, CO: Westview Press, 1989.

61   V. Nee, "Peasant Entrepreneurship and the Politics of Regulation in China," in V. Nee and D. Stark (eds), *Remaking the Economic Institutions of Socialism: China and Eastern Europe*, Stanford, CA: Stanford University Press, 1989, pp. 174–5.

62   D. Zweig, *Agrarian Radicalism in China, 1968–1981*, Cambridge, MA: Harvard University Press, 1989, p. 95.

63   Ibid., p. 97.

64   *Zibo Shizhi* (*Zibo Gazette*), 1995, Beijing: Zhonghua Shuju, pp. 4–5.

65   Zhonggong Zibo Shiwei Lishi Ziliao Zhengji Yanjiu Weiyuanhui (Chinese Communist Party Zibo Branch Party History Research Committee), *Zhonggong Zibo Lishi Dashiqi* (*Major Events of Zibo History*), Beijing: Zhonggong Dangshi Chubanshe, 1997, p. 39.

66   Ibid., p. 162.

67   Ibid., p. 628.

68   *ZTN* (*Zibo Statistical Yearbook*), 2001, p. 21.

69   *Zibo Shizhi*, p. 1323.

70   *Zibo Nianjian Erlinglingyi* (*Zibo Yearbook*), 2001, Jinan: Qilu Chubanshe, p. 23.

71   *Zibo Shizhi*, pp. 796–9.

72   *Zhonggong Zibo Lishi Dashiqi*, p. 213.

73   *Zibo Shizhi*, pp. 1457–9.

74   Ibid., p. 537.

75   Ibid., p. 678.

76   It does not, however, deny the progress made in education, public health, and, arguably, social order (contrasted with the pre-1949 period of civil war and turbulence) in the PRC. These improvements are, in many ways, contributing to the general development of the economy.

77   A. Watson, C. Findlay, and Du Juntang, "Who Won the 'Wool War?': A Case Study of Rural Product Marketing in China," *China Quarterly*, No. 11, June 1989, p. 236.

78   Hu Erhu and Zie Zhiqiang (eds), *Zhongguo Gongshangju, Xiangzhen Qiyeju Juzhang Tanjianli Tongyi Dashichang Yu Guifan Shichang Xingwei* (Chiefs of Management Bureau of Industry and Commerce and Management Bureau of Rural Enterprise in China Commenting on the Development of Unified Market and the Regulation of Market Behavior), Beijing: Dongfang Chubanshe, 1994, pp. 107–11 and 307–9.

79   Trade barriers were set up not only between provinces but also between different levels of government within the same region, in order to prevent the outflow of

valuable commodities such as wool, cotton and silk. In some cases, militias were even mobilized. A. Watson *et al.*, "Who Won the 'Wool War?'": a Case Study of Rural Product Marketing in China," op. cit.

3 The rise of enterprise managers in rural China

1 *Zhongguo Xiangzhen Qiyebao (ZGXZQYB)*, 10/12/1998, p. 1.
2 For instance, "Zhao Ziyang Tongzhi Yu Zuijia Nongmin Qiyejia Zuotan" (Zhao Ziyang Met the Best Peasant Entrepreneurs), *ZGXZQYB*, 9/14/1987, p. 1, "Rural Entrepreneurs Write a Letter to Deng," *FBIS* (China), No. 194, 1992, pp. 40–2; and "Li Peng Congratulates Inventor-Entrepreneurs," *FBIS* (China), No. 91, 1994, p. 27.
3 Here, this author agrees with the definition of elites suggested by Mills that power elites are those who are in the positions which enable them to transcend the ordinary environments of ordinary men and women; thus they are in positions to make decisions having major consequences. However, this author does not subscribe to his view on the homogeneity of the elites. C. Wright Mills, *The Power Elites*, New York: Oxford University Press, 1956, pp. 3–4.
4 Interview with enterprise manager.
5 See, for example, P. Drucker, *The Practice of Management*, Melbourne: William Heinemann, 1955, pp. 1–18 and 301–26.
6 J. Schumpeter, *Capitalism, Socialism and Democracy*, London: Unwin University Books, 1943, p. 132.
7 J. Berliner, "Entrepreneurship in the Soviet Period: An Overview," in G. Guroff and F. Carstensen (eds), *Entrepreneurship in Imperial Russia and the Soviet Union*, Princeton, NJ: Princeton University Press, 1983, pp. 194–5.
8 B. Richard, *Industrial Society in Communist China*, New York: Vintage Books, 1969, pp. 231–43.
9 D. Hay *et al.*, *Economic Reform and State-Owned Enterprise in China, 1979–1987*, Oxford: Clarendon Press, 1994, Chapter 3.
10 W. Brus and K. Laski, *From Marx to the Market: Socialism in Search of an Economic System*, Oxford: Clarendon Press, 1989, pp. 132–49.
11 Information provided by the Tangshan ETC.
12 For the debate, see, for example, R. Hebert and A. Link, *The Entrepreneur: Mainstream Views and Radical Critiques*, New York: Praeger, 1982.
13 Statistics provided by the Tangshan ETC.
14 Interview with enterprise manager.
15 Hong Yung Lee, *From Revolutionary Cadres to Party Technocrats in Socialist China*, Berkeley, CA: University of California Press, 1991, pp. 356–64, and K. W. Chow, "The Politics of Performance Appraisal," in M. K. Mill and S. S. Nagel (eds), *Public Administration in China*, Westport, CT: Greenwood Press, 1993, pp. 105–29.
16 Interview with official of county REA.
17 M. Edin, *Market Forces and Communist Power: Local Political Institutions and Economic Development in China*, Stockholm: Uppsala University, 2000, pp. 130–1.
18 It is interesting to realize that even in the collective farms in the Soviet Union – the socialist *sovkhozy* and *kolkhozy* in the villages in the 1930s – the farm managers were also under immense pressure in performing the entrepreneurial role. The risk involved in bad performance (impact on future career and personal income) propelled these managers to try to improve the efficiency of their farms by experimenting with different innovations. Some even went further in resisting direct instructions from their superiors that they thought were harmful to their farms. D. Roy and B. A. Laird, "The Soviet Farm Manager as an Entrepreneur," in G. Guroff and F. Carstensen (eds), *Entrepreneurship in Imperial Russia and the Soviet Union*, op. cit., pp. 259–83.

19   A. Rona-Tas, "The First Shall be Last? Entrepreneurship and Communist Cadres in the Transition from Socialism," *American Journal of Sociology*, Vol. 100, No. 1, July 1994, pp. 40–69.

20   In this chapter, political capital refers to the occupation of leading positions in local Party-state institutions.

21   V. Nee, "A Theory of Market Transition: From Redistribution to Markets in State Socialism," *American Sociological Review*, No. 56, 1989, p. 668.

22   I. Szelenyi, *Socialist Entrepreneurs: Embourgeoisement in Rural Hungary*, Madison, WI: University of Wisconsin Press, 1988, p. 18.

23   A. Rona-Tas, "The First Shall be Last?" op. cit., pp. 44–5. See also I. Szelenyi and S. Szelenyi, "Circulation or Reproduction of Elites During the Postcommunist Transformation of Eastern Europe," *Theory and Society*, No. 24, 1995, pp. 615–38.

24   In the countryside of Shandong, 95 percent of those who are involved in agricultural production have been educated only to junior high level or below, whereas among those who work in the Party-state and mass organizations, about two-thirds are educated to a higher level. *Shandong Tongji Nianjian* (*Statistical Yearbook of Shandong*), 1994, Beijing: Zhongguo Tongji Chubanshe, p. 35.

25   In addition to the *hukou* system, life chances for most peasants are confined to the local community. Few options available for peasants to get out of the local village: finding a job in the city, going to university, or joining the army. The first two are extremely difficult, though the third choice is popular among peasants. Huang Shuming, *The Spiral Road: Change in a Chinese Village Through the Eyes of a Communist Party Leader*, Boulder, CO: Westview Press, 1989, pp. 71–3.

26   J. Oi, "Fiscal Reform and the Economic Foundations of Local State Corporatism," *World Politics*, 45, October 1992, pp. 99–126.

27   For example, D. Wank, "Private Business, Bureaucracy, and Political Alliance in a Chinese City," *Australian Journal of Chinese Affairs*, No. 33, January 1995, pp. 55–71; and C. Francis, "Reproduction of *Danwei* Institutional Features in the Context of China's Market Economy: The Case of Haidian District's High-Tech Sector," *China Quarterly*, No. 147, September 1996, pp. 839–59.

28   For a discussion on the new content of Chinese enterprise management in the reform era, see D. Brown and M. Branine, "Adaptive Personnel Management: Evidence of an Emerging Heterogeneity in China's Foreign Trade Corporations," and M. Warner, "Beyond the Iron Rice-Bowl: Comprehensive Labour Reform in State Owned Enterprises in North-East China," in D. Brown and R. Porter (eds), *Management Issues in China: Vol. I: Domestic Enterprises*, London: Routledge, 1996, pp. 191–213 and 214–36.

29   For further discussion on the difficulty for communist cadres to adjust to the new market logic, see, for example, M. Kennedy and P. Gianoplus, "Entrepreneurs and Expertise: a Cultural Encounter in the Making of Post-Communist Capitalism in Poland," *East European Politics and Societies*, Vol. 8, No. 1, Winter 1994, pp. 58–93.

30   Zhang Gang's survey on rural enterprises in Zhejiang and Sichuan provinces found that fewer than one-fifth of enterprise managers in these enterprises had previously served as township/village cadres. It is interesting to see that similar pattern can be observed among their urban counterparts. The findings of a nationwide research conducted by the Chinese Entrepreneur Research Group – a joint task force composed of experts from the State Council Research Office and State Trade and Commerce Commission – revealed that only 23 percent of managers from enterprises of various ownership in the urban sector were cadres before. The majority of them had served as technical or managerial personnel before they came to the present manager posts. The state sector, unsurprisingly, employs the highest percentage of ex-cadres, although this category accounts for only 2 percent of the total number of incumbent managers. Both findings seem

to concur with the argument that professional management skills are crucial for the appointment of enterprise managers, and political capital is hardly the sole determinant for the choice. Based on the findings of his survey on the rural private sector, Odgaard also suggests that toward the end of the 1980s a new breed of entrepreneurs was emerging, increasingly comprising younger, technically trained people, and the proportion of cadres and former cadres among entrepreneurs may be less significant than some Chinese surveys would indicate. Zhang Gang, "Government Intervention vs Marketization in China's Rural Industries: the Role of Local Governments," *China Information*, Vol. VIII, No. 1/2, 1993, p. 56; Zhongguo Qiyejia Tiaocha Xitong (Chinese Entrepreneurs Research Group), "Zhongguo Qiyejia Xianzhuang Fenxi ji Qiyejia tui Qiye Jingying Huanjing di Pingjia," (Analysis of the Present Conditions of Chinese Entrepreneurs and Their Assessment of the Business Environment), *Guanli Shejie (Management World)*, No. 6, December 1993, pp. 128–9; and O. Odgaard, "Entrepreneurs and Elite Formation in Rural China," *Australian Journal of Chinese Affairs*, No. 28, July 1992, pp. 89–90.

31 Yunxiang Yan, "The Impact of Rural Reform on Economic and Social Stratification in a Chinese Village," *Australian Journal of Chinese Affairs*, No. 27, January 1992, pp. 1–23.

32 The national data are produced from the candidates' profiles published in *ZGXZQYB*, the co-organizer of the contest, between June and July 1987. The contest was organized by the newspaper and Central People's Radio and was the first event that signified official recognition of the role played by rural entrepreneurs. Official endorsement was well reflected in the dominance of senior officials, including the Deputy Minister of Agriculture and several state councillors (the equivalent of cabinet ministers in PRC). The eventual 100 winners of the contest were even granted a reception by Premier Zhao Ziyang. A total of 132 enterprise managers were nominated and were recommended by their local authorities all over the country. Of these, fifty were identified as managers in the collective sector at subcounty level. This contest was later formalized by the Ministry of Agriculture and has been held every three years since 1991. See "Quanguo Xiangzhen Qiyejia Pingxuan Banfa" (Regulation for the Adjudication of National Rural Entrepreneur, 4/26/1991), *ZXQN*, 1992, p. 90.

33 The Zibo data are extracted from the list of outstanding entrepreneurs of the prefecture published in the *Zibo Nianjian 1995*. This appears to be first attempt of the prefectural government to include such a detailed list of outstanding enterprise managers, who won the honor on the recommendation of their administrative superiors. A total of 121 managers were mentioned, and sixty-nine came from TVEs. See *ZN*, 1995, Jinan: Qilu Shushe, pp. 381–432.

34 In this analysis, two major categories of political capital will be identified: (1) leading position in Party-state institutions at county, township, and village levels and (2) membership in the people's Congress and People's Political Consultative Conference. It is, however, important to realize the different status of these political institutions, for it is misleading to treat them as of equal political significance. Although the People's Congress is constitutionally the law-making arm of the Chinese political system, and the Political Consultative Conference is always praised as an indispensable component of the decision-making process, their roles remain consultative and symbolic in reality. The cardinal principle of Party leadership implies that the Party organization is at the center of political power at all levels and that the administrative bureaucracy comes second in this hierarchy.

35 Robert Putnam suggested three different methods of identifying the powerful: positional analysis, decisional analysis, and reputational analysis. R. Putnam,

The Comparative Study of Political Elites, Englewood Cliffs, NJ: Prentice-Hall, 1976, pp. 15–19.

36 Unfortunately, a comparison with the Zibo and national data is not possible at this point, as these two lists do not provide enough information of individuals' service records in other enterprises to make a meaningful comparison with the Tangshan data.

37 Interview with enterprise manager.

38 *Huantai Nianjian* (*Huantai Yearbook*), 1988–1991, Jinan: Qilu Shushe, 1992, p. 238.

39 Ibid., pp. 71 and 238.

40 Eighty percent of them were educated to tertiary level, whereas the Zibo data show that only 20 percent of enterprise managers have similar qualifications.

41 Zhonggong Ziboshi Shiwei Xuanchuanbu (Chinese Communist Party Zibo Committee Propaganda Department) (ed.), *Fuqiangzhilu: Laizi Ershiwuge Jingjiqiang Xiangzhen di Baogao* (*Path to Prosperity: Report from Twenty-five Prosperous Townships in Zibo*), 1993.

42 Yasheng Huang, *Inflation and Investment Controls in China: The Political Economy of Central-Local Relations During the Reform Era,* New York: Cambridge University Press, 1996, p. 116.

43 Some of them are natives of a nearby town or township, but some come from another prefecture 100 kilometers away.

44 *ZTN,* 1991, Jinning: Shadong Tongjiju, 1992, p. 45. For the distinction between state cadre and local cadre, see the previous discussion in Chapter 1.

45 Local people describe people from the same community by using the phrase, *"he tongyi koujing di shui changdadi"* (growing up with others by drinking water from the same well). Local people believe that through these locally recruited cadres, their sentiments can be felt by the administration and they can maintain unofficial contact with the local state.

46 Interviews with enterprise workers.

47 It is interesting to see that most of these managers do not generate any profit for their enterprises after the fulfillment of all financial obligations, i.e. tax and management fees. However, these zero-profit enterprises somehow manage to maintain a financial balance after these extractions (except in case 11). The managers argue, in other words, that the financial situation of the local treasury is improved by their contribution of tax and management fees even though there is no net profit.

48 Interview with township ETC official.

49 Author's interview.

50 Ibid.

51 Ibid.

52 G. Eyal, I. Szelenyi, and E. Townsley, *Making Capitalism Without Capitalists: the New Ruling Elites in Eastern Europe,* New York: Verso, 1998, p. 8.

4 Where local government still matters

1 For instance, Tu Weiming warns against premature endorsement of the application of the classical liberal view in analyzing the dynamism of the Chinese market economy. David Wank goes further and emphasizes the beneficial nature of the close association with officialdom. This view is echoed by Boisot and Child, who believe that Chinese enterprise managers are eager to accept the protection and security offered by the state. Jean Oi's notion of local state corporatism is, of course, the dominant view advocating the persistence of bureaucratic influence in the rural setting. Tu Weiming, "Introduction: Cultural Perspectives," *Daedalus,* Vol. 122, No. 2, Spring 1993, pp. X–XI; D. Wank, "Private Business,

Bureaucracy, and Political Alliance in a Chinese City," *Australian Journal of Chinese Affairs*, No. 33, January 1995, pp. 67–8; M. Boisot and J. Child, "The Iron Law of Fiefs: Bureaucratic Failure and the Problem of Governance in the Chinese Economic Reforms," *Administrative Science Quarterly*, No. 33, December 1988, pp. 521–2; and J. Oi, "Fiscal Reform and the Economic Foundations of Local State Corporatism in China," *World Politics*, Vol. 45, October 1992, pp. 99–126.

2   Huang Yasheng, "Web of Interests and Patterns of Behavior of Chinese Local Economic Bureaucracies and Enterprises during Reforms," *China Quarterly*, No. 123, September 1990, p. 447.

3   It must be stressed that the analysis does not aim to provide a comprehensive overview of the external linkages of rural enterprises. Two important external linkages, supply of bureaucratic services and foreign investment, are not included in the analysis. The exclusion of the former is due, first, to the fact the role of the local state in this respect has been well documented in previous work, especially Oi's description of local state corporatism, and, second, to the fact that, as mentioned above, the nature of this linkage excludes any analysis of the impact of market or personal alternatives on dependence on the local state, and thus it does not fit our analytical purpose here. As for linkage with foreign investors, the aim of this research is to focus on the changing state–society relationship in rural China under a specific development pattern – evolution of the economy with a dominant collective component. For the development of those communities, which are strongly influenced by foreign capital, or predominantly steered by private business initiatives, separate research is needed.

4   S. Lubman, "Introduction: The Future of Chinese Law," *China Quarterly*, No. 141, March 1995, p. 3.

5   R. Keith, *China's Struggle for the Rule of Law*, London: St. Martin's Press, 1994, p. 125.

6   D. Clarke, "The Execution of Civil Judgments in China," *China Quarterly*, No. 141, March 1995, p. 68.

7   R. Keith, *China's Struggle for the Rule of Law*, op. cit., p. 125.

8   P. Potter, *The Economic Contract Law of China: Legitimation and Contract Autonomy in the People's Republic of China*, Seattle: University of Washington Press, 1992, pp. 90–111.

9   *ZTZ*, 1994, pp. 73 and 99.

10   O. Williamson, "Transaction-Cost Economics: The Governance of Contractual Relations," *Journal of Law and Economics*, Vol. XXII, No. 2, October 1979, p. 238.

11   It is interesting to see that business via network can also be found in certain business practices in the Western world; see, for example, S. Macaulay, "Non-Contractual Relations in Business: A Preliminary Study," *American Sociological Review*, Vol. 28, No. 1, 1963, pp. 55–67; and R. Waldinger, "Immigrant Enterprise in the United States," in S. Zukin and P. Dimaggio (eds), *Structure of Capital: The Social Organization of the Economy*, New York: Cambridge University Press, 1990, pp. 395–424.

12   This may not appear a particularly high ratio, and enterprises under the capitalist system may show a similar asset composition. However, if one considers the absence of a fully fledged capital market in rural China and the fact that the majority of these enterprises are not listed on the stock market, such a ratio is extraordinary. Chen Jianbo, "Fuzhai Jingying di Hongguan Xianying" (The Macro-Effect of Enterprises Operating with Large Debts) *ZGXZQYB*, 10/28/1992, p. 3. This is a survey conducted by the State Council's Development Research Center between 1986 and 1990. The analysis is based on data from the 200 large rural enterprises from ten provinces studied during this period.

13   *ZGTN*, 1992, p. 391.

14   Chen Jianbo, "'Fuzhai Jingying' di Hongguan Xianying," op. cit.

15   Estimate based on information obtained from interviews with officials from county RCC and ABC and *Huantai Bao* (Huantai News), 3/22/1996, p. 1.

16   Estimation based on the speech made by Director of Tangshan ETC in the Annual Enterprise Work Conference of Tangshan 1996.

17   Yuan Peng, "Capital Formation in Rural Enterprises," in Christopher Findlay, Andrew Watson, and Harry Xu (eds), *Rural Enterprises in China*, London: Macmillan, 1994, p. 108; and F. Montes-Negret, "China's Credit Plan: an Overview," *Oxford Review of Economic Policy*, Vol. 11, No. 4, 1995, pp. 25–42.

18   Interview with official of county ABC.

19   Interview with official of county RCC.

20   Interview with official of county ABC.

21   Hong Yung Lee, *From Revolutionary Cadres to Party Technocrats in Socialist China*, Berkeley, CA: University of California Press, 1991, pp. 329–84.

22   Interview with official of county RCC.

23   Only one manager interviewed disclosed that he had managed to get a loan from a bank in another township. However, he did not get the loan directly. Instead, he asked a friend in that area to get the loan and then passed it to him. Nevertheless, he was charged by his friend for the service. The amount is equivalent to the bank interest payment. In other words, his interest rate was doubled.

24   It is doubtful whether there is a formal regulation forbidding such transaction. However, it is generally true that cross-regional loans are rare. As pointed out in the 200 enterprises survey mentioned above, only 2.76 percent of loans released by local banks are given to outsiders. See Chen Jianbo, "Xiangzhen Qiye Xinyong di Zhidu Jichu" (Institutional Foundation of Rural Enterprise Credit), *ZGXZQYB*, 11/8/1992, p. 3.

25   Interviews with township ETC officials.

26   Interviews with bank officials.

27   Interviews with bank officials and township ETC officials.

28   An estimate based on information from an official of county Commission for Restructuring Economy.

29   A local stock exchange did exist until the early 1990s.

30   See *ZGXZQYB*, 6/16/1989, p. 3.

31   Deng Yingtao *et al.*, *Zhongguo Nongcun Jingrong di Biange yu Fazhan 1978–1990* (*The Changes and Development of the Chinese Rural Finance 1978–1990*), Hong Kong: Oxford University Press, 1994, pp. 109–18.

32   "Jiaqiang Guanli Guifen Xingwei Cujin Nongcun Hezuo Jijinhui Wending Jiankang Fazhan: Nongyebu Nongcun Hezuo Jijinhui Bangongshi Fuzeren da Jijie wen" (Strengthening Regulation and Promoting a Healthy and Steady Development of Rural Cooperative Funds: Official of the Rural Cooperative Fund Office of the Ministry of Agriculture Answering Questions from Reporters) *Nongcun Hezuo Jingji Jingying Guanli* (*Operation and Management of a Rural Cooperative Economy*), No. 10, 1995, p. 13. See also Deng Yingtao and Xi Xiaobo, Zhongguo Nongcun Jingrong, op. cit.

33   Wen Tiejun and Zhu Shouyin, "Nongcun Hezuo Jinrong Gaige Shiyan Yanjiu Baogao" (Research Report on the Experiment of Rural Cooperative Financial Reform), *Zhongguo Nongcun Jingji* (*China's Rural Economy*), No. 1, 1994, pp. 40–6.

34   *Huantai Nianjian 1988–1991* (*Huantai Yearbook 1988–1991*), Jinan: Qilu Shushe, 1994, p. 191.

35   Nongyebu (Ministry of Agriculture), Nongcun Hezuo Jijinhui Dengji Guanli Banfa (Method of Registration and Management of Rural Cooperative Funds), 4/19/1995; *Nongcun Hezuo Jingji Jingying Guanli* (*Operation and Management of a Rural Cooperative Economy*), No. 6, 1995, pp. 6–7. A research official of the Ministry of Agriculture specializing in the area of rural financial reform informs this author

that premier Zhu Rongji, in particular, believes that the funds are a potential danger to rural financial stability. In fact, most funds were closed down by the late 1990s.

36 Wang Yanxin, "Nongcun Jinrong Tizhi Gaige di Jige Wenti" (Several Problems Concerning Reform in the Rural Financial System), *Zhongguo Nongcun Jingji* (*China's Rural Economy*), No. 5, May 1995, pp. 45–50, and "Article on the Establishment of Commercial Banks," *FBIS* (China), No. 216, 1993, pp. 40–3.

37 N. Lardy (1998), *China's Unfinished Revolution*, Washington, DC: Brookings Institution, p. 181.

38 F. Montes-Negret, "China's Credit Plan: An Overview," op. cit., p. 37. See also "Agricultural Bank Plans to be More Market Oriented," *FBIS* (China), No. 7, 1993, p. 36.

39 Zhou Xiaochuan and Zhu Li, "China's Banking System: Current Status, Perspectives on Reform," *Journal of Comparative Economics*, No. 11, 1987, pp. 399–402.

40 Interview with county bank official.

41 *Huantai Bao* (*Huantai News*), 1/31/1996, p. 2.

42 Interviews with county bank official.

43 Interview with township ETC official.

44 Interview with county bank official.

45 *Huantai Bao* (*Huantai News*), 3/20/1996, p. 2; and 5/22/1996, p. 2.

46 S. Whiting (2001), *Power and Wealth in Rural China*, New York: Cambridge University Press, p. 40.

47 C. Wong (1991), "The Maoist Model Reconsidered: Local Self-Reliance and the Financing of Rural Industrialization," in W. Joseph, C. Wong and D. Zweig (eds), *New Perspectives on the Cultural Revolution*, Cambridge, MA: Harvard University Press, p. 185.

48 *Zibo Shizhi*, p. 1476.

49 Interview with the county REA official.

50 As stated by an ETC official, usually 20–30 percent of the total amount is required as a down-payment. This is required mostly by suppliers from outside Shandong.

51 Interview with enterprise manager.

52 Interview with enterprise manager.

53 A county official disclosed that the Tangshan government had intervened on at least in one occasion to postpone a planned power cut. This was at Dongyue's request; in that instance, the petrochemical plant was already behind a schedule with a major deal and further delay would have had disastrous financial consequences.

54 Qibao Petrochemical Factory, one of the major enterprises in Qifeng township, employs sixty people in its marketing department. Altogether, the factory employs 860 people. Interview with general manager of the factory.

55 Interview with enterprise manager.

56 Interview with enterprise manager.

57 Interview with enterprise manager.

58 *Huantai Nianjian* (*Huantai Yearbook*), 1988–1991, Jinan: Qilu Shushe, 1994, pp. 309–10.

59 Ibid., p. 309.

60 Shandongsheng Huantaixian Renmin FaYuan (People's Court of Huantai county of Shandong Province), *Minshi Panjueshu 1995 No. 60* (*Civil Case Verdict No. 60, 1995*), 12/30/1995. By 1998, Li had still received nothing from the offender.

61 Interview with township official.

62 Interviews with township ETC officials.

63   G. White, J. Howell, and Shang XiaoYuan, *In Search of Civil Society: Market Reform and Social Change in Contemporary China*, Oxford: Clarendon Press, 1996; and V. Shue, "State Sprawl: the Regulatory State and Social Life in a Small Chinese City," in Deborah D., D. Davis, Richard Kraus, Barry Naughton, and Elizabeth Perry (eds.), *Urban Spaces in Contemporary China: The Potential for Autonomy and Community in Post-Mao China*, New York: Cambridge University Press, 1995, pp. 90–112.

64   Author's interview.

65   Interview with county Entrepreneurs' Association official.

66   Interview with government officials.

67   Interview with Zibo Rural Entrepreneurs' Association official.

68   Interview with enterprise manager and township ETC official.

69   Interview with township ETC official.

70   *Shandongsheng Zibo Romu Zhutie Gufen Youxian Gongxi Jianjie* (*Profile of the Shandong Zibo Romu Metal Shareholding Company*). Zibo Romu Metal Shareholding Company, 1999.

71   Interview with enterprise manager.

72   Interview with enterprise manager.

73   Interview with enterprise manager.

74   Interview with official.

5 Accommodating managers' autonomy

1   Samuel Ho, for instance, stresses the difficulty in separating local governments from local enterprises. Similarly, Song Lina and Du He emphasize the township government's influence on local enterprises. Weitzman and Xu also point out that TVEs do not have genuine autonomy in business transactions and community government has a major influence in the determination of managerial personnel and appointment. The most elaborated view is of course, the notion of local state corporatism of Jean Oi. S. Ho, *Rural China in Transition: Non-agricultural Development in Rural Jiangsu, 1978–1990*, Oxford: Clarendon Press, 1994; Song Lina and Du He, "The Role of Township Governments in Rural Industrialization," in W. Byrd and Lin Qinsong (eds), *China's Rural Industry: Structure, Development, and Reform*, Oxford: Oxford University Press, a Publication for the World Bank, 1990, pp. 342–57; J. Oi, "Fiscal Reform and the Economic Foundations of Local State Corporatism in China," *World Politics*, No. 45, October 1992, pp. 99–126; and M. Weitzman and Chenggang Xu, "Chinese Township–Village Enterprises as Vaguely Defined Cooperatives," *Journal of Comparative Economics*, No. 18, 1994, pp. 121–45.

2   Chun Chang and Yijiang Wang, "The Nature of the Township–Village Enterprise," *Journal of Comparative Economics*, No. 19, 1994, pp. 437–9.

3   Surveys found that employment, revenue, and living standards are the major motivations for local governments' enthusiasm. See, for example, the survey conducted by the study team of the World Bank in the mid-1980s. W. Byrd and A. Gelb, "Why Industrialize? The Incentive for Rural Community Governments," in W. Byrd and Lin Qingsong (eds), *China's Rural Industry*, op. cit., pp. 358–87. More details of the survey findings on this matter can be found in Dui Haiyan, *Zhongguo Nongcun Gongyehua Yanjiu* (*Study of China's Rural Industrialization*), Beijing: Zhongguo Wujia Chubanshe, 1992, pp. 111–17.

4   J. Kai-sing Kung, "The Evolution of Property Rights in Village Enterprises: The Case of Wuxi County," in J. Oi and A. Walder (eds), *Property Rights and Economic Reform in China*, Stanford, CA: Stanford University Press, 1999, pp. 95–120.

5　Ma Rong, Wang Hanshang, and Liu Shiding (eds), *Jiushi Nandai Zhongguo Xiangzhen Qiye Tiaocha (Survey of China's Rural Enterprise in the Nineties)*, Hong Kong: Oxford University Press, 1994, p. 218.

6　R. Madsen, *Morality and Power in a Chinese Village*, Berkeley, CA: University of California Press, 1984, p. 142.

7　The emphasis on egalitarianism is further illustrated in cases in which income was earned from outside jobs. It was common for rural communities to send a contingent of male workers to nearby cities or towns where extra laborers were needed for temporary construction jobs. Under such circumstances, these laborers were treated as the property of their collective. They were paid in cash, which they handed over to their collective, and they received credit in the form of workpoints in return. S. Heins Potter and J. Potter, *China's Peasants: The Anthropology of a Revolution*, Cambridge: Cambridge University Press, 1990, pp. 67–8.

8　For a discussion of land distribution in post-Mao China, see Huang Shu-ming, *The Spiral Road: Change in a Chinese Village Through the Eyes of a Communist Party Leader*, Boulder, CO: Westview Press, 1989, pp. 169–73; and A. Rahman Khan, "The Responsibility System and Institutional Change," in K. Griffin (ed.), *Institutional Reform and Economic Development in the Chinese Countryside*, London: Macmillan, 1984, pp. 76–131; and J. Kung, "Equal Entitlement Versus Tenure Security Under a Regime of Collective Property Rights: Peasants' Preference for Institutions in Post-Reform Chinese Agriculture," *Journal of Comparative Economics*, Vol. 21, No. 2, 1995, pp. 82–111.

9　See for instance, R. Conroy, "Laissez-Faire Socialism? Prosperous Peasants and China's Current Rural Development Strategy," *Australian Journal of Chinese Affairs*, No. 12, July 1984, pp. 1–33.

10　See, for instance, S. Young, *Private Business and Economic Reform in China*, Armonk, NJ: M. E. Sharpe, an East Gate Book, 1995, pp. 33–66.

11　*XZGTN*, 2001, p. 279.

12　Chen Jianbo, "Zengjia Nongmin Shouru Feinong Chanye shi Zhongdian" (Non-farming Activities as the Focus of Increasing Peasants' Income), *Research Report of the State Council Research Center*, PRC, 2000, p. 1.

13　M. Weitzman and Chenggang Xu, "The Nature of the Township-Village Enterprise," op. cit., p. 132.

14　For examples, see "Township Enterprise Contract Responsibility System Viewed," *Journal and Periodical Research Service (JPRS)* (China), No. 14, 1987, pp. 24–9; "From Contract System to Share-System – Transformation of the Enterprise Operational Form and the Property Organizational Form," *JPRS* (China), No. 59, 1988, pp. 9–13; and "Reassessment of the Enterprise Ownership Responsibility System" *JPRS* (China), No. 115, 1989, pp. 29–34 and "*Nantongxian Qiye Chengbao Jingyi zhong di 'Fufangzhang Guiheshang Qiongmiaotang' Xianxiang*" (The Experience of Implementing the Contract Responsibility System in Enterprises in Nantong County: the Phenomenon of 'the Master Getting Rich at the Expense of the Temple and Monks'), *ZGXZQYB*, 7/20/1992, p. 1.

15　Interview with county REA official.

16　Maria Edin, *Market Forces and Communist Power: Local Political Institutions and Economic Development in China*, Uppsala: Uppsala University Press, 2000, pp. 131–2.

17　Interview with official of county Bureau of Finance.

18　The new system has not been rigorously implemented at local level. In Hubei province, for example, by the end of 1995, 58 percent of township administrations had not yet introduced the change. Jia Xiuxin and Han Mengyu, "Yuanshan Xiangzhen Fenshuizhi Caizheng Tizhi di Sikao" (Reflection on the Improvement of the Township Tax-Sharing Scheme) *Xiangzhen Caizheng (Township Finance)*, January 1997, pp. 13–15.

19 Interview with county Bureau of Finance official. See also Tsang Shu-ki and Cheng Yuk-shing, "China's Tax Reforms of 1994: Breakthrough or Compromise?" *Asian Survey*, Vol. XXXIV, No. 9, September 1994, pp. 769–88.

20 Ibid.

21 Ibid. See also *Huantai Bao* (*Huantai News*), 4/10/1996, p. 3.

22 Usually the growth rate is about 8 percent per year. In other words, if the quota is agreed to be one million, the amount will be automatically readjusted to 1.08 million in the second year and 1.17 in the third.

23 Interview with township Local Tax Office official. See also Huantaixiang Renmin Zhengfu Bangongshi (Office of the Huantai Count People's Government), "Huantaixiang Zhengfu Guanyu dui Xiangzhen Shixing Dinge Shangjiao, Beili Dizeng, Zengzhang Fencheng Caizheng Tizhi di Jueding" (Decision on the Implementation of the Financial System of "Fixed Quota Submission, Proportional Growth and Sharing of Above-Quota Amount" in Township Administrations, 5/26/1995.

24 Interview with township ETC official.

25 Interview with township ETC official.

26 Interview with enterprise manager.

27 Christine Wong tells a similar story in her general account of township finance in rural China in the 1990s. C. Wong, "Rural Public Finance," C. Wong (ed.), *Financing Local Government in the People's Republic of China*, Hong Kong: Oxford University Press, 1997, pp. 167–212.

28 Information provided by a township ETC. See also Tang Xinhua and Huang Yi (eds), *Xinbian Xiangzhen Qiye Huiji* (*New Edition of Rural Enterprise Accounting*), Beijing: Zhongguo Wuxi Chubanshe, 1995, pp. 378–405.

29 Information provided by Qifeng and Tangshan ETC.

30 J. Harding, "Hidden Compensations," *Financial Times*, 3/24/1997, p. 8.

31 Interview with county REA official. A similar view was given by officials from the ETCs of various townships.

32 Interview with township ETC official.

33 Interview with county REA official.

34 Interview with township ETC official.

35 Interview with township ETC official.

36 Interview with township ETC official.

37 Interview with enterprise manager.

38 Interview with enterprise manager.

39 Interview with township ETC official.

40 Interview with enterprise manager.

41 Interview with county REA official.

42 Interview with township ETC official and enterprise manager.

43 Interview with enterprise manager. This appears to be a common phenomenon across the country. TVEs throughout the countryside are all suffering from various kinds of extortion by administrative units. See, for example, ZGXZQYB, 4/13/1987, p. 1; and 7/1/1988, p. 1.

44 This does not, however, imply that their resident status has been changed. They remain rural residents.

45 Interview with county REA official.

46 There are reports of local government collaborating with enterprises in tax evasion in other parts of the country. In some cases, collective enterprises are keeping two different sets of accounts. One is the genuine record, which is kept away from outside inspection, whereas the other is a fake for tax purposes. The local government is reported to be aware of this and to have decided to turn a blind eye, as, although it may lose part of the tax return, the central treasury is the major victim. By tolerating this malpractice, more resources can be kept in the

community and the burden on enterprises can be reduced. These benefits can certainly offset the local state's direct financial loss.

47 This method is usually applied in private enterprises, but it is also extended to collective enterprises occasionally. According to this method, the amount payable is determined by the result of an assessment conducted by the relevant tax office. This is a subjective exercise; it is not based on the hard data of transaction volume or turnover but the official's impression of the business conditions of the enterprise concerned. This is a compromise as the management of many rural enterprises is still very primitive and a formal accounting system has not been fully established.

48 Interview with township local tax bureau official.

49 Interview with township local tax bureau official.

50 *Huantai Bao* (*Huantai News*), 3/18/1996, p. 1.

51 Interview with township ETC and county REA officials.

52 Interview with enterprise manager.

53 Interview with enterprise manager.

54 With the general paucity of management and technical talent in the rural area, and the endurance of the social bias against rural areas, the local state is, in fact, happy if managers can find any talent willing to join their enterprises. Local policy also allows enterprises to provide special bonus schemes to attract outside talent. Staff members who have made a significant contribution during three years' service in any collective enterprise which achieves a profit margin of a half- to one-million yuan are entitled to a 100-m² apartment, plus an imported Audi sedan. The task of talent scouting is predominantly the job of the enterprise manager. Zhonggong Huantai Xianwei, Huantaixian Renmin Zhengfu (Committee of Huantai county of the Chinese Communist Party and the People's Government of Huantai county), "Guanyu Jiakuai Jingji Fazhan di Ruogan Guiding" (Several Guidelines for Speeding up Economic Development), 3/1/1993.

55 *ZGXZQYB* 4/12/1986, p. 1, "Ministry To Send Cadres to Rural Areas," *FBIS* (China), No. 70, 1993, pp. 25–6; and "Official Urges Sending County Cadres to Front," *FBIS* (China), No. 124, 1992, pp. 30–1.

56 *ZN*, 1989, p. 112.

57 Extracted from *ZN*, 1987, p. 109; 1990, p. 79; 1992, p. 113; 1993, p. 114; 1994, p. 120; and 1998, p. 56.

58 *Zibo Shizhi*, 1995, p. 185.

59 *ZGXZQYB*, 2/4/1995, p. 1.

60 Extracted from *ZN* 1987, pp. 133–4; 1988, p. 120; 1990, pp. 96–7; 1992, p. 134; and 1998, pp. 102–3.

61 *ZN* 1987, p. 109.

62 Interview with enterprise manager.

6 Evaluating enterprise reform: a local perspective

1 S. Whiting, *Power and Wealth in Rural China*, New York: Cambridge University Press, 2001.

2 R. Bates, *Prosperity and Violence: The Political Economy of Development*, New York: W. W. Norton & Company, 2001, p. 102.

3 Y. Barzel, *Economic Analysis of Property Rights*, Cambridge: Cambridge University Press, 1997, pp. 3–5.

4 T. Rawski, "Progress Without Privatization: The Reform of China's State Industries," in V. Milor (ed.), *Changing Political Economies: Privatization in Post-Communist and Reforming Communist States*, London: Lynne Rienner, 1994, pp. 27–52; and Guowuyuan Yanjiushi Ketizu (State Council Research Office Task

Group), "Zengqiang Guoying Dazhongxing Qiye Huoli di Lishihuigu" (A Historical Review of the Attempts to Strengthen the Vitality of State-Owned Large and Medium-Sized Enterprises), *Guanli Shijie (Management World)* No. 6, December 1991, pp. 138–43.

5   A condition in which the budget constraints of an enterprise can be circumvented through subsidies or tax exemption. Any attempt to improve economic efficiency is undermined under such circumstances.

6   D. Hay *et al.*, *Economic Reform and State-Owned Enterprises in China, 1979–1987*, Oxford: Clarendon Press, 1994, pp. 5–6.

7   Qimiao Fan, "State-Owned Enterprise Reform in China: Incentives and Environment," in Qimiao Fan and P. Nolan (eds), *China's Economic Reforms: The Costs and Benefits of Incrementalism*, London: Macmillan, St. Martin's Press, 1994, pp. 137–56.

8   A phenomenon in which the operator tries to squeeze the full productive potential from the assets during the contract period regardless of the long-term negative consequences for those resources. A typical example is land. The fertility of a large amount of contracted land has been damaged as many contractors have paid no attention to irrigation and conservation and have used their plots in irresponsible ways.

9   Township Enterprise Contract Responsibility System Viewed" *JPRS* (China) No. 14, 7/2/1987, pp. 24–9; and "Reassessment of Enterprise Ownership Responsibility System," *JPRS* (China), No. 115, pp. 29–34.

10 In 1984, the Tinqiao Department Store in Beijing was chosen as the first testpoint for the shareholding experiment in the commercial sector, and the newly founded company, Shanghai Feile Stereo Shareholding Limited, established in the same year, was the first experiment in the industrial sector. Jia Heting, "Zhongguo Gufenzhi Gaizudi Youguan Zhengce" (The Related Policies of the Transformation of the Chinese Shareholding System) *Guanli Shijie (Management World)*, No. 3, June 1993, pp. 73–5.

11 The title of Zhao's report is "Advance Along the Road of Socialism with Chinese Characteristics" (1987). Quoted from Ajit Singh, "The Stock Market in a Socialist Economy," in P. Nolan and Dong Fureng (eds), *The Chinese Economy and its Future: Achievements and Problems of Post-Mao Reform*, Cambridge: Cambridge University Press, 1990, pp. 161–78.

12 "China to Overhaul Regulation of Markets," *Asian Wall Street Journal*, 10/20/1992.

13 *Zhonghua Renmin Gongheguo Gongxifa (The Company Law of the People's Republic of China)*. National People's Congress, 1993.

14 The regulations passed during the early 1990s include the "Gufenyouxian Gongxi Guifanyijian" (Guideline for the Limited by Shares Company) and "Youxiazeren Gongxi Gufenyijian" (Guideline for the Limited Liabilities Company), "Zhonghua Renmin Gongheguo Qiyefa"(Enterprise Law of the PRC) and the "Zhonghua Renmin Gongheguo Gongxifa" (Company Law of the PRC). Jia Heting, "Zhongguo Gufenzhi Gaige di Youguan Zhengce," op. cit.

15 The subsequent discussion is only intended to provide an extremely simplified version of the property rights theory. The discussion is cursory, with little elaboration of the possible complications if a different shareholding structure is involved. It should, however, provide a fair summary of the essential arguments of the theory.

16 T. Eggertsson, *Economic Behavior and Institutions*, Cambridge: Cambridge University Press, 1990, pp. 40–1; and O. Williamson, "Organization Form, Residual Claimants, and Corporate Control," *Journal of Law and Economics*, Vol. XXVI, June 1983, pp. 351–5.

17 The method of correcting managerial failure depends on the shareholding structure. A closed and concentrated shareholding structure implies a close communication within the enterprise and a lower cost of supervision; incompetent managers are likely to be replaced by shareholders, rather than through the market. However, with a dispersed structure and the existence of a secondary market, incompetent managers are likely to be replaced through market, i.e. through takeover or merger.

18 H. Demsetz, "The Structure of Ownership and the Theory of the Firm," *Journal of Law and Economics*, XXVI, June 1983, pp. 375–90.

19 E. Furubotn and S. Pejovich, "Property Rights and Economic Theory: A Survey of Recent Literature," *Journal of Economic Literature*, Vol. 10, 1972, pp. 1139–40; G. Libecap, *Contracting for Property Rights*, Cambridge: Cambridge University Press, 1989.

20 A. Alchian and H. Demsetz, "Production, Information Costs, and Economic Organization," *American Economic Review*, Vol. 62, No. 5, 1972, pp. 777–95.

21 For a summary of the positive appraisal of the merits of the shareholding system among Chinese economists, see Gufenzhi Yanjiuzu (Shareholding System Research Group), "Guoyou Dazhongxing Qiye Qufenzhi Wenti Yanjiu" (Research on the Question of the Shareholding System in Large and Medium Size State-Owned Enterprises) *Zhongguo Gongye Jingji Yanjiu (China Industrial Economic Research)*, No. 1, January 1992, pp. 26–30, and Wangguo and Shi Xia, "Gufenzhi: Gaohuo Dazhongxing Qiye di Zhengque Xuanze," (Shareholding System: The Correct Choice for Revitalizing Large and Medium Size Enterprises), *Zhongguo Gongye Jingji Yanjiu (China Industrial Economic Research)*, No. 11, November 1991, pp. 9–14.

22 The description of the shareholding enterprise is based on the organizational structure stipulated in the Company Law of the PRC.

23 For a discussion of the limitations of the impact of the shareholding system in reality, see, for example, K. Cowling, "Reflections on the Privatization Issue," and Dong He, "The Stock Market and Industrial Performance: Lessons from the West for Stock Market Development in China," in Ha-Joon Chang and P. Nolan (eds), *The Transformation of the Communist Economies: Against the Mainstream*, London: St. Martin's Press, 1995, pp. 162–76 and 191–217.

24 Dong Fureng, "Reform of the Economic Operating Mechanism and Reform of Ownership," in P. Nolan and Dong He (eds), *The Chinese Economy and its Future*, op. cit., p. 70.

25 *ZTZ*, 1994, p. 50.

26 *ZGTN*, 1995, p. 572.

27 The proportion of government revenue as a percentage of GNP fell from 34 percent to 19.8 percent between 1978 and 1988. World Bank, *China: Financial Sector Policies and Institutional Development*, Washington, DC: World Bank, 1990.

28 R. Brayshaw and Z. Teng, "Re-emergence of the Chinese Stock Market," in John Blake and Simon Gao (eds), *Perspectives on Accounting and Finance in China*, London: Routledge, 1995, p. 89.

29 In fairness, most of these enterprises are big enterprises and, in total, they constitute about 11 percent of the national total gross output value (at current prices); however, it is still clear that the progress of this reform is confined. *ZGTN*, 1995, p. 380.

30 D. E. Ayling and Z. Jiang, "Chinese and Western Stock Markets: International Influences and Development," in John Blake and Simon Gao (eds), *Perspectives on the Accounting and Finance in China*, op. cit., p. 76.

31 "Slow Introduction of Shareholding System Urged," and "Authorities Said 'Opposing' Third Stock Market," *FBIS* (China), No. 225, 11/20/1992, pp. 32–3.

32   Quotation cited from, Richard Baum, *Burying Mao: Chinese Politics in the Age of Deng Xiaoping*, Princeton, NJ: Princeton University Press, 1996, p. 358.

33   D. E. Ayling and Z. Jiang, "Chinese and Western Stock Markets," op. cit., p. 80.

34   For the academic debate concerning the urgency and desirability of full-scale privatization of the Chinese economy, see Louis Putterman, "The Role of Ownership and Property Rights in China's Economic Transition," *China Quarterly* No. 144, December 1995, pp. 1047–64, Andrew Walder, "Corporate Organization and Local Government Property Rights in China," and T. Rawski, "Progress Without Privatization," in Vedal Milor (ed.), *Changing Political Economy*, pp. 53–66 and 27–52; D. Hay *et al.*, *Economic Reform and State-Owned Enterprises in China;* and K. Cowling, "Reflections on the Privatization Issue," in Ha-Joon Chang and P. Nolan (eds), *The Transformation of the Communist Economies*, op. cit., pp. 162–76. For a general discussion of the socialist economy, see L. Haddad, "On the Rational Sequencing of Enterprise Reform," *Journal of Communist Studies and Transition Politics*, Vol. 11, No. 1, March 1995, pp. 91–109.

35   R. Baum, *Burying Mao*, op. cit., pp. 360–2.

36   *ZTZ*, 1994, p. 50.

37   Cui Zhiyuan Cui is one of those who have advocated the application of such a "disintegrated view" of property relations in understanding the property right issue in China. He argues that "phrasing the problem as identifying the owner is fundamentally wrong. Cui Zhiyuan, *Di er ci Si xiang Jiefang yu Zhidu Chuangxin* (*The Second Ideological Liberation and Institutional Innovation*), Hong Kong: Oxford University Press, 1997.

38   A. Walder, "Corporate Organization and Local Government Property Rights in China," op. cit.

39   C. Elizondo, *Property Rights in Mexico: Government and Business After the 1982 Bank Nationalization*, unpublished PhD thesis, Nuffield College, University of Oxford, 1992, p. 19.

40   Furubotn and Pejovich, "Property Rights and Economic Theory," op. cit., p. 1140.

41   D. C. North, *Institutions, Institutional Change and Economic Performance*, Cambridge: Cambridge University Press, 1990, pp. 83–91; and "Five Propositions about Institutional Change," J. Knight and I. Sened (eds), *Explaining Social Institutions*, Ann Arbor, MI: University of Michigan Press, 1995, pp. 15–26.

42   Here, it is assumed that the local government commands only a minority share. Such an assumption is made because it makes the impact of reform more discernible for the comparative purposes.

43   Interview with an officialsof the prefecture CRE. He disclosed that there have been disputes between administrative units over the collection of management fees. Under the present commercial registration regulations in China, no enterprise can register as a shareholding cooperative enterprise. It has to opt for either a private or collective status. This is the reason leading to the controversy over the distribution of management fees. Also, Yuan Peng, "Guanyu Nongcun Gufenhezuozhi Qiye Fazhanzhong di Wenti yu Jianyi," (Problems and Recommendations concerning the Development of Rural Shareholding Enterprises) *Guanli Shijie* (*Management World*), No. 3, 1994, p. 150.

44   S. R. Munzer, *A Theory of Property*, Cambridge: Cambridge University Press, 1990, p. 29.

45   D. C. North, *Institutions, Institutional Change and Economic Performance*, op. cit., p. 33.

46   K. Firmin-Sellers, "The Politics of Property Rights," *American Political Science Review*, Vol. 89, No. 4, December 1995, pp. 867–81.

7 Managers cashing in: shareholding reform in rural China

1 Interview with officials of the Zibo prefecture Commission for Restructuring Economy (CRE).

2 "Zhonggong Zhongyang Guanyu 1984 nian Nongcun Gongzuo de Tongzhi" (Notice of the Central Committee Concerning Rural Work in 1984), in Guojia Gongshang Xingzheng Guanliju Xinxi Zhongxin (Information Center of the Bureau of Industry and Commerce) (ed.), *Geti Laodongzhe Shouce* (*Individual Laborers' Handbook*), Beijing: Beijing Ribao Chubanshe and Gongshang Chubanshe, 1984, pp. 188–201.

3 E. B. Vermeer, "Experiments with Rural Industrial Shareholding Cooperatives: The Case of Zhoucun District, Shandong Province," *China Information*, Vol. 10, No. 3/4, Winter 1995/Spring 1996, pp. 75–107.

4 Nongyebu (Ministry of Agriculture), "Nongmin Gufenhezuo Qiye Zanxing Guiding" (Tentative Regulation for Rural Shareholding Cooperative Enterprise), in Guowuyuan Fazhiju Bangongshi (Office of the Legal Bureau of the State Council)(ed.), *Jiti, Geti, Xiying Jingji Kaiye Jingying Zhengce Fagui Xuanbian* (*Selection of Regulations and Policies for the Operation of Collective, Individual and Private Economy*), Beijing: Zhongguo Minzhi Fazhi Chubanshe, 1993, pp. 42–50.

5 The minimum capital requirement of ten million yuan also shows the caution of the central government in implementing shareholding reform. It reveals its intention to confine the experiment to relatively established and efficient enterprises.

6 Interviews with officials of the Zibo prefecture CRE and the deputy director of the Zhoucun Office of the National Rural Reform Experiment Office. Central documents were issued on this matter, for instance Nongyebu (the Ministry of Agriculture), "Guanyu Tuixing he Wanshan Xiangzhen Qiye Gufenhezuozhi di Tongji" (Notice on the Implementation and Improvement of the Cooperative Shareholding System among Rural Enterprises), 12/24/1992.

7 Huantaixian Tizhigaige Weiyuanhui (Huantai county CRE), "Guyuan Zhuanfa Ziboshi Tigaiwei, Gongshangju, Gongziju Yuangufeng Youxiangongsi Guifangongzuo ji Zhongxin Dengjizhuce di Shishixize di Tongji" (Notice of Relaying the Document of the Details for the Implementation of the Standardization and Re-registration of Limited by Shares Companies from the CRE, Bureau of Industry and Commerce and State Asset Management Bureau of Zibo Prefecture), 1/3/1996; and Zhoucun Nongcungaige Shiyan Bangongshi (Zhoucun Office of National Rural Reform Experiment Office), "Guanyu Jiading Gufenhenzuo Qiye Guifenhua Jianshe di Shixing Yijian" (Tentative Views Concerning the Strengthening of Standardization of Cooperative Shareholding System), 11/10/1991.

8 Interview with an enterprise manager.

9 Wang Taiji, "Xiangzhenqiye Rencaijie Wenti Heshi Caineng Jiejue?" (When Can the Problem of Shortage of Human Resources in Rural Enterprise be Solved?) *ZGXZQYB*, 2/4/1995, p. 1; and Xiao Yue, "Dao Xiangzhenqiye Qu: Zhongguo Chengzhen Qingnian Jiuye Xindongxiang," (Going to Rural Enterprises: The New Pattern of Employment of Urban Youth in China) *ZGXZQYB*, 2/24/1994. p. 1.

10 This view was echoed in many of the author's formal and informal encounters with local officials of townships ETCs.

11 Interview with an enterprise manager. The story was also confirmed by interviews with local officials.

12 A term used by James Scott to describe the social tactics, ranging from gossiping to social ostracism, used by peasants to show their disapproval of the powerful people who break the community code of legitimate conduct. J. C. Scott, *Weapons*

of the Weak: Everyday Forms of Peasant Resistance, New Haven, CT: Yale University Press, 1985.

13   Interview with workers. This appears to be more than an isolated case. According to press reports, some enterprises have even tried to persuade workers to buy company shares by appealing to the ideological superiority of shareholding. Buying shares is honored as a virtue of the advanced worker – a new addition to the four virtues identified by Deng Xiaoping as the requirements for an individual to meet the task of socialist modernization in 1980. This may show how desperate the effort is. "Stockholder as Virtue Criticized," *JPRS* (China), No. 43, 7/9/1993, p. 1; and Wang Xinglung, "Zhigong Weihebuyuan Rugu?"(Why are Workers Unwilling to Buy Shares?), *ZGXZQYB*, 8/28/1995, p. 2.

14   Restricted circulation of shares means that the returns to this investment will be confined mainly to dividends and interest. The major financial attraction of share investment, the prospect of a rise in market value, is unlikely in this situation.

15   Comments made by one worker in Tangshan township are revealing. Working in a shareholding company, he said he had no complaint against those who earned more income from shares because he thought that these people had to take some risks, first, because these share investments cannot be withdrawn (though transferable), and, second, because the dividend rate, though high in general, is not guaranteed. Most important to him, he claimed, this income is "distribution according to capital" (*anzi fenpei*) but not "distribution according to labour" (*anlao fenpei*). "These are two different matters and have nothing to do with fairness," he argued.

16   *Company Law of the People's Republic of China.*

17   Zhonggong Zhoucunquwei Zhoucunqu Renmin Zhengfu (Zhoucun District Committee of the Chinese Communist Party and the Zhoucun District People's Government), "Zhoucunqu Nongcun Gaige Shiyanqu 1987–1995 Nian Gaige Shiyan Baogao" (Zhoucun Office of National Rural Reform Experiment Office's Report of 1987–1995, 6/20/1995, p. 9.

18   Pengyangxiang Dangwei Zhengfu (The Party Committee and People's Government of Pengyang Township), "Shenruchijiu di Tuidong Gufenhezuozhi Gaige Wei Pengyang Jingji di Zhenxing he Tengfei er Fendou" (Intensification of Shareholding Cooperative Reform as a Means to Revitalize the Economy of Pengyang County), 6/11/1992; and also Zhoucun Shiyanqu Bangongshi (Zhoucun Office of National Rural Experiment Office), "Gufenhezuozhi shi Shenhua Nongcun Gaige di Xinchangshi" (Shareholding Cooperative Reform is the New Experiment in the Intensification of Rural Reform), in Zhoucunqu Nongcun Gaige Shiyan Bangongshi (Zhoucun Office of National Rural Experiment Office) (ed.), *Zhoucun Xianxiang (The Zhoucun Phenomenon)*, 1995, p. 13 and pp. 49–50.

19   Interview with the manager of a district collective asset management company.

20   D. E. Ayling and Z. Jiang, "Chinese and Western Stock Markets: International Influences and Development," in J. Blake and S. Gao (eds), *Perspectives on the Accounting and Finance in China*. London: Routledge, 1995, p. 92.

21   Nongyebu Xiangzhen Qiyeju (TVE Bureau of the Ministry of Agriculture), "Xiangzhen Qiye Zichanpingu Banfa" (Method of Asset Valuation For TVEs), *ZGXZQYB*, 9/6/1994, p. 3.

22   Huantaixiang Tigaiwei (Huantai county CRE), "Huantaixiang Tigaiwei Jiuwunian Gongzuo Zongjie" (Summary of the Works of the Huantai county CRE in 1995), 1/26/1996.

23   Interview with CRE official.

24   See Zhoucun Shiyanqu Bangongshi, "Gunfenhezuozhi shi Shenhua Nongcun Gaige di Xinchangshi," 4/94, p. 11; and "Zhoucunqu Xiangzhen Gufenhezuozhi Zichanpingu Zhegu Shixing Banfa" (Provisional Method of Asset Valuation

of Rural Shareholding Cooperative System in Zhoucun District), 10/30/1991. Improper valuation practices have also been highlighted in the progress report of shareholding reform in Huantai County.

25 In contrast to the shareholders' assembly, workers' participation in this institution is based on their being employees of the enterprise rather than the number of shares they hold. The committee is composed mainly of representatives of the trade union and Party branch in the company.

26 Interviews with CRE officials, 3/20/1996, and the Economic Commission of Zhoucun District Government. Private conversations with workers of shareholding companies in Huantai are also consistent with this picture.

27 Nongyebu Nongcun Gufenhezuo Ketizu, "1992 Nian Nongcun Gufenhezuo Zuzhi Fazhan Baogao: Quanguo Qishiwuge Xian de Tiaochafenxi" (Report of Rural Shareholding Cooperative Organization Development in 1992: National Survey of 75 Counties), op. cit.

28 Ibid., p. 48.

29 "Gufenhezuozhi shi Shenhua Nongcun Gaige di Xinchangshi," op. cit., p. 25.

30 Interview with Zibo prefecture CRE official.

31 Zhonggong Zhoucunqu Weiyuanhui, Zhoucunqu Renmin Zhengfu (Zhoucun District Committee of the Chinese Communist Party and the Zhoucun District People's Government), "Guanyu Jinyibu Shenhua Gufenhezuozhi Gaige Jiaquai Jianli Xiandai Qiye Zhidu di Shixing Fangan" (The Provisional Plan for the Intensification of Shareholding Cooperative Reform and the Building of Modern Enterprise Structure), 5/4/1994; and "Xianwei Shuji Wumingjun Tan Qiyegaige" (County Secretary Wumingjun on Enterprise Reform), 11/2/1993 in Zhonggong Huantai Xianwei Bangongshi (The Office of the Huantai county Committee of the Chinese Communist Party) (ed.), *Huantaixian Qiye Chanquanzhidu Gaige Cailiao Huibian* (*Selection of Documents on Enterprise Ownership Reform in Huantai County*), 1994, pp. 1–4.

32 Huantaixian Teigaiwei (Huantai county CRE), "Huantaixian Teigaiwei Jiuwunian Gongzuo Zongjie" (Report of the Huantai county CRE 1995), 1/26/1996, pp. 4–5.

33 Zhonggong Huantai Xianwei Bangongshi (ed.), *Huantaixian Qiye Chanquanzhidu Cailiao Huibian*, 1994, op. cit., pp. 46–72.

34 Interview with official of Zibo prefecture CRE.

35 Several articles of the *Provisional Regulation of Rural Shareholding Cooperative Enterprise,* a blueprint for the structure of shareholding cooperative enterprises in the countryside, passed by the Ministry of Agriculture in 1990, are noteworthy. For instance, it is stipulated that 60 percent of the after-tax profits of the enterprise are required for further development of the enterprise, of which 50 percent has to be saved as "public inventory" that cannot be divided among shareholders. This guarantees that this "collective" element will not be lost shortly after the conversion. Nongyebu (Ministry of Agriculture), "Nongmin Gufenhezuoqiye Zanxingguiding" (Provisional Regulation of Rural Shareholding Cooperative Enterprise), 1 2/2/1990, and *ZGXZQYB*, 3/2/1990, p. 3.

36 "Zhoucunqu Gufenzhiqiye Laodong Guanli Zanxingguiding" (Provisional Regulation of Labour Management in Shareholding Enterprises in Zhoucun District). Zhoucunqu Renmin Zhengfu (Zhoucun District People's Government), 1994.

37 "Zhoucunqu Xiangzhen Gufenhezuozhi Qiye Guanlibanfa" (Provisional Method of Management of Shareholding Cooperative Enterprises in Zhoucun District), 1991.

38 Interview with the manager of Wangcunzhen Collective Asset Management Company. This company is entrusted with the responsibility of managing shareholding enterprises on behalf of the town government in Wangcunzhen. The

manager admitted that the pre-reform quota system is basically still in force for those ex-collective enterprises under its management.

39 Jiang Zemin, "Gaoju Deng Xiaoping Lilun Weida Qizhi Ba Jianshe Shehui Chuyi Shiye Quanmian Tuixiang ershiyi Shiji" (Uphold the Great Banner of Deng Xiaoping's Theory and Promote the Cause of Socialist Development with Chinese Characteristics to the Twenty-First Century), Report at the CCP's Fifteenth National Congress, Beijing, 9/12/1997, *Beijing Wanbao* (*Beijing Evening News*), 9/22/1997, pp. 1–7.

40 Ibid.

41 Tongming Li, "Guanyu Xiangzhen Qiye Gufen Hezuozhi Ruogan Lilun Wenti de Sikao" (Reflections on the Theoretical Issues Concerning the Shareholding Cooperative Reform in Rural Enterprises) *Nongye Jingji Wenti* (*Problems of Agricultural Economy*), No. 7, 1999, pp. 14–17.

42 The rate dropped from 0.058 to 0.048 from 1995 to 1997. Calculated from *ZXQN*, 1996, pp. 114 and 118; and 1998, pp. 110 and 112.

43 *ZTN*, 1993, p. 51; 1996, p. 53; 1997, p. 49; 1998, p. 67; and 1999, p. 67.

44 Nongyebu (Ministry of Agriculture), Xiangzhen Qiye Zujian he Fazhan Qiye Jituan Zanxing Banfa (Provisional Method for the Formation and Development of Rural Enterprise Groups), *ZGXZQYB*, 24 January 1992, p. 3.

45 Author's interview with township government official.

46 *ZN*, 1995, 1996, 1997, and 1998.

47 Author's interview.

48 *ZR*, 10/27/1999, p. 1.

49 *Huantaixian Renmin Zhengfu Gongzuo Baogao* (*Annual Report of the Huantai County People's Government*), 1/16/1998, p. 16.

50 Wang Shuwu Tongzhi cai Xianzhengfu Disanci Quanti Chengyuan (Kuoda) Huiyi shang de Jianghua (speech made by Comrade Wang at the third full meeting of the township government), op. cit.

51 *ZN*, 1998, p. 116.

52 Interview with township mayor.

53 For instance, see *Maqiaozhen Zhengfu Gongzuo Baogao* (*Annual Report of Maqiao Township Government*), 1/9/1999.

54 *Guolizghen Zhengfu Gongzuo Baogao* (*Government Report of Guoli Township Government*) 1999.

55 T. Rawski, "Progress without Privatization: The Reform of China's State Industries," in Velat Milor (ed.), *Changing Political Economy: Privatization in Post-Communist and Reforming Communist State*, Boulder, CO: Lynne Reinner, 1994, pp. 27–51.

8 Prospects of the local state–manager alliance

1 D. North, *Institutions, Institutional Change and Economic Performance*, New York: Cambridge University Press, 1990, pp. 93–104.

2 Tremendous progress in privatization has been achieved in these countries since the late 1980s. A substantial portion of the industrial capacity of these post-socialist regimes has been put into private hands either through a voucher system or through cash sales. For example, in Russia roughly 900,000 employees move from the public to the private sector each month, and by mid-1994 two-thirds of the Russian manufacturing labor force had already joined privatized firms. M. Boycko, A. Shleifer and R. Vishny, *Privatizing Russia*, Cambridge, MA: MIT Press, 1996, p. 105.

3 See, for instance, D. Kelliher, *Peasant Power in China: The Era of Rural Reform, 1979–1989*, New Haven, CT: Yale University Press, 1992; and K. Zhou, *How the Farmers Changed China: Power of the People*, London: Westview Press, 1996.

4　D. Yang, "Local Government and Rural Industrialization in China," *Peasant Studies*, Vol. 18, No. 2, Winter 1991, pp. 131–41.

5　For a discussion of the prevalence of clientelism in rural politics, one of the best works is Jean Oi's study of village government. See J. Oi, *State and Peasant in Contemporary China: The Political Economy of Village Government*, Berkeley, CA: University of California Press, 1989.

6　M. Shafer, "The Political Economy of Sectors and Sectoral Change: Korea Then and Now," in S. Maxfield and B. Ross Schneider, (eds), *Business and the State in Developing Countries*, Ithaca, NY: Cornell University Press, 1997, pp. 88–121.

7　C. Lindblom, *Politics and Markets: The World's Political-Economic Systems*, New York: Basic Books, 1977, pp. 172–3 and 175.

8　The theory of "three representation" states that the Chinese Communist Party represents the advanced culture, advanced production force, and fundamental interests of the people of China.

9　Several factories this author visited had bars on the windows, and the only door of the workshop was locked while the workers were operating inside. The managers regard these as important measures against theft, particularly by workers. Unsurprisingly, these are responsible for the numerous death by fire throughout the country, as hundreds of panicking workers simply cannot get out through the single exit in time.

10　Although workers in state-owned enterprises are entitled to a comprehensive welfare package, including a wide range of medical, housing, education, and retirement benefits, most workers employed in the rural enterprises this author visited received no benefits other than subsidized meals.

11　Interview with factory workers.

12　Lianjiang Li and K. O'Brien, "Villagers and Popular Resistance in Contemporary China," *Modern China*, Vol. 22, No. 1 (January 1996), pp. 28–61; and K. O'Brien, "Rightful Resistance," *World Politics*, No. 49, October 1996, pp. 31–55.

13　J. Scott, *Weapons of the Weak: Everyday Forms of Peasant Resistance*, New Haven, CT: Yale University Press, 1985.

14　Jiang Zhingyi *et al.*, "Pingdushi: Liangtianzhi Gaige di Zhengce Xiaoguo Fenxi" (Two-Farms System: Analysis of the Experience of Pengdu City), *Zhongguo Nongcun Jingji* (Chinese Rural Economy), No. 4, April 1994, pp. 26–30; and Nongyebu Nongcun Hezuo Jingji Yanjiu Ketizu (Research Group for Rural Cooperative Economy of the Ministry of Agriculture), "Zhongguo Nongcun Tudi Chengbao Jingying Zhidu yu Hezuo Zuzhi Yunxing Kaocha" (Survey on Land Contract System and the Functioning of Cooperative Organizations in Rural China), *Nongye Jingji Wenti* (Problems of Agricultural Economy), No. 11, November 1993, pp. 45–53.

15　The low cost factor is also crucial for attracting potential overseas investors. In particular, the laxity of controls on industrial safety and pollution make rural enterprises in China ideal venues for investors whose host countries have stricter restrictions on such matters.

16　B. Naughton, "Implications of the State Monopoly Over Industry and Its Relaxation," *Modern China*, Vol. 18, No. 1, January 1992, pp. 14–41.

17　Chen Xiwen, "Jiegou Biange yu Baoju Tiaozheng: Xiangzhen Qiye Fazhan di Xinjieduan" (Structural Readjustment: the New Stage of Rural Enterprise Development), *Nongye Jingji Wenti* (*Problems of Chinese Agriculture*), No. 1, January 1993, pp. 31–5; and Lu Wen, "Xiangzhen Qiye Mianlin di Xinxingshi he Fazhan di Xinyaoqiu" (The New Stage of Rural Enterprise Development), *Zhongguo Nongcun Jingji* (*Chinese Rural Economy*), No. 1, January 1993, pp. 47–51.

18　There has, in fact, been a growing concern over rural stability in the Party leadership in recent years. Great emphasis has been placed on the importance of strengthening the Party machinery at the rural grass-roots level and on social order. In the Fourth Plenary Session of the 14th CPC Central Committee held in 1994, this theme was again highlighted by top Party officials, and a central document, "The Circular of the CPC Central Committee on Strengthening the Construction of Rural Grassroots Party Organizations" was issued. Two months later, the Party Organization Department issued another document, "Suggestions on Further Rectifying Party Branches That are Weak and Lax in Discipline or in a State of Paralysis," providing guidelines for how these ideas can be implemented. "Advice on Reorganizing Rural Party Branches," *JPRS* (China), No. 247, 1994, pp. 16–18.

19 *ZXQN*, 1999, p. 111; and *Zhongguo Xiangzhen Qiye* (*China's Rural Enterprise*), No. 10, 1998, p. 28.
20 *ZXQN*, 1998, p. 198; and *ZGTN*, 1998, p. 594.
21 R. Yep and Louie Kin-shuen, "Interest Articulation of Rural Businesses 1984–1999: A Preliminary Analysis," paper presented at the Sixth European Conference on Agricultural and Rural Development in China, Leiden University, The Netherlands, 5–7 January 2000.
22 *ZGXZQYB*, 4/18/1988, p. 1.
23 *Zhonghua Renmin Gongheguo Xiangcun Jiti Suoyouzhi Qiye Tiaoli* (*The PRC Regulation of Rural Collective Enterprise*), 1990.
24 *ZGXZQYB*, 3/29/1993, p. 1; and 3/15/1995, p. 1.
25 *Nongmin RiBao* (*Peasant Daily*) 3/26/1992, p. 1; and *Zhongguo Xiangzheng Qiyebao*, 3/23/1992, p. 1.
26 *ZGXZQYB*, 9/18/1992, p. 1.
27 *ZGXZQYB*, 4/1/1987, p. 1.
28 *ZGXZQYB*, 10/14/1994, p. 3.
29 *ZGXZQYB*, 11/14/1994, p. 4.
30 "Rural Entrepreneurs Write Letter to Deng," *FBIS* (China), No. 194, 6 October 1992, pp. 40–2.
31 *Nongmin Ribao,* 6/30/1994, p. 1.
32 *ZGXZQYB*, 4/21/1994, p. 1.
33 *ZGXZQYB*, 11/14/1994, p. 4.

Bibliography

"Advice on Reorganizing Rural Party Branches," *JPRS* (China), No. 247, 1994, pp. 16–18.

"Agricultural Bank Plans to be More Market Oriented," *FBIS* (China), No. 7, 1993, p. 36.

Alchian, A. and H. Demsetz, "Production, Information Costs, and Economic Organization," *American Economic Review*, Vol. 62, No. 5, 1972, pp. 777–95.

Almond, G., "The Return to the State," *American Political Science Review*, Vol. 82, No. 3, 1988, pp. 853–73.

Arato, A. and J. Cohen, *Civil Society and Political Theory*, Cambridge, MA: MIT Press, 1992.

"Article on the Establishment of Commercial Banks," *FBIS* (China), No. 216, 1993, pp. 40–3.

Ash, R., "The Evolution of Agricultural Policy," *China Quarterly: Special Issue on Food and Agriculture in China During the Post-Mao Era*, No. 116, December 1988, pp. 529–55.

"Authorities Said 'Opposing' Third Stock Market," *FBIS* (China), No. 225, 11/20/1992, pp. 32–3.

Aziz, S., *Rural Development: Learning From China*, London: Macmillan, 1978.

Barnett, D., *Cadres, Bureaucracy, and Political Power in Communist China*, New York: Columbia University Press, 1967.

Barzel, Y., *Economic Analysis of Property Rights*, New York: Cambridge University Press, 1997.

Bates, R., *Beyond the Miracle of the Market: The Political Economy of Agrarian Development in Kenya*, Cambridge: Cambridge University Press, 1989.

—— *Prosperity and Violence: the Political Economy of Development*, New York: W. W. Norton, 2001.

Baum, R., *Burying Mao: Chinese Politics in the Age of Deng Xiaoping*, Princeton, NJ: Princeton University Press, 1996 edition.

Benewick, R. and P. Wingrove (eds), *China in the 1990s*, London: Macmillan, 1995.

Blake, J. and S. Gao (eds), *Perspectives on the Accounting and Finance in China*, London: Routledge, 1995.

Blecher, M. and V. Shue, *Tethered Deer: Government and Economy in a Chinese County*, Stanford, CA: Stanford University Press, 1996.

Boisot, M. and J. Child, "The Iron Law of Fiefs: Bureaucratic Failure and the Problem of Governance in the Chinese Economic Reforms," *Administrative Science Quarterly*, No. 33, December 1988, pp. 507–27.

—— "From Fiefs to Clans and Network Capitalism: Explaining China's Emerging Economic Order," *Administrative Science Quarterly*, No. 41, 1996, pp. 600–28.

Bonnin, M. and Y. Chevrier, "The Intellectual and the State: Social Dynamics of Intellectual Autonomy during the Post-Mao Era," *China Quarterly*, No. 127, 1991, pp. 569–93.

Boycko, M. *et al.*, *Privatizing Russia*, Cambridge, MA: MIT Press, 1996.

Brown, D. and R. Porter (eds), *Management Issues in China: Volume – Domestic Enterprises*, London: Routledge, 1996.

Brunn, O., *Business and Bureaucracy in a Chinese City: an Ethnography of Private Business Households in Contemporary China*, Berkeley, CA: Institute of East Asian Studies, University of California, 1993.

Brus, W. and K. Laski, *From Marx to the Market: Socialism in Search of an Economic System*, Oxford: Clarendon Press, 1989.

Burns, J., *Political Participation in Rural China*, Berkeley, CA: University of California Press, 1988.

Byrd, W. and Lin Qinsong (eds), *China's Rural Industry: Structure, Development, and Reform*, New York: Oxford University Press, 1990.

Cawson, A., *Corporatism and Political Theory*, Oxford: Basil Blackwell, 1988.

Chan, A. *et al.*, *Chen Village: The Recent History of a Peasant Community in Mao's China*, Berkeley, CA: University of California Press, 1984.

Chang Chun and Wang Yijiang, "The Nature of the Township-Village Enterprise," *Journal of Comparative Economics*, No. 19, 1994, pp. 437–9.

Chang, Ha-Joon and P. Nolan (eds), *The Transformation of the Communist Economies: Against the Mainstream*, London: St. Martin's Press, 1995.

Chen Baisong and Zhang Bun, "Nongmin Fudan Xianzhuang, Chengyin and Duice," (The Development, Causes and Remedies for the Problem of Peasants' Burden) *Nongye Jingji Wenti* (*Problems of Agricultural Economy*), No. 3, March 1993, pp. 37–41.

Chen, Jianbo, "Fuzhai Jingying di Hongguan Xianying" (The Macro-Effect of Enterprises Operating with Large Debts) *Zhongguo Xiangzhen Qiyebao*, 10/28/1992, p. 3.

—— "Xiangzhen Qiye Xinyong di Zhidu Jichu" (Institutional Foundation of Rural Enterprise Credit), *Zhongguo Xiangzhen Qiyebao*, 11/8/1992, p. 3.

Chen, Xiwen, "Jiegou Biange yu Baoju Tiaozheng: Xiangzhen Qiye Fazhan di Xinjieduan," (Structural Readjustment: the New Stage of Rural Enterprise Development) *Nongye Jingji Wenti* (*Problems of Chinese Agriculture*), No. 1, January 1993, pp. 31–5.

"China to Overhaul Regulation of Markets," *Asian Wall Street Journal*, 10/20/1992, p. 2.

Clarke, D., "The Execution of Civil Judgments in China," *China Quarterly*, No. 141, March 1995, pp. 65–81.

Conroy, R., "Laissez-Faire Socialism? Prosperous Peasants and China's Current Rural Development Strategy," *Australian Journal of Chinese Affairs*, No. 12, July 1984, pp. 1–33.

Corinna-Barbara, F., "Reproduction of *Danwei* Institutional Features in the Context of China's Market Economy: The Case of Haidian District's High-Tech Sector," *China Quarterly*, No. 147, September 1996, pp. 839–59.

Cui, Zhiyuan, *Di er ci Si xiang Jiefang yu Zhidu Chuangxin* (*The Second Ideological Liberation and Institutional Innovation*), Hong Kong: Oxford University Press, 1997.

Davis, D., R. Kraus, B. Naughton, and E. Perry (eds), *Urban Spaces in Contemporary China: the Potential for Autonomy and Community in Post-Mao China*, Cambridge: Cambridge University Press and Washington, DC: Woodrow Wilson Center Press, 1995.

Demsetz, H., "The Structure of Ownership and the Theory of the Firm," *Journal of Law and Economics*, XXVI, June 1983, pp. 375–90.

Deng Yingtao and Zu Ziaobo, *Zhongguo Nongcun Jingrong di Biange yu Fazhan 1978–1990 (The Changes and Development of the Chinese Rural Finance 1978–1990)*, Hong Kong: Oxford University Press, 1994.

Donnithorne, A., "China's Cellular Economy: Some Economic Trends Since the Cultural Revolution," *China Quarterly*, No. 52, October/December 1972, pp. 605–19.

Dou Xianjun, "Guanyu Nongcun Shengyu Laodongli Zhuanyi Wenti di Yanjiu," (Study on the Issue of Transferring Surplus Rural Labor), *Nongye Jingji Wenti (Problems of Agricultural Economy)*, No. 172, April 1994, pp. 10–14.

Drucker, P. , *The Practice of Management*, Melbourne: William Heinemann, 1955.

Duara, Prasenjit, *Culture, Power and the State: Rural North China, 1900–1942*, Stanford, CA: Stanford University Press, 1988.

Dui Haiyan, *Zhongguo Nongcun Gongyehua Yanjiu (Study of China's Rural Industrialization)*, Beijing: Zhongguo Wujia Chubanshe, 1992.

Easton, D., "The Political System Besieged by the State," *Political Theory*, Vol. 9, No. 3, 1981, pp. 305–25.

Eckstein, H., "On the Science of the State," *Daedalus*, Vol. 108, No. 4, 1979, pp. 1–20.

Edin, M., *Market Forces and Communist Power: Local Political Institutions and Economic Development in China*, Uppsala: Uppsala University Press, 2000.

Eggertsson, T., *Economic Behavior and Institutions*, Cambridge: Cambridge University Press, 1990.

Elizondo, C., *Property Rights in Mexico: Government and Business After the 1982 Bank Nationalization*, unpublished PhD thesis, Nuffield College, University of Oxford, 1992.

Esherick, J. and M. Backus Rankin (eds), *Chinese Local Elites and Pattern of Dominance*, Berkeley, CA: University of California Press, 1990.

Evans, P., *Embedded Autonomy: States and Industrial Transformation*, Princeton, NJ: Princeton University Press, 1995.

Eyal, G., I. Szelenyi, and E. Townsley, *Making Capitalism without Capialists: the New Ruling Elites in Eastern Europe*, London: Verso, 1998.

Falkenheim, V. (ed.), *Citizens and Groups in Contemporary China*, Ann Arbor, MI: Center for Chinese Studies, University of Michigan, 1987.

Fan Fang, "Xin di Siluan Xianxiang Renxin Sizou Zhuangkuang" (Phenomenon of Four New Sources of Chaos and Situation of Desertion), *Nongcun Gongzuo Tongxun (Rural Work Newsletter)*, No. 5, May 1993, pp. 38–9.

Fan Qimiao and P. Nolan (eds), *China's Economic Reforms: The Costs and Benefits of Incrementalism*, London: Macmillan, St. Martin's Press, 1994.

Fine, R. and S. Rai (eds), *Civil Society: Democratic Perspectives*, London: Frank Cass, 1997.

Findlay, C., A. Watson, and H. Wu (eds), *Rural Enterprises in China*, London: Macmillan, 1994.

Firmin-Sellers, K., "The Politics of Property Rights," *American Political Science Review*, Vol. 89, No. 4, December 1995, pp. 867–81.

Fligstein, N., "The Economic Sociology of the Transitions from Socialism," *American Journal of Sociology*, Vol. 101, No. 4, January 1996, pp. 1074–81.

Friedman, E., P. Pickowicz, and M. Selden, *Chinese Village, Socialist State*, New Haven, CT: Yale University Press, 1991.

"From Contract System to Share-System – Transformation of the Enterprise

Operational Form and the Property Organizational Form," *JPRS* (China), No. 59, 1988, pp. 9–13.

Fukuyama, F., *The End of History and the Last Man*, London: Penguin Books, 1992.

Furubotn, E. and S. Pejovich, "Property Rights and Economic Theory: A Survey of Recent Literature," *Journal of Economic Literature*, Vol. 10, 1972, pp. 1137–62.

Gold, T., "The Resurgence of Civil Society in China," *Journal of Democracy*, Vol. 1, No. 1, 1990, pp. 18–31.

Goodman, D. and G. Segal (eds), *China Deconstructs: Politics, Trade and Regionalism*, London: Routledge, 1994.

Griffin, K. (ed.), *Institutional Reform and Economic Development in the Chinese Countryside*, London: Macmillan, 1984.

Gufenzhi Yanjiuzu (Shareholding System Research Group), "Guoyou Dazhongxing Qiye Qufenzhi Wenti Yanjiu" (Research on the Question of the Shareholding System in Large and Medium Size State-Owned Enterprises) *Zhongguo Gongye Jingji Yanjiu* (*China Industrial Economic Research*), No. 1, January 1992, pp. 26–30.

Guldin, G. (ed.), *Farewell to China's Peasantry: Rural Urban and Social Change in the Late Twentieth Century*, Armonk, NY: M. E. Sharpe, 1997.

Guojia Gongshang Xingzheng Guanliju Xinxi Zhongxin (Information Center of the Bureau of Industry and Commerce) (ed.), *Geti Laodongzhe Shouce* (*Individual Laborers' Handbook*), Beijing: Beijing Ribao Chubanshe and Gongshang Chubanshe, 1984.

Guolizghen Zhengfu Gongzuo Baogao (*Government Report of Guoli Township Government*) 1999.

Guowuyuan Fazhiju Bangongshi (Office of the Legal Bureau of the State Council) (ed.), *Jiti, Geti, Xiying Jingji Kaiye Jingying Zhengce Fagui Xuanbian* (*Selection of Regulations and Policies for the Operation of Collective, Individual and Private Economy*), Beijing: Zhongguo Minzhi Fazhi Chubanshe, 1993.

Guowuyuan Yanjiushi Ketizu (State Council Research Office Task Group), "Zengqiang Guoying Dazhongxing Qiye Huoli di Lishihuigu" (A Historical Review of the Attempts to Strengthen the Vitality of State-owned Large and Medium-sized Enterprises) *Guanli Shijie* (*Management World*), No. 6, December 1991, pp. 138–43.

Guroff, G. and F. Carstensen (eds), *Entrepreneurship in Imperial Russia and the Soviet Union*, Princeton, NJ: Princeton University Press, 1983.

Haddad, L., "On the Rational Sequencing of Enterprise Reform," *Journal of Communist Studies and Transition Politics*, Vol. 11, No. 1, March 1995, pp. 91–109.

Hall, J. (ed.), *Civil Society: Theory, History and Comparison*, Cambridge: Polity Press, 1995.

Hall, P. and R. Taylor, "Political Science and the Three New Institutionalisms," *Political Studies*, XLIV, 1996, pp. 936–57.

Hann, C. and E. Dunn (eds), *Civil Society: Challenging Western Models*, London: Routledge, 1996.

—— "Second Economy and Civil Society," *Journal of Communist Studies*, Vol. 6, No. 2, 1990, pp. 21–44.

Harding, J., "Hidden Compensations," *Financial Times*, 3/24/1997, p. 8.

Hay, D. *et al.*, *Economic Reform and State-Owned Enterprises in China, 1979–1987*, Oxford: Clarendon Press, 1994.

He Baogang, *The Democratic Implications of Civil Society in China*, London: St. Martin's Press, 1997.

Herbert, R. and A. Link, *The Entrepreneur: Mainstream Views and Radical Critiques*, New York: Praeger Publisher, 1982.

Ho, S., *The Asian Experience in Rural Non-Agricultural Development and Its Relevance for China*, World Bank Staff Working Papers, No. 75, Washington, DC: The International Bank for Reconstruction and Development/The World Bank, 1986.

—— *Rural China in Transition: Non-Agricultural Development in Rural Jiangsu, 1978–1990*, Oxford: Clarendon Press, 1994.

Hu Erhu and Zu Zhiqiang (eds), *Zhongguo Gongshangju, Xiangzhen Qiyeju Juzhang Tanjianli Tongyi Dashichang Yu Guifan Shichang Xingwei* (*Chiefs of Management Bureau of Industry and Commerce and Management Bureau of Rural Enterprise in China Commenting on the Development of Unified Market and the Regulation of Market Behavior*), Beijing: Dongfang Chubanshe, 1994.

Huang, S., *The Spiral Road: Change in a Chinese Village Through the Eyes of a Communist Party Leader*, Boulder, CO: Westview Press, 1989.

Huang, Y., "Web of Interests and Patterns of Behavior of Chinese Local Economic Bureaucracies and Enterprises during Reforms," *China Quarterly*, No. 123, September 1990, p. 431–58.

—— *Inflation and Investment Controls in China: The Political Economy of Central-Local Relations During the Reform Era*, New York: Cambridge University Press, 1996.

Huantai Nianjian 1988–1991 (*Huantai Yearbook 1988–1991*), Jinan: Qilu Shushe, 1992.

Huantaixian Renmin Zhengfu Gongzuo Baogao (*Annual Report of the Huantai County People's Government*), 1/16/1998.

Huantaixian Teigaiwei (Huantai county CRE), "Guyuan Zhuanfa Ziboshi Tigaiwei, Gongshangju, Gongziju Yuangufeng Youxiangongsi Guifangongzuo ji Zhongxin Dengjizhuce di Shishixize di Tongji" (Notice of Relaying the Document of the Details for the Implementation of the Standardization and Re-registration of Limited by Shares Companies from the CRE, Bureau of Industry and Commerce and State Asset Management Bureau of Zibo Prefecture), 1/3/1996.

—— *Huantaixian Teigaiwei Jiuwunian Gongzuo Zongjie* (*Report of the Huantai county CRE 1995*), 1/26/1996.

Huantaixiang Renmin Zhengfu Bangongshi (Office of the Huantai county People's Government), "Huantaixiang Zhengfu Guanyu dui Xiangzhen Shixing Dinge Shangjiao, Beili Dizeng, Zengzhang Fencheng Caizheng Tizhi di Jueding" (Decision on the Implementation of the Financial System of "Fixed Quota Submission, Proportional Growth and Sharing of Above-Quota Amount" in Township Administrations), 5/26/1995.

Jia Heting, "Zhongguo Gufenzhi Gaizudi Youguan Zhengce" (The Related Policies of the Transformation of the Chinese Shareholding System) *Guanli Shijie* (*Management World*), No. 3, June 1993, pp. 73–5.

Jia Xiuxin and Han Mengyu, "Yuanshan Xiangzhen Fenshuizhi Caizheng Tizhi di Sikao" (Reflection on the Improvement of the Township Tax-Sharing Scheme) *Xiangzhen Caizheng* (*Township Finance*), January 1997, pp. 13–5.

Jiang Zemin, "Gaoju Deng Xiaoping Lilun Weida Qizhi Ba Jianshe Shehui Chuyi Shiye Quanmian Tuixiang ershiyi Shiji" (Uphold the Great Banner of Deng Xiaoping's Theory and Promote the Cause of Socialist Development with Chinese Characteristics to the Twenty-First Century) (Report at the CCP's Fifteenth National Congress, Beijing, 9/12/1997), *Beijing Wanbao* (*Beijing Evening News*), 9/22/1997, pp. 1–7.

Jiang Zhingyi, Chen Ziguang, and Jia Yanhai, "Pingdushi: Liangtianzhi Gaige di Zhengce Xiaoguo Fenxi," (Two-Farms System: Analysis of the Experience of Pengdu City) *Zhongguo Nongcun Jingji* (*Chinese Rural Economy*), No. 4, April 1994, pp. 26–30.

"Jiaqiang Guanli Guifen Xingwei Cujin Nongcun Hezuo Jijinhui Wending Jiankang Fazhan: Nongyebu Nongcun Hezuo Jijinhui Bangongshi Fuzeren da Jijie wen" (Strengthening Regulation and Promoting a Healthy and Steady Development of Rural Cooperative Funds: Official of the Rural Cooperative Fund Office of the Ministry of Agriculture Answering Questions from Reporters), *Nongcun Hezuo Jingji Jingying Guanli* (*Operation and Management of a Rural Cooperative Economy*), No. 10, 1995, p. 13.

"Jiuxiniandai Nongcun Gaige di Zhuti: Fang Nongyebu Nongcun Jingji Yanjiu Zhongxin Fuzhuren Du Ying" (Theme of the Rural Reform in the 1990s: Interview with Du Ying, Deputy Director of the Rural Economy Research Center of the Ministry of Agriculture), *Zhongguo Nongcun Jingji* (*Chinese Rural Economy*), No. 109, January 1994, pp. 1–8.

Johnson, C., *MITI and the Japanese Miracle: The Growth of Industrial Policy, 1925–1975*, Stanford, CA: Stanford University Press, 1982.

Keane, J., *Democracy and Civil Society*, London: Verso, 1988.

—— (ed.), *Civil Society and the State: New European Perspectives*, London: Verso, 1988.

Keith, R., *China's Struggle for the Rule of Law*, London: St. Martin's Press, 1994.

Kelliher, D., *Peasant Power in China: The Era of Rural Reform, 1979–1989*, New Haven: Yale University Press, 1992.

—— "Chinese Communist Political Theory and the Rediscovery of the Peasantry," *Modern China*, Vol. 20, No. 4, December 1994, pp. 387–415.

Kennedy, M. and P. Gianoplus, "Entrepreneurs and Expertise: a Cultural Encounter in the Making of Post-Communist Capitalism in Poland," *East European Politics and Societies*, Vol. 8, No. 1, Winter 1994, pp. 58–93.

Knight, J., *Institutions and Social Conflict*, Cambridge: Cambridge University Press, 1992.

Knight, J., and I. Sened (eds), *Explaining Social Institutions*, Ann Arbor, MI: University of Michigan Press, 1995.

Kojima, R., "Agricultural Organization: New Forms, New Contradictions," *China Quarterly* No. 116, December 1988, pp. 706–35.

Kornai, J., *The Economics of Shortage*, Amsterdam: North Holland Publishing Company, 1980, two volumes.

Krasner, S., "Approaches to the State: Alternative Conceptions and Historical Dynamics," *Comparative Politics*, Vol. 16, No. 2, 1984, pp. 223–46.

Kueh, Y. Y., "China's Second Land Reform," *China Quarterly*, No. 101, March 1985, pp. 122–31.

Kung, J., "Equal Entitlement Versus Tenure Security Under a Regime of Collective Property Rights: Peasants' Preference for Institutions in Post-Reform Chinese Agriculture," *Journal of Comparative Economics*, Vol. 21, No. 2, 1995, pp. 82–111.

Lee, H. Y., *From Revolutionary Cadres to Party Technocrats in Socialist China*, Berkeley, CA: University of California Press, 1991.

Li Lianjiang and K. O'Brien, "Villagers and Popular Resistance in Contemporary China," *Modern China*, Vol. 22, No. 1, January 1996, pp. 28–61.

"Li Peng Congratulates Inventor-Entrepreneurs," *FBIS* (China), No. 91, 1994, p. 27.

Li Qin, "Dui Woguo Nongmin Fudan Xianzhuang di Fenxi," (The Analysis of the Peasants' Burden in China) *Zhongguo Nongcun Jingji* (*Chinese Rural Economy*), No. 8, August 1992, pp. 47–51.

Li Tongming, "Guanyu Xiangzhen Qiye Gufen Hezuozhi Ruogan Lilun Wenti de Sikao" (Reflections on the Theoretical Issues Concerning the Shareholding Cooperative Reform in Rural Enterprises) *Nongye Jingji Wenti* (*Problems of Agricultural Economy*), No. 7, 1999, pp. 14–7.

Libecap, G., *Contracting for Property Rights*, Cambridge: Cambridge University Press, 1989.

Lieberthal, K. and D. Lampton (eds), *Bureaucracy, Politics, and Decision Making in Post-Mao China*, Berkeley, CA: University of California Press, 1992.

Lieberthal, K. and M. Oksenberg, *Policy Making in China: Leaders, Structures and Processes*, Princeton, NJ: Princeton University Press, 1988.

Lin, Nan, "Local Market Socialism: Local Corporatism in Action in Rural China," *Theory and Society*, No. 24, 1995, pp. 301–54.

Lindblom, C., *Politics and Markets: The World's Political-Economic Systems*, New York: Basic Books, 1977.

Lipset, S., *Political Man*, Baltimore: Johns Hopkins University Press, 1981.

Lu Wen, "Xiangzhen Qiye Mianlin di Xinxingshi he Fazhan di Xinyaoqiu," (The New Stage of Rural Enterprise Development) *Zhongguo Nongcun Jingji* (*Chinese Rural Economy*), No. 1, January 1993, pp. 47–51.

Lubman, S., "Introduction: The Future of Chinese Law," *China Quarterly*, No. 141, March 1995, pp. 1–21.

Ma, Rong, Wang Hanshang, and Liu Shiding (eds), *Jiushi Nandai Zhongguo Xiangzhen Qiye Tiaocha* (*Survey of China's Rural Enterprise in the Nineties*), Hong Kong: Oxford University Press, 1994.

Macaulay, S., "Non-Contractual Relations in Business: A Preliminary Study," *American Sociological Review*, Vol. 28, No. 1, 1963, pp. 55–67.

Madsen, R,, *Morality and Power in a Chinese Village*, Berkeley, CA: University of California Press, 1984.

Maqiaozhen Zhengfu Gongzuo Baogao (*Annual Report of Maqiao Township Government*), 1/9/1999.

March, J. and J. Olsen, "The New Institutionalism: Organizational Factors in Political Life," *American Political Science Review*, Vol. 78, No. 3, 1984, pp. 737–49.

Migdal, J., *State in Society: Studying how States and Societies Transform and Constitute One Another*, New York: Cambridge University Press, 2001.

Migdal, J., A. Kohli, and V. Shue (eds), *State Power and Social Forces: Domination and Transformation in the Third World*, Cambridge: Cambridge University Press, 1994.

Mill, M. and S. S. Nagel (eds), *Public Administration in China*, Westport, CT: Greenwood Press, 1993.

Miller, R. (ed.), *The Development of Civil Society in Communist Systems*, Australia: Allen and Unwin, 1992.

Mills, C. W., *The Power Elites*, New York: Oxford University Press, 1956.

Milor, V. (ed.), *Changing Political Economies: Privatization in Post-Communist and Reforming Communist States*, London: Lynne Rienner, 1994.

"Ministry To Send Cadres to Rural Areas," *FBIS* (China), No. 70, 1993, pp. 25–6.

Montes-Negret, F. "China's Credit Plan: An Overview," *Oxford Review of Economic Policy*, Vol. 11, No. 4, 1995, pp. 25–42.

Moore, B., *Social Origins of Dictatorship and Democracy*, Boston: Beacon Press, 1966.

Munzer, S. R., *A Theory of Property*, Cambridge: Cambridge University Press, 1990.

Naguin, S. and E. Rawski, *Chinese Society in the Eighteenth Century*, New Haven, CT: Yale University Press, 1987.

"Nantongxian Qiye Chengbao Jingyi zhong di 'Fufangzhang Guiheshang Qiongmiaotang' Xianxiang," (The Experience of Implementing the Contract Responsibility System in Enterprises in Nantong County: the Phenomenon of `the Master Getting Rich at the Expense of the Temple and Monks'), *Zhongguo Xiangzhen Qiyebao*, 7/20/1992, p. 1.

Naughton, B., "Implications of the State Monopoly Over Industry and Its Relaxation," *Modern China*, Vol. 18, No. 1, January 1992, pp. 14–41.

—— "Chinese Institutional Innovation and Privatization from Below," *American Economic Review, Papers and Perspectives*, Vol. 84, No. 2, 1994, pp. 266–75.

Nee, V., "A Theory of Market Transition: From Redistribution to Markets in State Socialism," *American Sociological Review*, Vol. 54, October 1989, pp. 663–81.

Nee, V. and D. Stark (eds), *Remaking the Economic Institutions of Socialism: China and Eastern Europe*, Stanford, CA: Stanford University Press, 1989.

Nee, V. and Su Sijin, "Institutional Change and Economic Growth in China: The View from the Villages," *Journal of Asian Studies*, Vol. 49, No. 1, February 1990, pp. 3–25.

—— "Social Inequalities in Reforming State Socialism: Between Redistribution and Markets in China," *American Sociological Review*, Vol. 56, June 1991, pp. 267–82.

—— "Organizational Dynamics of Market Transition: Hybrid Forms, Property Rights, and Mixed Economy in China," *Administrative Science Quarterly*, No. 37, 1992, pp. 1–27.

—— "Institutions, Social Ties, and Commitment in China's Corporatist Transformation," Russell Sage Foundation and Cornell University, Working Paper No. 64, 1994.

Nolan, P. and Dong Fureng (eds), *The Chinese Economy and its Future: Achievements and Problems of Post-Mao Reform*, Cambridge: Cambridge University Press, 1990.

Nongmin Ribao (Peasant Daily).

Nongyebu (Ministry of Agriculture), "Guanyu Tuixing he Wanshan Xiangzhen Qiye Gufenhezuozhi di Tongji" (Notice on the Implementation and Improvement of the Cooperative Shareholding System among Rural Enterprises), 12/24/1992.

—— "Nongmin Gufenhezuoqiye Zanxingguiding" (Provisional Regulation of Rural Shareholding Cooperative Enterprise), 2/12/1990.

—— Nongcun Hezuo Jijinhui Dengji Guanli Banfa (Method of Registration and Management of Rural Cooperative Funds), 4/19/1995.

—— Xiangzhen Qiye Zujian he Fazhan Qiye Jituan Zanxing Banfa (Provisional Method for the Formation and Development of Rural Enterprise Groups), *Zhongguo Xiangzhen Qiyebao*, 1/24/1992, p. 3.

Nongyebu Nongcun Gufenhezuo Ketizu, "1992 Nian Nongcun Gufenhezuo Zuzhi Fazhan Baogao: Quanguo Qishiwuge Xian de Tiaochafenxi" (Report of Rural Shareholding Cooperative Organization Development in 1992: National Survey of 75 Counties).

Nongyebu Nongcun Hezuo Jingji Yanjiu Ketizu (Research Group for Rural Cooperative Economy of the Ministry of Agriculture), "Zhongguo Nongcun Tudi Chengbao Jingying Zhidu yu Hezuo Zuzhi Yunxing Kaocha," (Survey on Land Contract System and the Functioning of Cooperative Organizations in Rural China), *Nongye Jingji Wenti (Problems of Agricultural Economy)*, No. 11, November 1993, pp. 45–53.

Nongyebu Xiangzhen Qiyeju (TVE Bureau of the Ministry of Agriculture), "Xiangzhen Qiye Zichanpingu Banfa" (Method of Asset Valuation For TVEs), *Zhongguo Xiangzhen Qiyebao*, 9/6/1994, p. 3.

North, D. and R. Thomas, *The Rise of the Western World: A New Economic History*, Cambridge: Cambridge University Press, 1973.

—— *Institutions, Institutional Change and Economic Performance*, New York: Cambridge University Press, 1990.

O'Brien, K., "Rightful Resistance," *World Politics*, No. 49, October 1996, pp. 31–55.

Odgaard, O., "Entrepreneurs and Elite Formation in Rural China," *Australian Journal of Chinese Affairs*, No. 28, July 1992, pp. 89–108.

O'Donnell, G. and P. Schmitter (eds), *Transition from Authoritarian Rule: Tentative Conclusions about Uncertain Democracies*, Baltimore: Johns Hopkins University Press, 1986.

"Official Urges Sending County Cadres to Front," *FBIS* (China), No. 124, 1992, pp. 30–1.

Oi, J., *State and Peasant in Contemporary China: The Political Economy of Village Government*, Berkeley, CA: University of California Press, 1989.

—— "Fiscal Reform and the Economic Foundations of Local State Corporatism in China," *World Politics*, No. 45, October 1992, pp. 99–126

—— "The Role of the Local State in China's Transitional Economy," *China Quarterly*, No. 144, December 1995, pp. 1132–49.

—— *Rural China Takes Off: Institutional Foundations of Economic Reform*, Berkeley, CA: University of California Press.

Oi, J. and A. Walder (eds), *Property Rights and Economic Reform in China*, Stanford, CA: Stanford University Press, 1999.

Olson, M., *The Logic of Collective Action*, Cambridge MA: Harvard University Press, 1965.

Parish, W. and E. Michelson, "Politics and Markets: Dual Transformations," *American Journal of Sociology*, Vol. 101, No. 4, January 1996, pp. 1042–59.

Park, A., S. Rozelle, C. Wong and Changqing Ren, "Distributional Consequences of Reforming Local Public Finance in China," *China Quarterly*, No. 147, September 1996, pp. 751–78.

Pearson, M., "The Janus Face of Business Associations in China: Socialist Corporatism in Foreign Enterprises," *Australian Journal of Chinese Affairs*, No. 31, January 1994, pp. 25–46.

—— *China's New Business Elite: The Political Consequences of Economic Reform*, Berkeley, CA: University of California Press, 1997.

Pengyangxiang Dangwei Zhengfu (The Party Committee and People's Government of Pengyang township), "Shenruchijiu di Tuidong Gufenhezuozhi Gaige Wei Pengyang Jingji di Zhenxing he Tengfei er Fendou" (Intensification of Shareholding Cooperative Reform as a Means to Revitalize the Economy of Pengyang County), 6/11/1992.

Pike, F. and T. Stritch, *The New Corporatism: Social-Political Structures in the Iberian World*, Notre Dame, IN: University of Notre Dame Press, 1974.

Polanyi, K., *The Great Transformation: the Political and Economic Origins of Our Time*, Boston: Beacon Press, 1957.

Potter, P. , *The Economic Contract Law of China: Legitimation and Contract Autonomy in the People's Republic of China*. Seattle: University of Washington Press, 1992.

Potter, S. H. and J. Potter, *China's Peasants: The Anthropology of a Revolution*, Cambridge: Cambridge University Press, 1990.

Powell, W. and P. Dimaggio (eds), *The New Institutionalism in Organizational Analysis*, Chicago, IL: Chicago University Press, 1991.

Putnam, R., *The Comparative Study of Political Elites*, Englewood Cliffs, NJ: Prentice-Hall, 1976.

Putterman, L., "The Role of Ownership and Property Rights in China's Economic Transition," *China Quarterly* No. 144, December 1995, pp. 1047–64.

Qian Ying, "Defang Zhengfu Jingji Xingwei Guifanhua Wenti Yanjiu" (Research on the Problem of Routinization of the Economic Behavior of Local Government), *Nongcun Jingji Shehui* (*Rural Economy and Society*) No. 4, 1989, pp. 28–31.

Qin Guangwu, "Ganqun Quanxi Beiwanlu" (Memorandum of the Relationship Between

Cadres and the Masses), *Nongcun Gongzuo Tongxun (Rural Work Newsletter)*, No. 11, 1988, pp. 30–1.

Quanguo Xiangzhen Qiyejia Pingxuan Banfa" (Regulation for the Adjudication of National Rural Entrepreneur), *Zhongguo Xiangzhen Qiye Nianjian 1992*, 4/26/1991.

Rau, Z. (ed.), *The Re-emergence of Civil Society in Eastern Europe and the Soviet Union*, Boulder, CO: Westview Press, 1991.

"Reassessment of the Enterprise Ownership Responsibility System" *JPRS* (China), No. 115, 1989, pp. 29–34.

Redfield, M. P. (ed.), *China's Gentry: Essays in Rural Urban Relations by Fei Xiaotong*, Chicago: University of Chicago Press, 1953.

Richard, B., *Industrial Society in Communist China*, New York: Vintage Books, 1969.

Riskin, C., "Political Conflict and Rural Industrialization in China," *World Development*, Vol. 6, No. 5, 1978, pp. 681–92.

—— *China's Political Economy: The Quest for Development Since 1949*, Oxford: Oxford University Press, 1988.

Rona-Tas, A., "The First Shall be Last? Entrepreneurship and Communist Cadres in the Transition from Socialism," *American Journal of Sociology*, Vol. 100, No. 1, July 1994, pp. 40–69.

Rosenbaum, A. (ed.), *State and Society in China: The Consequences of Reform*, Boulder, CO: Westview Press, 1992.

"Rural Entrepreneurs Write Letter to Deng," *FBIS* (China), Vol. 92, No. 194, 10/6/1992, p. 41.

Schmitter, P., "Ten Propositions Concerning Civil Society and the Consolidation of Democracy," unpublished paper, Stanford University, 1996.

Schumpeter, J., *Capitalism, Socialism and Democracy*, London: Unwin University Books, 1943.

Scott, J., *Weapons of the Weak: Everyday Forms of Peasant Resistance*, New Haven, CT: Yale University Press, 1985.

—— *Seeing Like a State: How Certain Schemes to Improve the Human Condition Have Failed*, New Haven: Yale University Press, 1998.

Seligman, A., *The Idea of Civil Society: Resolving the Battle of Private Interests and the Common Good*, New York: Free Press, 1992.

Shandong Tongji Nianjian (Statistical Yearbook of Shandong), 1994, Beijing: Zhongguo Tongji Chubanshe, 1994.

Shue, V., *Peasant China in Transition*, Berkeley, CA: University of California Press, 1980.

—— *The Reach of the State: Sketches of the Chinese Body Politic*, Stanford, CA: Stanford University Press, 1988.

Skinner, W., "Marketing and Social Structure in Rural China," *Journal of Asian Studies*, Vol. 24, No. 1, 1964, pp. 3–24; Vol. 24, No. 2, 1964, pp. 195–228; and Vol. 24, No. 3, 1965, pp. 363–99.

"Slow Introduction of Shareholding System Urged," *FBIS* (China), No. 225, 11/20/1992, pp. 32–3.

Smith, A., *The Wealth of Nations*, London: Penguin, 1986.

Solinger, D., *Chinese Business Under Socialism: The Politics of Domestic Commerce, 1949–1980*, Berkeley, CA: University of California Press, 1984.

—— *China's Transients and the State: A Form of Civil Society*, Hong Kong: Hong Kong Institute of Asia-Pacific Studies, Chinese University of Hong Kong, 1991.

Stark, D., "Recombinant Property in East European Capitalism," *American Journal of Sociology*, Vol. 101, No. 4, January 1996, pp. 993–1027.

Steinmo, S., K. Thelen and F. Longstreth (eds), *Structuring Politics: Historical Institutionalism in Comparative Analysis*, Cambridge: Cambridge University Press, 1994.

"Stockholder as Virtue Criticized," *JPRS* (China), No. 43, 7/9/1993, p. 1.

Sun Zhonghua, "Nonghu Jingji Mianlin di Xinqinkuang: Quanguo Nongcun Guding Guancha Tiaocha Fenxi," (New Economic Development Faced by Rural Households: The Analysis of the National Fixed-Point Survey of Rural Households) *Nongye Jingji Wenti (Problems of Agricultural Economy)*, November 1992, pp. 9–12.

Swain, N., "Small Cooperatives and Economic Work Partnership in the Computing Industries: Exception that Proves the Rule," *Journal of Communist Studies,* Vol. 6, No. 2, 1990, pp. 85–109.

"Symposium on 'Public Sphere'/'Civil Society' in China," *Modern China*, Vol. 19, No. 2, April 1993.

Szelenyi, I., *Socialist Entrepreneurs: Embourgeoisement in Rural Hungary*. Madison, WI: University of Wisconsin Press, 1988.

Szelenyi, I., and E. Kostello, "The Market Transition Debate: Toward a Synthesis?" *American Journal of Sociology*, Vol. 101, No. 4, January 1996, pp. 1082–96.

Szelenyi, I., and S. Szelenyi, "Circulation or Reproduction of Elites During the Postcommunist Transformation of Eastern Europe," *Theory and Society*, No. 24, 1995, pp. 615–38.

Tang Xinhua and Huang Yi (eds), *Xinbian Xiangzhen Qiye Huiji* (New Edition of Rural Enterprise Accounting), Beijing: Zhongguo Wuxi Chubanshe, 1995.

"Township Enterprise Contract Responsibility System Viewed" *JPRS* (China), No. 14, 1987, pp. 24–9.

Tsang, E., "The Changing Role of Supply and Marketing Co-operatives in China," *Small Enterprise Development*, Vol. 5, No. 3, September 1994, pp. 35–42.

Tsang, Shu-ki and Cheng Yuk-shing, "China's Tax Reforms of 1994: Breakthrough or Compromise?" *Asian Survey*, Vol. XXXIV, No. 9, September 1994, pp. 769–88.

Tu Weiming, "Introduction: Cultural Perspectives," *Daedalus*, Vol. 122, No. 2, Spring 1993, pp. X–XI.

Unger, J. and A. Chan, "China, Corporatism, and the East Asian Model," *Australian Journal of Chinese Affairs*, No. 33, January 1995, pp. 29–53.

Vermeer, E. B., "Experiments with Rural Industrial Shareholding Cooperatives: The Case of Zhoucun District, Shandong Province," *China Information*, Vol. 10, No. 3/4, Winter 1995/Spring 1996, pp. 75–107.

Wade, R., *Governing the Market: Economic Theory and the Role of Government in East Asian Industrialization*, Princeton, NJ: Princeton University Press, 1990.

Walder, Andrew, "Local Governments as Industrial Firms: An Organizational Analysis of China's Transitional Economy," *American Journal of Sociology*, Vol. 101, No. 2, September 1995, pp. 263–301.

—— "Markets and Inequality in Transitional Economics: Toward Testable Theories," *American Journal of Sociology*, Vol. 101, No. 4, January 1996, pp. 1060–73.

Walker, K., "Trends in Crop Production, 1978–86," Special Issue on Food and Agriculture in China During the Post-Mao Era, *China Quarterly,* No. 116, December 1988, pp. 592–633.

Wang Guo and Shi Xia, "Gufenzhi: Gaohuo Dazhongxing Qiye di Zhengque Xuanze," (Shareholding System: The Correct Choice for Revitalizing Large and Medium Size Enterprises) *Zhongguo Gongye Jingji Yanjiu (China Industrial Economic Research)*, No. 11, November 1991, pp. 9–14.

Wang Yanxin, "Nongcun Jinrong Tizhi Gaige di Jige Wenti" (Several Problems

Concerning Reform in the Rural Financial System), *Zhongguo Nongcun Jingji (China's Rural Economy)*, No. 5, May 1995, pp. 45–50.

Wang Zhonghui, "Township Public Finance and Its Impact on the Financial Burden of Rural Enterprises and Peasants in Mainland China," *Issues & Studies*, No. 31, August 1995, pp. 103–21.

Wank, D., "Private Business, Bureaucracy, and Political Alliance in a Chinese City," *Australian Journal of Chinese Affairs*, No. 33, January 1995, pp. 55–71.

—— *Commodifying Communism: Business, Trust and Politics in a Chinese Society*, New York: Cambridge University Press, 1999.

Watson, A., C. Findlay and Du Juntang, "Who Won the 'Wool War?': A Case Study of Rural Product Marketing in China," *China Quarterly*, No. 118, June 1989, pp. 213–41.

Weitzman, M. and Chenggang Xu, "Chinese Township–Village Enterprises as Vaguely Defined Cooperatives," *Journal of Comparative Economics*, No. 18, 1994, pp. 121–45.

Wen Tiejun and Zhu Shouyin, "Nongcun Hezuo Jinrong Gaige Shiyan Yanjiu Baogao" (Research Report on the Experiment of Rural Cooperative Financial Reform), *Zhongguo Nongcun Jingji (China's Rural Economy)*, No. 1, 1994, pp. 40–6.

White, G. (ed.), *Developmental States in East Asia*, London: Macmillan Press, 1988.

—— (ed.), *The Chinese State in the Era of Economic Reform: The Road to Crisis*, London: Macmillan, 1991.

—— "Prospects for Civil Society in China: A Case Study of Xiaoshan City," *The Australian Journal of Chinese Affairs*, No. 29, 1993, pp. 63–87.

—— *Riding the Tiger: The Politics of Economic Reform in Post-Mao China*, London: Macmillan, 1993.

White, G., Jude Howell, and Xiaoyuan Shang, *In Search of Civil Society: Market Reform and Social Change in Contemporary China*, Oxford: Clarendon Press, 1996.

Whiting, S., *Power and Wealth in Rural China: the Political Economy of Institutional Change*, New York, Cambridge University Press, 2001.

Williamson, O., "Transaction-Cost Economics: The Governance of Contractual Relations," *Journal of Law and Economics*, Vol. XXII, No. 2, October 1979, pp. 233–61.

—— "Organization Form, Residual Claimants, and Corporate Control," *Journal of Law and Economics*, Vol. XXVI, June 1983, pp. 351–66.

Wong, C. (ed.), *Financing Local Government in the People's Republic of China*, Oxford: Oxford University Press, 1997.

Wong, C., C. Heady and Wing T. Woo, *Fiscal Management and Economic Reform in the People's Republic of China*, Hong Kong: Oxford University Press, 1995.

World Bank, *China: Financial Sector Policies and Institutional Development*, Washington, DC: World Bank, 1990.

Xiangzhen Qiye (Rural Enterprise) (Zibo).

Xiao, Yue, "Dao Xiangzhenqiye Qu: Zhongguo Chengzhen Qingnian Jiuye Xindongxiang," (Going to Rural Enterprises: The New Pattern of Employment of Urban Youth in China), *Zhongguo Xiangzhen Qiyebao*, 2/24/1994, p. 1.

Yan, Yunxiang, "The Impact of Rural Reform on Economic and Social Stratification in a Chinese Village," *Australian Journal of Chinese Affairs*, No. 27, January 1992, pp. 1–23.

Yang Zhongyi, "Qianxi Cunganbu di Bazhong Xintai" (Analysis of Eight Kinds of Mentality of Village Cadres) *Xiangzhen Luntan (Township Forum)*, No. 8, August 1991, p. 33.

Yang, C. K., *The Chinese Family in the Communist Revolution*, MIT, Cambridge, MA: Technology Press, 1959.

——*A Chinese Village in the Early Communist Transition*, MIT, Cambridge, MA: Technology Press, 1959.

Yang, D., "Local Government and Rural Industrialization in China," *Peasant Studies*, Vol. 18, No. 2, Winter 1991, pp. 131–41.

—— *Calamity and Reform in China: State, Rural Society, and Institutional Change since the Great Leap Famine*, Stanford, CA: Stanford University Press, 1996.

Yep, R., "Towards a Symbiotic State–Enterprise Relationship in Rural China: Changes and Prospect," *Hong Kong Journal of Social Science*, No. 17, Autumn 2000, pp. 1–18.

—— "The Limitations of Corporatism in Understanding Reforming China," *Journal of Contemporary China*, Vol. 9, No. 25, 2000, pp. 547–66. The journal can be found on line at http://www.tandf.co.uk

—— "Bring the Managers in: A Case of Rising Influence of Enterprise Managers in Rural China," *Issues & Studies*, Vol. 36, No. 4, July/August 2000, pp. 132–65.

—— "Evolution of Shareholding Enterprise Reform in Rural China: A Manager Empowerment Thesis," *Pacific Affairs*, Vol. 74, No. 1, Spring 2001, pp. 53–73.

Yep, R. and Louie Kin-shuen, "Interest Articulation of Rural Businesses 1984–1999: A Preliminary Analysis," paper presented in the 6th European Conference on Agricultural and Rural Development in China, 5–7 January, 2000, Leiden University, The Netherlands.

Young, S., *Private Business and Economic Reform in China*, Armonk, NY: M. E. Sharpe, an East Gate Book, 1995.

Yuan Peng, "Guanyu Nongcun Gufenhezuozhi Qiye Fazhanzhong di Wenti yu Jianyi," (Problems and Recommendations concerning the Development of Rural Shareholding Enterprises), *Guanli Shijie (Management World)*, No. 3, 1994, p. 50.

Zeitin, M., "Corporate Ownership and Control: the Large Corporation and the Capitalist Class," *American Journal of Sociology*, Vol. 79, No. 5, 1974, pp. 107–19.

ZGXZQYB, "Xiangzhenqiye Rencaijie Wenti Heshi Caineng Jiejue?" (When Can the Problem of Shortage of Human Resources in Rural Enterprise be Solved?), 2/4/1995, p. 1.

ZGXZQYB, "Zhigong Weihebuyuan Rugu?" (Why are Workers Unwilling to Buy Shares?), 8/28/1995, p. 2.

Zhang Gang, "Government Intervention vs. Marketization in China's Rural Industries: The Role of Local Governments," *China Information*, Vol. VIII, 1993, pp. 45–73.

"Zhao Ziyang Tongzhi Yu Zuijia Nongmin Qiyejia Zuotan" (Zhao Ziyang Met the Best Peasant Entrepreneurs), *Zhongguo Xiangzhen Qiyebao*, 9/14/1987, p. 1.

Zhonggong Huantai Xianwei Bangongshi (The Office of the Huantai county Committee of the Chinese Communist Party) (ed.), *Huantaixian Qiye Chanquanzhidu Gaige Cailiao Huibian (Selection of Documents on Enterprise Ownership Reform in Huantai County)*, 1994.

Zhonggong Huantai Xianwei, Huantaixian Renmin Zhengfu (Committee of Huantai county of the Chinese Communist Party and the People's Government of Huantai county), "Guanyu Jiakuai Jingji Fazhan di Ruogan Guiding" (Several Guidelines for Speeding up Economic Development), 3/1/1993.

Zhonggong Zhoucunqu Weiyuanhui, Zhoucunqu Renmin Zhengfu (Zhoucun District Committee of the Chinese Communist Party and the Zhoucun District People's Government), "Guanyu Jinyibu Shenhua Gufenhezuozhi Gaige Jiaquai Jianli Xiandai Qiye Zhidu di Shixing Fangan" (The Provisional Plan for the Intensification of Shareholding Cooperative Reform and the Building of Modern Enterprise Structure), 5/4/1994.

Zhonggong Zhoucunquwei Zhoucunqu Renmin Zhengfu (Zhoucun District Committee of the Chinese Communist Party and the Zhoucun District People's Government), "Zhoucunqu Nongcun Gaige Shiyanqu 1987–95 Nian Gaige Shiyan Baogao" (Zhoucun Office of National Rural Reform Experiment Office's Report of 1987–1995), 6/20/1995.

Zhonggong Ziboshi Shiwei Xuanchuanbu (Chinese Communist Party Zibo Committee Propaganda Department) (ed.), *Fuqiangzhilu: Laizi Ershiwuge Jingjiqiang Xiangzhen di Baogao* (Path to Prosperity: Report from Twenty-five Prosperous Townships in Zibo), 1993.

Zhongguo Jingji Tizhi Gaige Yanjiuzuo Shehui Yanjiuzhi, Shehui Yulun Tiaochazhi (Social Research Division and Social Opinion Research Division of China's Economic Reform Research Institute), *Gaige de Shehui Xinli Bianqian yu Xuanze* (*The Social Psychology of Reform: Change and Choice*), Chengdu: Sichuan Renmin Chubanshe, 1988.

Zhongguo Nongye Nianjian 1989 (*China's Agricultural Yearbook 1989*), Beijing: Zhongguo Nongye Chubanshe, 1989.

Zhongguo Qiyejia Tiaocha Xitong (Chinese Entrepreneurs Research Group), "Zhongguo Qiyejia Xianzhuang Fenxi ji Qiyejia tui Qiye Jingying Huanjing di Pingjia" (Analysis of the Present Conditions of Chinese Entrepreneurs and Their Assessment of the Business Environment), *Guanli Shejie* (*Management World*), No. 6, December 1993, pp. 128–9.

Zhongguo Tongji Nianjian (*China's Statistical Yearbook*), 1992–3, 1995, 1998.

Zhongguo Tongji Zhaiyao (*China's Statistical Digest*), 1993–4.

Zhongguo Xiangzhen Qiye Nianjian (*China's Rural Enterprise Yearbook*), 1992–3, 1995–6, and 1998–9.

Zhongguo Xiangzhen Qiyebao (*China's Rural Enterprise News*).

Zhonghua Renmin Gongheguo Gongxifa (*The Company Law of the People's Republic of China*).

Zhonghua Renmin Gongheguo Xiangcun Jiti Suoyouzhi Qiye Tiaoli (*The PRC Regulation of Rural Collective Enterprise*), 1990.

Zhou Xiaochuan and Zhu Li, "China's Banking System: Current Status, Perspectives on Reform," *Journal of Comparative Economics*, No. 11, 1987, pp. 399–402.

Zhou Yimiao and Zhang Yulin (eds), *Zhongguo Chengxiang Xietiao Fazhan Yanjiu* (Research on the Rural–Urban Coordinated Development in China), Hong Kong: Oxford University Press, 1994.

Zhou, K., *How the Farmers Changed China: Power of the People*, Boulder, CO: Westview Press, 1996.

Zhoucun Nongcungaige Shiyan Bangongshi (Zhoucun Office of National Rural Reform Experiment Office), "Guanyu Jiading Gufenhenzuo Qiye Guifenhua Jianshe di Shixing Yijian" (Tentative Views Concerning the Strengthening of Standardization of Cooperative Shareholding System), 11/10/1991.

Zhoucunqu Gufenzhiqiye Laodong Guanli Zanxingguiding" (Provisional Regulation of Labour Management in Shareholding Enterprises in Zhoucun District), 1994.

Zhoucunqu Nongcun Gaige Shiyan Bangongshi (Zhoucun Office of National Rural Experiment Office) (ed.), *Zhoucun Xianxiang* (The Zhoucun Phenomenon), 1995.

"Zhoucunqu Xiangzhen Gufenhezuozhi Qiye Guanlibanfa" (Provisional Method of Management of Shareholding Cooperative Enterprises in Zhoucun District), 1991.

"Zhoucunqu Xiangzhen Gufenhezuozhi Zichanpingu Zhegu Shixing Banfa" (Provisional Method of Asset Valuation of Rural Shareholding Cooperative System in Zhoucun District), 10/30/1991.

Zibo Nianjian (*Zibo Yearbook*), 1987–9, 1990, and 1992–8.

Zibo Ribao (*Zibo Daily*).

Zibo Shizhi (*Zibo Gazette*), 1995.

Zibo Tongji Nianjian (*Zibo Statistical Yearbook*) 1997, 1993, and 1996–9.

Zucker, L. (ed.), *Institutional Patterns and Organizations: Culture and Environment*, Cambridge, MA: Ballinger, 1988.

Zukin, S. and P. Dimaggio (eds), *Structure of Capital: The Social Organization of the Economy*, New York: Cambridge University Press, 1990.

Zweig, D., *Agrarian Radicalism in China, 1968–1981*, Cambridge, MA: Harvard University Press, 1989.

Index

MEMORIAL UNIVERSITY OF NEWFOUNDLAND

3 1162 01309160 9